A Grammar of Speech

Oxford University Press
Walton Street, Oxford OX2 6DP

Oxford New York Toronto
Delhi Bombay Calcutta Madras Karachi
Petaling Jaya Singapore Hong Kong Tokyo
Nairobi Dar es Salaam Cape Town
Melbourne Auckland

and associated companies in Berlin Ibadan

Oxford and *Oxford English* are trade marks of Oxford University Press

ISBN 0 19 437 193 X

© David Brazil 1995

Typeset by Wyvern Typesetting Ltd, Bristol
Printed in Hong Kong

Contents

Acknowledgements   xi

The author and series editors   xii

Foreword   xiii

Transcription notations   xv

Introduction

An exploratory grammar   1
Starting assumptions   2
Why do we want a linear grammar?   4
Discourse analysis   4
What is a sentence grammar?   7
Product and process   10
Why speech?   11
Who is it for?   12

1 The argument and organization of the book

Communicating in time   15
Immediate constituent grammars   17
Finite state grammars   20
Summary of the argument   21
Development of the description   22

2 Used language

Sample of data   24
Used speech is purposeful   26
    Going through the motions   28
Interaction   29
    What can be told or asked?   30
    Communicative need   31
Participants co-operate   31
    Dealing with mismatches   32
    Projecting a need   32
Existential values   33

Contents

Meaning and value   33
Existential antonyms   34
Scholarly background   36
Process and product   37
The purposeful increment   38

3 Telling and asking exchanges

The telling increment   41
Minimum requirements for telling: syntactic   42
Minimum requirements for telling: intonational   44

4 The simple chain

Initial, Intermediate, and Target States   47
Three-element chains   48
Four- and five-element chains   50
A set of sequencing rules   51
Some implications of the sequencing rules   51
The simple chain   55
Sample of data   55

5 Non-finite verbal elements

Non-finite forms   57
Extensions   57
Chains representing more than one telling increment   61
Suspension   61
Suspension in simple chains   62
Characteristics of suspensions   64
Suspensive non-finite verbal elements   64
Suspensive elements before chain-initial N   66
Extensions and suspensions compared   67
Sample of data   67

6 The relationship between elements

The relationship among constituents   69
Post-verbal and post-nominal functions   70

Contents

Indeterminacy and ambiguity 71
Non-significant differences 73
Indeterminacy in chains with non-finite verbal elements 74
Unrestricted reference 76
A finite-state account 76
Non-finite verbal elements as suspensions 77

7 The timing of events

The two time continua 79
Event time and moment of utterance 79
Differentiated and undifferentiated time reference 80
Perfective and imperfective verbs 81
Exploitation 82
Non-finite verbal elements 84
    Event time with the *-ing* form 85
    Event time with the *to* form 85
    Event time with the pp form 86
Linearity 87
The effect of suspension 88
Non-finite verbal elements with post-nominal function 88

8 Selection and communication

Prominence and selection 90
Existential values 92
Tone units with two prominent syllables 95
The nature of prominence 95
Selection in two-prominence tone units 96
Sample of data 99

9 More on verbal elements

Analysis of multi-word elements 101
Selectional possibilities of auxiliary *have* 102
    Communicative deficiency 104
    Auxiliary *have* followed by non-finite forms 105
Auxiliary *be* 107
    Events and conditions 108
    Auxiliary *be* followed by non-finite forms 109
Longer verbal sequences 111

Contents

10 Modals and the plain infinitive

Modals   113
Base form of non-finite elements   114
Modals in sequence with non-finite forms   115
Conversational use of modals   116
Verbal element *do*   119
Plain infinitives following other verbal elements   120
Sample of data   120

11 More extensions and suspensions

Reduplication   121
   The + symbol   122
Preposition/nominal elements   123
Indeterminacy resulting from reduplication   123
Same or different referent?   127
Reduplicative N as extension or suspension   128
Finite second predication   128
Summary   130

12 Zero realization

Second mention   131
The Ø symbol   132
Zero realization in finite second predications   133
Who   134
Optional elements   136
Uses of zero realization compared   137

13 Open selectors

The pertinence of selection   139
Open selectors in telling increments   140
Functional indeterminacy of open selectors   141
Selection by equation   143
Prominent and non-prominent W   144
Selection by predication   145
Suspensions   146
Slot-filling *who*   147
Sample of data   150

14 Nominal elements

Events and things   151
Characterizing and identifying   151
Speaker's choice   153
Post-nominal specification   155
  Other kinds of post-specifiers   157
Pre-nominal specification   159
  Ordering of adjectival elements   161
  Intonation of pre-specified nominal elements   164

15 Talk about talk

What does the discourse count as?   167
Retrospective labelling   170
Unlabelled intentions   171
Essential and incidental items   171
Secondary purposes of increments   172
Illocutionary force   173
Explicit and implicit purposes   175
What is the discourse about?   176
Discrete labelling   178

16 More talk about talk

Non-discrete labelling   179
Pre-empting the purpose   180
Tone choice   182
Suspensions at the beginning of the chain   183
Theme   187
Temporal precedence   187

17 Asking exchanges

Who knows what?   190
Initiating increments   192
  Finding out or making sure?   193
Question types   195
Responses   197
Extended responses   200

18 What can go wrong?

Chains that do not occur   203
Categories of constraint   204
Absolute constraints   207
Probable constraints associated with particular words   208
Category 3 constraints   209
On-line amendments   211

19 A version of the story analysed   214

A linear analysis   215
   Comments   218

20 Uses of a linear account of grammar

Principles   222
The sentence   225
A user's model?   228
Psychological reality?   229
Purposeful language and psycholinguistics   230
Language acquisition   232
Language learning and teaching   234
   Seeing the wood for the trees   235
   Learning to use a language or learning about it? 239

Appendix   240

Glossary   247

Bibliography   256

Index   259

Acknowledgements

I am indebted to my storytellers for providing me with a corpus to work on but must keep the promise of anonymity that I made them.

The book has had a lengthy gestation and most of my former colleagues in the School of English at Birmingham University have been involved at some time or other in the exchange of ideas without which I could never have completed it. I should like to mention three in particular: Richard Cauldwell, Martin Hewins, and Dave Willis.

Anna Mauranen and Laurence Schourup were both kind enough to read an early version of the manuscript and offer invaluable comments and advice.

I am grateful to the series editors, John Sinclair and Ronald Carter, for their help and generous promotion of the book; and to Antoinette Meehan of Oxford University Press for efficiently steering it through the editorial process.

The author and publishers would like to thank the following for permission to reproduce material that falls within their copyright:

Cambridge University Press for extracts from *An Introduction to Theoretical Linguistics* (1968) by John Lyons.

Every effort has been made to trace the owners of copyright material in this book, but we should be pleased to hear from any copyright holder whom we have been unable to contact.

The author
and series editors

David Brazil, a Fellow of the Institute of Advanced Research in the Humanities at the University of Birmingham, joined the English Department there in 1975 to work on discourse intonation. Since taking early retirement in 1986, he has been visiting professor at universities in Brazil and Japan, where the main thrust of his work has been to apply the principles that informed his intonation studies to a fresh examination of grammar.

John Sinclair has been Professor of Modern English Language at the University of Birmingham since 1965. His main areas of research are discourse (both spoken and written) and computational linguistics — with particular emphasis on the study of very long texts. He has been consultant/adviser to a number of groups, including, among others, the Bullock Committee, The British Council, and the National Congress for Languages in Education. He holds the title of Adjunct Professor in Jiao Tong University, Shanghai. Professor Sinclair has published extensively, and is currently Editor-in-Chief of the Cobuild project at Birmingham University.

Ronald Carter is Professor of Modern English Language in the Department of English Studies at the University of Nottingham where he has taught since 1979. He is Chairman of the Poetics and Linguistics Association of Great Britain, a member of CNAA panels for Humanities, and a member of the Literature Advisory Committee of The British Council. Dr Carter has published widely in the areas of language and education, applied linguistics, and literary linguistics. He is Director of the Centre for English Language Education at the University of Nottingham and from 1989 to 1992 was National Co-ordinator for Language in the National Curriculum.

Foreword

Describing English Language

The Describing English Language series provides much-needed descriptions of modern English. Analysis of extended naturally-occurring texts, spoken and written, and, in particular, computer processing of texts have revealed quite unsuspected patterns of language. Traditional descriptive frameworks are normally not able to account for or accommodate such phenomena, and new approaches are required. This series aims to meet the challenge of describing linguistic features as they are encountered in real contexts of use in extended stretches of discourse. Accordingly, and taking the revelations of recent research into account, each book in the series will make appropriate reference to corpora of naturally-occurring data.

The series will cover most areas of the continuum between theoretical and applied linguistics, converging around the mid-point suggested by the term 'descriptive'. In this way, we believe the series can be of maximum potential usefulness.

One principal aim of the series is to exploit the relevance to teaching of an increased emphasis on the description of naturally-occurring stretches of language. To this end, the books are illustrated with frequent references to examples of language use. Contributors to the series will consider both the substantial changes taking place in our understanding of the English language and the inevitable effect of such changes upon syllabus specifications, design of materials, and choice of method.

John Sinclair, *University of Birmingham*
Ronald Carter, *University of Nottingham*

A Grammar of Speech

This is a courageous and innovative book. For many years, its author has expressed dissatisfaction at the poor representation of speech in conventional grammars, and now he offers a grammar that puts the organization of the spoken language in central position.

For David Brazil, the most important feature of speech is its inter-active character. Whether in intimate conversation or public per-formance, anyone communicating through speech must be engaged in shaping an interaction through co-operative verbal behaviour, in real time. With writing, things are different, and the interactive nature of the communication may be obscured at times. The seg-mentation into units, especially sentences, is usually clearer, how-ever, and there is not normally any need to pay minute attention to the passage of real time while one is composing a written piece.

Small wonder, then, given these differences, if grammars concen-trate on either the spoken or the written form, and tend to neglect the other. Almost all grammars focus on the written language, and the few that claim to deal with speech make only modest concessions to the special character of speech.

David Brazil starts from a firm position: that speech will be exam-ined for its grammatical structure without reference to the received conventions of grammatical description, since these arise mainly from the study of written language. This perspective gives a new look to the grammar, and a rich role to the intonation choices that we make, and that have little place in other grammars. The new model turns out to be more general than was envisaged, and could form the basis of a genuine integrated grammar of speech and writing.

The brilliant analysis of intonation that forms the powerhouse of this description has been evolving for some twenty years, and has been the inspiration for many other studies, some of which are listed in the bibliography. Here, it accounts for interactive meaning in the broader perspective of a grammar, and combines with a phrase generator to create the specifications for meaningful uttterances.

I commend this fascinating book to anyone with an interest either in the spoken language or the grammar of English; they will profit from studying it. For David Brazil's close colleagues, there will be an end to waiting for him to articulate this valuable model.

John Sinclair

Transcription notations

The following notations are used throughout the book:

A	adverbial element
E	adjectival element
N	nominal element
P	preposition
P/N	preposition/nominal element
V	verbal element
V¹	non-finite verbal element
W	open selector
a	suspensive adverbial element
d	article
d°	article with zero realization
e	suspensive adjectival element
n	suspensive nominal element
p	suspensive preposition
v	suspensive verbal element
v¹	suspensive non-finite verbal element
w	suspensive open selector
// //	tone unit boundary
//P//	proclaiming tone
//R//	referring tone
//0//	level tone
//r//	referring tone (non-dominant)
//p//	proclaiming tone (non-dominant)
//r+//	referring tone (dominant)

//p+//	proclaiming tone (dominant)
+	reduplication
Ø	element with zero realization
#	end of increment
&	*and* or *so*

Introduction

An exploratory grammar

Grammars are of many kinds, and it is important to say something at the outset about what kind of grammar this is. There are many ways of describing the differences between them, but one particular way will be useful for present purposes: they may aspire to be definitive or they may be avowedly exploratory. A definitive grammar is helpful if one is in search of what passes for a fact about the way a language works: for instance, if one needs guidance on a question of grammatical correctness or an explanation of something more theoretical—for instance, why certain sentences seem to be capable of two or more quite different interpretations. Such a grammar starts from the assumption that canons of correctness have somehow been established, and/or that well-founded explanations are actually there to be found. Existing definitive grammars do not explain everything, however.

An exploratory grammar is useful if one is seeking possible explanations of some of the many still unaccounted-for observations one may make about the way language works. It accepts uncertainty as a fact of the linguist's life. Its starting-point can be captured in the phrase 'Let us assume that ...' and it proceeds in the awareness that any assertions it makes are based on nothing more than assumptions; the aim is to test these assumptions against observable facts.

The distinction just made is not, of course, so clear-cut in practice, or so well recognized as we may have seemed to suggest. It is, for instance, a hazard of the grammarian's business that users frequently accord definitive status to grammars which their writers have intended to be exploratory: carefully formulated hypotheses are all too likely to be misinterpreted as expressions of God-given truth. It is partly for this reason that the present writer's intentions are emphasized at this point. The book will be of the 'Let us assume ...' kind.

1

Starting assumptions

This book differs from most of the current work in the field of grammar in the rather different set of assumptions it invites readers to entertain. As its title indicates, moreover, it does so specifically in relation to English speech. And for reasons that will be given later, its main focus is upon speech that is produced as monologue.

A common assumption that underpins much comtemporary grammar can be crudely expressed like this:

> Let us assume that the mechanisms whereby words are assembled to make larger units will be revealed to us if we begin by thinking of speakers as aiming, in everything that they do linguistically, at the production of objects which we call 'sentences'.

The alternative that this book explores can then be equally crudely expressed like this:

> Let us assume that the mechanisms whereby words are assembled to make larger units will be revealed to us if we begin by thinking of speakers as pursuing some useful communicative purpose and as aiming, at any one time, at the successful accomplishment of that purpose.

If we say we are seeking to develop a grammar of communication to put alongside existing grammars of sentence-making, we shall have a working description of our intention which will do service until we are able to refine it.

The notion of the sentence is so much part and parcel of what we take grammar to be about that it is not immediately obvious how we can dispense with it as a key part of our conceptual apparatus. It may, indeed, seem perverse to try to do so. At this point it is possible to do no more than give two closely related reasons for making so fundamental a break with tradition.

The first reason is that the notion of sentencehood brings with it the idea of a self-contained object. We think we know where a sentence begins and ends; it has a special kind of completeness that makes it seem to be in some way separable, both from any other speech that may precede or follow it and from the unique background of speaker–hearer understanding against which every sample of purposeful speech operates. To a very large extent, the sentence which has no special context, either of a linguistic or of a 'real world' kind, has been taken to be the proper object of the grammarian's attentions. But it is not characteristic of language users to produce such free-standing objects; they produce pieces of language in the performance of some communicative activity which is meaningful in the situation they presently occupy. The concern of this book is with the language that such users do produce, so it is probably better not to put ourselves in the way of being tempted to entertain the idea of a sentence — that is, a potentially free-standing and unused object — at all.

The second, and in some way more important, reason arises from the first. It is very widely agreed, among those who have approached the task of formulating grammars, that in order to explain how the parts of a sentence are related to each other, a structural model of a rather special kind is necessary. It is the kind of model that enables us to show how small constituents combine with others to make larger constituents, which then combine with others to make even larger ones, and so on — the complete sentence is viewed as a kind of Chinese box assembly. We are not concerned at this point with the many different ways in which this apparently fundamental fact about linguistic structure has been represented, but with the received belief that no grammar of the sentence can do without it. We will enter once more into the realm of supposition:

> Let us suppose that the need for this particular kind of structural description arises directly from the common preoccupation with the potentially free-standing object.

It may be only because we want to be able to abstract away from all the conditions surrounding an act of purposeful speech that such descriptive apparatus is necessary. But language users, engaged as they are with some particular communicative task, can reasonably be expected to take into account what grammarians have so often elected systematically to ignore. Seen from the user's point of view, the notion of an unused and context-free object makes little sense. We may reasonably ask whether the form that the solution takes, that is to say the whole nature of the resulting grammatical description, is simply an inevitable consequence of the peculiar nature of the problem we set out to solve.

Let us therefore further suppose, then, that by taking into account the conditions and circumstances that are accessible to the user, we shall be able to manage without invoking the 'consituent-within-constituent' view of grammar.

Why do we want a linear grammar?

It is essentially the above supposition that this book sets out to explore. It develops one tentative view of how a purpose-driven grammar—as opposed to a sentence-oriented one—might be constructed; and, crucially, it does so without having recourse to any notion of constituency of the hierarchically organized kind.

The reasons for wanting to make such an exploration are discussed at greater length throughout the book. A brief statement will be sufficient here.

Speech is an activity that takes place in time: speakers necessarily say one word, follow it with another and then with another, and so on. There are obvious and well-recognized difficulties in reconciling this increment-by-increment presentation of speech with a hierarchical constituent-within-constituent account of how language is organized. But many aspects of verbal communication can scarcely be investigated at all except in the context of a view of speech as an ongoing event, and there is no need to labour the point that an account of grammar which dispensed with the Chinese box image would be more readily adaptable for use in such investigations.

Users of the book will, therefore, need to be willing to read it in the same exploratory spirit as that in which it was written. It is not directly concerned with specific applications, either to the solution of theoretical problems or to those practical matters in which language teachers and others might be interested but its relevance to such problems and to such pedagogical matters will, it is hoped, become apparent to all who are engaged with them. Its reason for existing is that, given the present state of linguistic knowledge, a serious attempt to take into account the fact that speech proceeds *linearly* is patently desirable.

Discourse analysis

Among the many reasons for this, we might note some of the questions that engage the attention of scholars working in fields that we can broadly describe as discourse analysis and conversational analysis. Very much of the work that has been done in these fields has been described as analysis 'above the sentence', a description which not only takes sentence grammar for granted, as something already described, but also often implies the existence of some kind of barrier or discontinuity. Practitioners on both sides of the barrier tend to take little note of what those on the other side are doing. Yet it is self-evident that those configurations of words that the grammarian calls sentences are, in some inescapable sense, part of the communicative activity that the discourse analyst commonly attends to.

One influential approach to discourse analysis (Sinclair and Coulthard 1975), has used a hierarchically conceived grammatical model as an analogue for 'discourse structure': the various units of discourse are visualized as being in a relationship which parallels the units that a Hallidayan model posits for the relationship among the constituent parts of the sentence (Halliday 1961). This approach has the advantage of recognizing that the two kinds of organization are likely to be essentially of the same kind—that is, language users are unlikely to be operating two distinct organizational systems at the same time. It does not, however, avoid the problem of assuming that they are discontinuous. The units of one mode of analysis can only be described as having a tendency to coincide with those of the other:

> The units of the lowest rank of discourse are acts and correspond most nearly to the grammatical unit clause, but when we describe an item as an act we are doing something very different from when we describe it as a clause. Grammar is concerned with the formal properties of an item, discourse with the functional properties, with what the speaker is using the item for.
> (Sinclair and Coulthard 1975: 27)

The particular kind of discourse that Sinclair and Coulthard had in mind when devising this model was that which teachers and pupils jointly construct in the pursuance of a certain kind of classroom lesson. Modifications of it have been applied to other kinds of discourse. A criticism sometimes voiced is summarized by Stubbs: not all discourse is as highly structured as that of the classroom; such an approach 'is primarily applicable to relatively formal situations in which a central aim is to formulate and transmit pieces of information' (Stubbs 1983: 146); it is less obviously applicable to 'casual conversation between social equals, where the general function of much of the discourse may be phatic and social' (ibid.: 146).

We might add that it is less obviously applicable, too, to the analysis of spoken monologue, since the use made of the central concept of the exchange depends upon there being frequent changes of role as between speaker and listener(s). As Coulthard points out, even within the classroom this presents problems:

> ...at the simplest level there is the question of whether a two-minute lecture by the teacher is one inform or a series.
> (Coulthard 1985: 134)

Although some kinds of discourse can undoubtedly be analysed in accordance with a constituent-within-constituent model, it is less clear that such a model is necessary, in the way that one is considered to be necessary to deal with sentence structure. The constituent parts of events of many kinds can, of course, be perceived to partake in this kind of relationship; but at least some of those events might be equally amenable to description along increment-by-increment lines. When we turn to researchers who have taken conversation, whether casual or otherwise, as their starting-point, we find greater reliance upon a far simpler kind of organization. The concept of the adjacency pair which we owe to Sacks (1967–71) says little about the relationship between certain utterances that is not covered by the observation that one follows the other in time: that answers follow questions, greetings follow greetings, and so on. A particular interest of those who have followed the conversational analysis line has been the efficient management of speaker change. This would seem necessarily to demand attention to what can properly happen at successive moments in the temporal development of the conversation.

This is not the place to speculate about how much of what Sinclair and Coulthard have presented in the context of a hierarchical approach could be re-presented, without serious loss, in terms of a simple linear one. There is good reason to suppose, however, that many of the questions we want to ask about spoken discourse could be sensibly addressed on the basis of the rather unremarkable fact that the events that comprise such discourse occur one after the other.

The task of reconciling two seemingly incompatible accounts of how language is organized at a sub-sentential level, and how discourse is organized at a supra-sentential one can, in fact, be visualized in a way which reverses Sinclair and Coulthard's solution. If discourse can be described in terms of a purely linear apparatus, can grammar—not the grammar of the sentence, but the grammar of the functional increments of which discourse is composed—be described in a similar way? In asking this question we are, of course, questioning the need for the distinction between formal properties and functional properties which Sinclair and Coulthard find it necessary to make. What we are saying is that it is the entity operating as a functional increment in the discourse whose grammatical organization we want to describe. Can we show that word-like objects are arranged in sequences which perform discoursal functions without first showing that they comprise non-functional sentence-like objects? In so doing, can we show how such sequences operate as contributions—which are themselves sequentially arranged—to a discourse? Can we, in other words, dispense with the notion that language users rely upon one set of principles when they are organizing the essential building blocks of their speech—their sentences—but make use of another set in arranging them to meet perceived communicative needs?

What is a sentence grammar?

Before seeking to embark upon an answer to the questions we have just posed, we must look briefly at what the term 'sentence grammar' implies. Anyone familiar with contemporary linguistic scholarship will know that no account is likely to satisfy everyone who is involved in it. Having noted that the term 'grammar', or rather its Greek equivalent, was once used to make very wide reference to 'the art of writing', Lyons goes on to say:

> The history of western linguistic theory until recent times is very largely a history of what scholars at different times held to fall within the scope of 'grammar' taken in this wider sense.
> (Lyons 1968: 133)

What has happened in recent times is that the term has come to have more restricted application:

7

Grammar, we will say, gives rules for combining words to form sentences. It thus excludes, on the one hand, the phonological description of words and sentences, and on the other, an account of the meaning that particular words and sentences bear.
(Lyons 1968: 133)

Lyons is at pains to underline the provisional nature of what he says by pointing out that our notions of 'sentence' and 'word' are not unproblematical: but, in order to proceed we must, for the time being at any rate, take these notions for granted.

If we continue in the spirit of Lyons' tentative formulation, we have also to recognize, as he does, that the mechanisms whereby words are presumed to combine to make sentences can be represented in various ways. Contemporary linguists tend to work in the light of differing views of those mechanisms, views which derive from differing sets of tenets: we have a number of schools of linguistics. We are likely to describe what we practise variously as transformational, systemic, stratificational, functional grammar, and so on. Debate occurs, of course, across the boundaries that these differences create; but it has, to a very much greater extent, occurred between members of one or other of the schools. That is to say, discussion has been carried on within certain assumptions which members of the school have, to use Lyons' words, agreed to 'take for granted'.

We have already said that a fundamental difference that separates the work of some linguists from that of others is the status they confer upon the mechanism, or formalism, that they see themselves as seeking to perfect. A dominant tradition, which owes its inspiration and many of its basic tenets to the work of Chomsky, aspires to what we may think of as a definitive account of natural language. The search is for a formalism which will relate the observable evidence provided by all such language to certain universal features. These features will then be seen to be related to invariable attributes of the human mind. In this view, the goal of linguistics is to be seen as an advance in our understanding of the properties and functions of mind:

At the level of universal grammar, he [the linguist] is trying to establish certain general properties of human intelligence.

Linguistics so characterised is simply the subfield of psychology
that deals with these aspects of the mind.
(Chomsky 1968: 24).

We may note in passing that, in so far as such a grammar makes
the sentence its starting-point, any deductions one may make about
psychological processes will depend for their validity on users
actually using sentences. This is something that this book calls into
question. The claim that Chomsky makes can be expressed roughly
thus:

Knowledge of one's language comprises one's knowledge of how
all the sentences of the language are recognized as sentences, and
of how to make and interpret them as such.

Alongside this, we might propose an alternative claim:

Knowledge of one's language comprises one's ability to engage in
those communicative events with which one is from time to time
confronted.

We can properly speculate as to whether it is only because of the way
the description is set up that the first of these seems to be a logical
prerequisite for the second.

Chomsky acknowledges that other aims may be pursued:

I do not, by any means, intend to imply that these are the only
aspects of linguistic competence that deserve serious study.
(Chomsky 1962: 530)

There seems to be little doubt in his mind, however, that
grammars which do not address the central psychological issue, as he
formulates it, will be intrinsically less interesting than those which
do.

Halliday takes a different position. He sees a grammar as
essentially a tool for the examination of a piece of language with a
particular analytical purpose in mind; the nature of the grammar
may be due then, in part at least, to the nature of the task:

We should not, perhaps, take it for granted that a description in
terms of a formalised model, which has certain properties lacking
in those derived from models of another kind, will necessarily be
the best description for all of the very diverse purposes for which

the descriptions of languages are needed. In assessing the value of a description, it is reasonable to ask whether it has proved useful for the purposes for which it was intended.
(Halliday 1964: 13)

The steps toward a description that are presented in this book are offered in the spirit of Halliday's pluralistic approach. Its primary motivation is, as has been said, the belief that there are many tasks currently facing the student of language, whether within linguistics or in one of the neighbouring disciplines, that might well be tackled more productively with the aid of a grammatical description differing quite radically from any of those that are presently on offer.

Product and process

A hint as to the nature of such a description is provided by Halliday himself:

Traditionally, grammar has always been a grammar of written language: and it has always been a product grammar. ['Product' is here used as one term of the Hjelmslevian pair process/product.] A process/product distinction is a relevant one for linguists because it corresponds to that between our experience of speech and our experience of writing: writing exists whereas speech happens.
(Halliday 1985: xxiii)

Halliday makes the distinction in order to define more clearly the aims of the text-explicating description that he presents. Since 'text' is self-evidently a product, he can properly exclude from consideration those factors which a process-oriented approach would need to take into account. But, there are many other reasons for which we might need to have recourse to a grammatical description; and for some of them, at least, a view of language as something happening might be a more promising starting-point than the more common one—a view of it as something which exists as an object available for *post hoc* examination.

Halliday properly says that such an undertaking involves 'going back to the beginning'. Many of the most basic concepts upon which product grammars have been erected will require re-examination. This will sometimes require comparisons: we may want to compare the way a new kind of formalism might deal with a certain phenomenon to how a previous model would deal with it. Readers trained in the use of one or other of the existing grammars will doubtless find themselves making such comparisons. When this happens some important considerations should be kept in mind. One is that what is said should not be interpreted as a claim that one way of doing the analysis is better than another in any absolute sense. The only way in which 'better' can be used is to say that one solution to a problem is more consistent than another with the principles upon which the present style of analysis is based. Furthermore, the purpose for examining certain instances in this book is simply to demonstrate that the principles underlying a purpose-driven grammar can be applied consistently, and provide worthwhile insights into how users proceed when assembling speech.

Why speech?

Part of the answer to this question has been anticipated in previous paragraphs. Our 'experience of speaking', to use Halliday's term, is of something that begins, continues, and ends in time: it happens. As speakers, we know that causing it to happen is not always without its problems: our ability to put together what we want to say may not always be equal to the pressure to keep up with ourselves, so to speak, in the delivery of our message. As listeners, too, we frequently feel ourselves under similar pressure. The fact that time is passing makes it imperative to decode what we hear promptly so as not to miss what comes next.

Our experience of writing on the other hand is often of something that has been worked out in detail beforehand: the act of careful composition, at least, consists in visualizing more or less clearly what we want to say, assembling the language we need in order to say it, and only then embarking upon the mechanical business of putting it down.

Such a comparison of two distinct modes of proceeding is, of course, far too simple to represent the truth. Much spoken language is pre-planned in considerable detail, and can therefore be expected to exhibit 'product' characteristics. Much writing is done in the kind of unprepared way that we have associated with speech, and left unedited: it can thus be viewed as 'process'. It is no part of the aim of this book to describe how and why speech and writing differ in

11

the way that Halliday (1985) does—though having available a real-time grammar might well be found advantageous by anyone attempting such a task. Speech has been chosen for examination principally because its general nature as an activity happening in time makes it a more transparently suitable object for a 'process' approach. To this we might add two further reasons. Firstly, as we have said, the need for a real-time grammar seems to be most urgent in work upon various kinds of spoken data. Secondly, using spoken data enables us to take into account from the outset a feature which is absent from written data—intonation.

This book is, then, a 'grammar of speech' in that it is a grammar which gives due consideration to those circumstances in which speech is characteristically produced. There is no intended implication in the title that the resulting formalism will be any less capable of accommodating written English than spoken English. It is rather that, by striving to remain aware of the circumstances in which people usually speak, we can more easily escape, so to speak, from some of the suppositions that underlie the various kinds of product grammar available. It is an attempt to describe the word-by-word assembly of speech in a way which takes into account some aspects of what we can, perhaps, agree is the 'reality of speaking'.

Who is it for?

As we have made clear, this book is concerned with some very basic and general considerations that affect our view of how the grammatical organization of speech should be perceived. It stops short of discussing detailed applications. It amounts to an examination of the starting-point at which much of our thinking about linguistic matters originates, and might be considered as dealing with matters that relate to the interests of a number of different kinds of reader.

Firstly, there are those whose interest is in the analysis of spoken data, and in particular those who are concerned in some way with relating recent and current investigations into what happens 'above the sentence' to detailed descriptions of how language is organized 'below' this hypothetical watershed.

Secondly, there are wide-ranging implications in what is proposed here for those who are engaged in teaching English, whether as the mother tongue or as second or foreign language.

In the latter connection, the apparent difference between learning a language and learning *about* it has often made for difficulties in deciding upon appropriate classroom practices. The conflicting demands of learning to communicate and learning grammar have led to a great deal of debate, not all of it well informed. In the mother-tongue situation, the seeming paradox that schoolbook grammar with which students are presented can often seem so difficult to master, even though they have a perfectly adequate working command of their native language, is one of the reasons for a similar longstanding dispute. Opinions vary widely about the usefulness of teaching explicit grammar to such students at all. In both cases, dogmatism has had an unfortunate tendency to take the place of enquiry into why these apparent conflicts exist. The possibility, as this book suggests, that the rule systems purposeful speakers habitually work with are of a quite different kind from those that they find in sentence grammars, might be one which is at least worth entertaining. One might reasonably ask whether difficulties arise because learners of both kinds are being asked to regard as a *product* something which, from their perspective as users, most obviously partakes of the nature of a real-time *process*.

Thirdly, the attempt to adopt a user's perspective might make the book interesting to another kind of reader. The question of the psychological reality of a grammar of a Chomskyan kind has been central to the arguments that followers of that tradition advance. The present book avoids involvement in this kind of argument. It does, however, seek to represent speaker's progress through an utterance—hence, by implication, the listener's interpretation of the utterance—in ways which might reasonably be said to accord with how they would report what they think they are doing; they might, for instance, say that they were telling or asking someone something rather than generating sentences of a declarative or interrogative kind. The terminology is selected, as far as possible, to reflect this. The exposition is couched largely in terms of moment-by-moment decisions. Although there is, of course, no suggestion that these are always, even often, conscious decisions, the method relies upon the convention that they are in some sense real to the users. Whether this convention is anything more than a metaphor, or whether users really are psychologically engaged with the mechanisms in anything like the way suggested, is necessarily an open question. It is a question to which psycholinguists might find it worthwhile addressing themselves.

Finally, the question of the feasibility of a linear, real-time description of syntax is one which currently occupies the attention of those who are engaged in man/machine interaction. If such interaction is to replicate purposeful language, it would seem to be important to get a clear view, not only of how a real-time grammar of such language might be represented, but also of the extent to which participants in a person-to-person interaction are dependent upon pre-existent understandings to appreciate what is going on.

1

The argument and organization of the book

Communicating in time

The starting-point of this book is the commonplace observation that people use speech in the course of their dealings with other people; that it is, moreover, the outcome of those dealings — whether it be, let us say, the successful negotiation of some kind of agreement, or the pleasant passage of a social encounter — that is likely to be most vividly present to their consciousness. The same could be said, of course, of much writing, but reasons were given in the Introduction for restricting our attention to speech.

We can think of anyone who is engaged in, for instance, reporting a sequence of events, or making an enquiry of another party, as being concerned primarily with such matters as what needs to be told or asked at the point in time when the report or enquiry occurs, and with how best to manipulate the available linguistic resources to tell or ask it. We can, moreover, think of the rules that govern that manipulation as being rules for telling or asking things. In other words, we do not necessarily have to assume that the consideration of such abstract notions as 'sentences' enters into the user's scheme of things at all. This does not mean, of course, that trained grammarians, or even informed schoolchildren, will not be able to recognize things they have learnt to call 'sentences' in the outcome; we can suppose, however, that the ability to do this is something over and above the ability to pursue successfully the perceived purpose. The grammar which accounts for how they do it will be a grammar of used speech. It will offer one possible explanation of how speakers manage to do what they think it needful to do linguistically in all the multifarious situations in which they are called upon to operate as communicators.

We can compare this stance with the one which is commonly

adopted: instead of making the initial assumption that competent speakers are first able to make sentences and then proceed to making use of them, we are saying that their competence comprises simply their ability to do what is needful to be done communicatively. If the outcome can then be analysed, using the methods of the sentence grammarian, that is an additional fact about it; but such analysis arises from an after-the-event examination of a sample of language which is no longer serving a here-and-now purpose in any communicative activity. The user does not necessarily have to be proficient in this kind of *post hoc* analysis in order to communicate successfully. Indeed, it has to be learned as a separate, and to many, an irksome and baffling, skill. Neither is it necessary to assume that the 'knowledge of the language system' which such analysis claims to make explicit is actually implicit in what users do. There is no reason why we should not start from a different assumption, namely that the rules that successful speakers obey are rules for doing all the things they need to use language to do.

When people take part in a real speech event, they are manifestly doing much more than stringing words together to make longer entities. The organization of speech events has received a lot of attention during the last twenty years or so; elaborate descriptive schema have evolved to show how the interactive and pragmatic behaviour of participants can result in coherent discourse. Such work has generally been conceived of as extra-grammatical. Indeed, the contention has sometimes been that it was necessary to set up separate procedures for discourse analysis to avoid over-complicating the grammar. Grammar could then concentrate upon describing the unused and uncontextualized sentence. The proposal in this book is: the practice of abstracting away from context and use leads the grammarian into describing a hypothetical system which is far more complex than is necessary if our interest is in how language works in real life. Knowledge that one is pursuing certain communicative ends relative to another party, in a context of which the other party is cognizant, and on the basis of an understanding that participants to an interaction normally co-operate in seeking to understand each other's intentions, provides an enormously rich background to even the most commonplace remark. If we view this understanding as something that one user can rely upon the other bringing to the interpretation of whatever is said, we can remove from the description of grammar the mechanisms that account for many of the differences of meaning we find among unused sentences.

The resulting simplification enables us to give due consideration to one fact about speech that can scarcely be accommodated in a sentence grammar, but which, as we have suggested, is an important consideration in the analysis of spoken discourse: the inescapable fact of the real-time, step-by-step assembly of a spoken utterance.

Immediate constituent grammars

We have already recognized that anyone who tries to describe the organization of natural languages is confronted at the outset by two seemingly contradictory considerations. On the one hand, language is characteristically produced and perceived one increment at a time. Anyone embarking upon a narrative, with, for instance,

My friend told me an amazing story . . .

is bound, by obvious constraints, to say one word and then go on to say the next. Although the act of writing allows more opportunity for re-examining what has been set down, and reshaping larger stretches like sentences or paragraphs, there remains a sense in which even the linear presentation of writing across the page parallels, in space, the occurrence of speech in real time.

But set over against all this is the fact that any understanding of how language works as a system often seems to require that we think in terms of what has come to be known as a 'constituent structure' model. The fundamentals of such a model are perhaps most readily seen in the work on immediate constituency analysis that was carried out in the 1930s. Bloomfield, who introduced the term, says:

> Any English-speaking person who concerns himself with this matter, is sure to tell us that the immediate constituents of *Poor John ran away* are the two forms *Poor John* and *ran away*; and that each of these is, in turn, a complex form; that the immediate constituents of *ran away* are *ran* and *away*; that the constituents of *poor John* are *poor* and *John*.
> (Bloomfield 1933: 161)

Lyons points out the close relationship between this method of analysis and the traditional procedure of parsing sentences into subject and predicate:

> Underlying both approaches to grammatical analysis is the view
> that sentences are not just linear sequences of elements, but are
> made up of 'layers' of *immediate constituents*, each lower-level
> constituent being part of a higher-level constituent. The analysis of
> a sentence into its several 'layers' of constituents can be
> represented graphically in a number of ways. We may use
> brackets: *[(Poor John) (ran away).]* Or we may construct a *tree-
> diagram.* (Lyons 1968: 210–11)

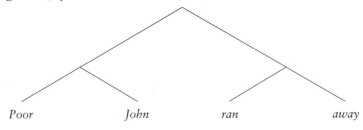

(adapted from Lyons ibid.: 211)

The opening of the narrative to which we shall make frequent
reference in this book can be represented as a number of constituents
which coalesce to form larger constituents, which in turn unite with
others to form larger ones still, and so on, using either of these
conventions:

[(A friend) (of mine)] [(told) (me) (an amazing story)]

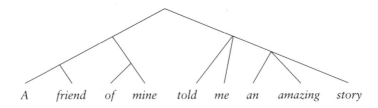

The concept of immediate constituency has been developed and
refined considerably since Bloomfield's day. The various sentence
grammars that are currently available differ in the way they identify
the constituents, in the way the structure-within-structure arrangement is conceptualized, and hence in the details of how the brackets

or the tree diagrams are set out. Some grammarians, like Halliday (1961 etc.) postulate intermediate units between sentence and word such as phrase, group, and clause. There is virtually universal agreement, however, that some such arrangement must be assumed, and a consequence is that there has been a tendency for the linear or real-time presentation of speech to be thought of as having only secondary interest for the grammarian.

All immediate constituency approaches, and all those that have developed from them imply the existence of classes of constituents and some kind of relationship between them. As Robins put it:

> Grammar is concerned with . . . the grouping and classification of recurrent elements of utterance by virtue of the functional places they occupy and the relations they contract with one another in the structures.
> (Robins 1964: 180)

Thus, *poor* and *John* might be classified as adjective and noun respectively because of the places they occupy relative to each other and to the other constituents of the sentence, a classification which involves saying that they stand in some kind of special relationship one with the other of a different kind from the relationships between *ran* and *away* and between the 'higher' constituents *poor John* and *ran away*.

Characterizing these various relationships in readily interpreted terms is not easy. The relationship holding between the 'highest' constituents of a sentence, the first cut into noun phrase and verb phrase is a case in point. A glance at the various attempts that have been made to give conceptual substance to notions like 'the subject of . . .' and 'the predicate of . . .' in teaching grammars and elsewhere makes it clear that Chomsky is right in saying that relationships like these can only be explained by making reference to the formalism that identifies them: thus, in non-technical terms, the subject is one of the 'higher level' constituents of the sentence and the predicate is the other, and that is all there is to be said. In other words, thinking in terms of grammatical relationships commits us to recognizing abstract relationships, which depend for their understanding upon our being familiar with the total system of which they are said to be part (Chomsky 1968).

It has been claimed that an appreciation of how language works depends upon our recognizing the existence of such abstract mechanisms, that is to say mechanisms which can be made accessible to us only if we follow the special procedures that linguistic science provides.

> I think that in order to achieve progress in the study of language and human cognitive faculties in general it is necessary first to establish 'psychic distance' from the 'mental facts' . . . , and then to explore the possibilities for developing explanatory theories, whatever they may suggest with regard to the complexity and abstractness of the underlying mechanisms. We must recognise that even the most familiar phenomena require explanation and that we have no privileged access to the underlying mechanisms . . .
> (Chomsky 1968: 23)

We need neither reject Chomsky's contention outright, nor enter into the largely philosophical argument on which it is based, in order to indulge the right we have claimed to make a contrary supposition: let us suppose that the abstraction we find in so many discussions of how language works is simply a consequence of starting the enquiry in a particular way. We can then go on to ask whether an alternative approach can provide an account of relationships which more nearly reflects a language user's commonsense apprehension of what is happening when we speak.

Finite state grammars

In his highly influential book *Syntactic Structures* (1957), Chomsky provides a technical demonstration of the truth that the sentences of a natural language cannot be accounted for by assuming that speakers make use of a simple left-to-right, or real-time mechanism. Such a mechanism, or finite state grammar, can be described informally as follows: after the first element of a sentence has been chosen and produced, it sets up a state in which only certain ways forward are possible; the subsequent element sets up another set of constraints upon what can come next, and so on. So, for instance, if a sentence begins with *The* . . . , we should not expect any of the words *an*, *strongly* or *walked* to follow immediately after it, and might reasonably conclude that this was because the rules prevented it. Writing such a grammar would involve us in arranging all the words of the language in classes such as verbs, nouns and pronouns, and discovering rules which would determine what might come after what in the increment-by-increment presentation of a sentence.

It is easy to show that such a rule system would be immensely complicated, even if it had to deal only with fairly simple sentences. Complication is scarcely an issue, however, if we accept Chomsky's contention that the nature of language is such that it would be impossible to achieve. His demonstration of this fact (Chomsky 1957: 21–24) is probably one of the least questioned arguments in the literature of linguistics. We neither question nor seek to expound it here. The point is that it is intended and is to be understood as a contribution to the elaboration of sentence-oriented grammars. Since our concern is with purpose-driven language, and since we are supposing that this operates on an essentially increment-by-increment basis, we shall have to show that in the circumstances we visualize for the production of used language, a finite state grammar is a possibility.

Summary of the argument

The position we have reached can be summarized provisionally as follows:

1 Since speakers manifestly *do* put their speech together piecemeal and in real time, we might expect to get closer to an understanding of what language is like for the user (as opposed to the sentence grammarian) if we take this into account from the outset.
2 If we approach used speech as purpose-driven activity, it may no longer be necessary to give priority in our grammar to a non-linear view of linguistic organization.
3 It might then be possible, by starting with a different set of assumptions about what it is we are describing, to develop an alternative grammar which fits more comfortably with our commonsense apprehension that, in some far from negligible sense, speakers assemble their utterances a bit at a time as they go along.
4 We might expect there to be advantages, in some of those areas of linguistic enquiry where grammars are needed, to seeking a clearer understanding of what language might be said to be like to speakers and hearers, operating, as they characteristically do,

in the context of a need to meet some specific communicative need.

Development of the description

Chapter 2 looks more closely at what we shall describe as 'used speech' and particularly at the circumstances in which it characteristically occurs. The purpose is to show how the activity of communicating verbally differs from what sentence grammarians do when they analyse specimens in order to display the working of the system.

In Chapter 3 we shall narrow our focus to the kind of speech that this book is primarily about: that is to say, language which serves a 'telling' purpose. Besides distinguishing formally between 'telling' and 'asking', we shall ask what are the least features that a stretch of speech must display, both syntactically and intonationally, in order to tell someone something.

Chapter 4 outlines the basic requirements of a grammar which assumes that speech is assembled increment by increment in real time to form a chain, viewing the process of assembly as a step-by-step modification of a State—as a progress from an Initial State to a Target State.

The descriptive mechanism is developed further in Chapter 5, where the use of non-finite verbal elements is considered as one way of extending the range of chains that the finite state grammar can produce without destroying its crucial finite state properties.

In Chapter 6 we begin to address the question of why many pairs of chains which have identical descriptions when viewed simply as sequences of items seem nevertheless to require different kinds of interpretation. The concept of 'indeterminacy' is introduced, and the argument is advanced that such differences generally derive from the particular communicative task the speaker is engaged in, rather than from abstractly conceived relationships.

Chapters 7, 9, and 10 are concerned with the details of how verbal elements are used. In particular, a general account is given of how these elements work together within the linear framework to indicate the timing of events, conditions, and other considerations. Chapter 8, which interrupts this sequence, does so in order to provide a necessary discussion of the here-and-now selective potential of certain stretches of language, and so make possible the introduction of the notion of communicative sufficiency.

Chapter 11 describes more procedures which enable the finite state mechanisms that have been proposed to produce chains which have not yet been taken into the analysis. Chapters 12 and 13 respectively then add to this two further features of those mechanisms, namely zero realization and open selection, which will further increase the ability of the grammar to describe the multiplicity of chains found in real speech.

In Chapter 14 there is more detailed attention to nominal elements, sequences of words which have so far been left unanalysed.

Chapters 15 and 16 focus upon those parts of the talk whose function is to characterize the discourse itself in some way rather than to contribute directly to that which the discourse is communicating. Such talk is represented as serving one of two purposes: indicating what (some part of) the discourse counts as, or indicating what it is about.

Chapter 17 provides a brief discussion of how a method of analysis which has been applied almost exclusively to telling can be extended to deal with what speakers do when they are asking.

The question of why certain kinds of utterance are not encountered in used speech—some of which would be said to be ungrammatical in a sentence-based framework—is raised in Chapter 18, the aim being to show how non-occurrence can be explained by reference to a linear mode of analysis. A short sample analysis, in which the tools we have proposed are applied, word by word, is provided in Chapter 19.

Chapter 20 provides a retrospective summary of the kind of grammar we have presented, and concludes with a general discussion of its main features and its wider implications for linguistics and language teaching. A summary of the intonation system referred to in the book is given in the Appendix.

2
Used language

We have already said that we shall be concerned with used language: that is to say, language which has occurred under circumstances in which the speaker was known to be doing something more than demonstrate the way the system works. We are concerned also with language which has been produced as speech rather than as writing. In this chapter we will look, in an informal and preliminary way, at some of the more obvious facts about the kind of naturally occurring spoken discourse that we are interested in.

Clearly it will be more satisfactory if we do this while having in mind a sample of speech which actually has been produced under the circumstances we have specified. There follows a written transcription of an oral narrative, let us call it the Little Old Lady, a discourse type that is a not untypical outcome of a common kind of social activity: a single offering in the sort of anecdote-swapping session that makes up a significant part of many people's everyday, relaxed, conversation.

Sample of data

(Dots are used to indicate hesitations in the narrative.)
A friend of mine told me this amazing story the other day she was a . . . she'd been shopping and she came back to this multi-storey car park that she's been in and it was kind of deserted . . . erm . . . and as she was walking towards her car she saw this figure sitting in the passenger seat . . . she thought what's that I've been burgled and as she walked towards the car feeling a bit scared this person got out of the car and it was a little old lady . . . so she thought oh well probably it's not a burglar and . . . er . . . anyway she asked her and the woman said . . . er . . . apparently she'd been sitting there waiting for her daughter to arrive and the daughter hadn't turned up and she was feeling a bit giddy and faint and so she went and sat in the car . . . it seems a very strange thing to do . . . I mean . . . apparently she'd been trying all the door handles one

was open so she sat in it . . . so anyway . . . this friend of mine . . . erm . . . said . . . you know . . . what are you going to do now . . . when are you meant to be meeting your daughter and the woman said half an hour ago so she said well . . . what are you going to do now and anyway . . . finally this woman asked her if . . . er . . . she could possibly give her a lift home because it was freezing and this old lady looked really ill and my friend thought oh . . . I'd better be nice and it was a bit out of her way but she thought she'd better do the . . . do the . . . do the right thing . . . so she piles her in the car and they go off . . . and as they're driving along she just happens to look across and sees her hands . . . and they weren't woman's hands at all . . . they were man's hands . . . it's got hairy big hairy hands . . . the little old dear's clothes on . . . a funny little hat and everything . . . but these big man's hands God . . . what am I going to do now and she looked down . . . and she'd got men's shoes on . . . and she looked again at the face . . . and it was a man's face and she thought God . . . he's a maniac . . . what am I going to do so very cleverly she got to this roundabout and she missed the turning that she should have gone off and she went down the next turning and the little old lady said where are you going dear we've . . . missed my turning so this friend of mine said well I'm sorry I'm . . . I don't know this area very well . . . I'd better turn round so she went up to . . . found a driveway and it was dark by this time and so she said . . . she pretented to be . . . you know . . . a hopeless female driver and said oh . . . I'm terribly sorry I'm not very good at this sort of thing would you mind getting out of the car and directing me at the back so this bloke . . . the little old lady gets out of the car and the moment he's out of the car she slams the door and shoots straight off and leaves her behind . . . so . . . anyway . . . this isn't the end of the story she then drives to a police station and reports the whole thing tells them all about it and the police sort of nod to each other and look a bit knowing . . . you know would you mind if I just borrowed your car keys as we'd like to search your car they went outside and when they came back a quarter of an hour later they asked her what is in the car she says oh . . . a handbag . . . and my shopping . . . and this and that so he says anything else she says no . . . no . . . there's the tools . . . and the spare tyre . . . and she goes through everything she can think of in the car and they said anything else and she said no and it's then they tell her do you know what's in the back seat of the car . . . underneath the back seat of the car . . . an axe.

The circumstances in which this tale was told and recorded are relevant to our present concerns. It was, in fact, retold to someone who hadn't yet heard it, shortly after the teller had heard it from someone else. In the version given here most of the substantive details of the first telling were faithfully preserved, though a few were omitted and others were added. It was evident that the teller had a good grasp of the complete story before he started, and was indeed able to make rather sophisticated use of what he remembered in order to give an effective shape to his retelling.

A comparison of his version with the version he had just heard shows, however, that in so far as the word-by-word organization of the language was concerned, he was, as one would expect, largely making up what he said as he went along. There was no question of his repeating *verbatim* the language of the other teller. This circumstance of now-coding is, as we shall see, of considerable importance for the argument of the book.

We will say no more for the moment about the adequacy of this anecdote as data upon which to base generalizations. It is enough to say that its use will be in keeping with an important principle: that our primary interest is in providing a way of describing such samples, rather than in discussing examples invented for the purpose. And it represents, beyond any reasonable doubt, a stretch of language which results from piecemeal, or incremental, composition.

Let us proceed now to some fairly commonplace observations. Although they could all be truthfully made of either speech or writing, it is in relation to the former mode that their implications will be considered here.

Used speech is purposeful

We have already said that speech is characteristically used in pursuit of a purpose. That is to say, it has some non-exemplificatory function in what we may broadly call the management of human affairs. The practice of inventing a sentence or of taking some real-life sentence out of its context in order to pose questions about its grammaticality, its structure or its meaning is a practice of the sentence grammarian, not the user.

There are, of course, many ways of describing the purpose that a particular utterance might be intended to serve. We have referred to the speaker of the Little Old Lady narrative as the 'teller', and might therefore be seen to have pre-empted the decision as to what his purpose is: it is to *tell* whoever is listening about his friend's alarming experience. But this judgement is unlikely to recognize the whole truth: such a tale might well have been intended to warn listeners against giving lifts to strangers; or, in the context of a convivial evening, its purpose might have been to entertain them; or, if it were one of those competitive events in which each person tries to go one better than the other, its purpose might have been to outdo them, or 'cap' another's offering. Clearly, attending to purpose in a commonsense way like this does not enable us to put an unquestionably appropriate label on many stretches of speech.

The fact that we do not know whether the purpose is to warn, entertain, or outdo the listener does, however, help us to resolve the problem, at least provisionally. For these ways of describing what the speaker sets out to do are of a different level of generality from telling. We could properly say that he warns, entertains, or outdoes his listener *by telling* the story. Our present interest is in describing the linguistic mechanisms — those mechanisms we refer to collectively as 'grammar' — that he has available for his use in doing all these things. Knowing whether the anecdote is intended, for instance, to warn is not a matter of recognizing its grammatical features: it is rather a matter of taking due note of the complexity of circumstances in which the tale is told: essentially, are the participants in a situation and in a relationship where offering such a warning is an appropriate thing to do? We will take it, for the time being at least, that if we describe the mechanisms speakers use in telling, we shall have thereby described the mechanisms they require for all those other purposes they pursue by telling. To put the matter slightly differently: if we know how people manage to tell, we know how they do all those other things they do by telling.

This position will have to be reviewed later, and in Chapters 15 and 16 we will look more closely at what, on this view of the matter, count as secondary purposes. Meanwhile, we shall take telling to be one of the primary purposes which speakers need the means to pursue.

The act of telling implies a certain distribution of knowledge as between speaker and hearer; and if the knowledge is assumed to be distributed differently—if it is the hearer who knows and the speaker who doesn't—the purpose of the utterance might be said to be to ask rather than to tell. Understanding whether one is being told or asked is much like understanding whether one is being warned or entertained. It depends upon one's judgment of present circumstances: specifically, in this case, upon who is supposed to know what. There is, however, another way in which asking and telling differ: they involve a different deployment of our grammatical resources. The distinction is, therefore, one that properly attracts the grammarian's attention.

We shall refer to the act of asking in most of this book only in order to help provide a working definition of the complementary act of telling. This will be our first task in the next chapter. Thereafter asking will not be examined until Chapter 17. Neither will the pursuit of other possible primary purposes be considered until then. The main concern in this book will be with the grammar of telling. This is dictated partly by the need to make the most economical use of available space, but there is a more important reason. Adopting this procedure enables us to go a long way towards showing how the mechanisms work in circumstances where their working is most obvious. The findings then provide a convenient base from which to go on to take in other possibilities.

Going through the motions

There is just one other aspect of what we have said in the last few paragraphs that ought perhaps to be enlarged upon before we proceed. A distinction is often made between speech which actually results in a transfer of information (I tell you the time) and speech which serves rather to oil the wheels of social intercourse (I ask you how you are, or invite you to agree that it is unseasonably warm for February). Although this difference is of considerable importance to language users, it does not, in fact, appear to be marked in any regular way in the organization of the utterance. There is, for instance, no predictable difference between the form taken by a genuine enquiry about your health and that taken by an enquiry made simply to make you feel noticed or to re-establish contact with you before launching upon the serious business of the encounter. Once more, we can say that speakers do one thing by doing another: we pursue an unspecified social purpose by going through the motions of telling or asking, and it is the latter account of the event that we shall want to concentrate upon here.

The importance of the point does, in fact, go well beyond those utterances that have a clearly phatic or social function. Although we have just associated telling and asking with an implicit distribution of knowledge, we must keep in mind that what is implicit in people's behaviour does not always correspond to the real situation at all: a teller might easily know less than the listener, or an asker might know more than the listener. The motives for going through the motions of telling and asking are multifarious; perhaps only in a minority of cases is it to bring about a straightforward transfer of knowledge. But it is enough for our present purposes to say that participants in a speech event regularly behave as if transfer of knowledge were their intention.

In the final analysis we cannot, of course, attribute to either of the parties to a conversation definitive and comprehensive knowledge of what the other party knows. They must nevertheless proceed for the most part as if they had such knowledge; and we can say that the narrative about the Little Old Lady would have been in no way different for us if the person to whom it was being told just happened to have heard it first-hand from the friend but was too polite to say so!

Interaction

Speech is interactive. This word is often used to indicate the observable participation of two parties: thus, according to this usage, conversation might be said to be interactive, because both parties contribute, while a spoken lecture, or an uninterrupted narrative, is not. Its use here, in relation to what we are calling 'monologue' is obviously different. It acknowledges that speakers characteristically pursue their purposes with respect to a second party. Acts of telling and asking both presuppose the existence of someone to tell or someone to ask. Moreover, they presuppose that someone has his or her own separate perspective upon the situation, and this perspective is systematically taken into account by the teller or asker; for each situation there are in-built constraints upon what could reasonably be told or asked.

What can be told or asked?

The friend is said to respond positively to the policeman's request to borrow her car keys and this seems likely because, according to her view of the prevailing circumstances, it would probably seem a reasonable thing for him to ask; and we can take it that his making of the request took account of the fact that she would be likely to take this view. To take another case, we are not told exactly what the old lady said when the friend found her sitting in her car, but we can be pretty sure that it would be an immediate explanation of what she was doing there; on any reasonable analysis, that would be what the circumstances demanded. She would answer the question that could be assumed to be in the friend's mind, even if the latter had not yet articulated it. We can say, indeed, that at any point in any verbal encounter, there are more or less binding restrictions upon what, in the light of the present circumstances, it would be appropriate to say to the particular person one is addressing. Sensitivity, both to situation and to the viewpoint of the other person within that situation, is constantly demanded of the speaker, and it is in this sense that we shall say that used language is interactive, even when one participant makes no observable contribution.

To consider the matter in a little more detail, let us imagine the conversation after the old lady has asked to be taken to her daughter's home. At some point, she must have been asked for, or perhaps have volunteered, information about where her daughter lived. A large number of perfectly truthful ways of giving it would doubtless have been available, as perhaps:

opposite the Rose and Crown

thirteen Mulberry Road

next to the Parkers

The choice she made from some such heterogeneous collection as this would depend upon her assessment of what, at the present moment, and taking into account what little she knew of the friend's knowledge of the town, it would be most useful to say.

Communicative need

We can use this constructed example to introduce a notion we will call 'communicative need'. For each occasion on which we speak, there are certain requirements we must seek to satisfy. It is our perception of these requirements that lies behind our purposeful utterances: we pursue a purpose that is in some sense imposed upon us by our reading of the present situation *vis-à-vis* our listener; and our listener's perception of that situation provides a framework within which to interpret what we say.

Participants co-operate

Both the concept of interaction, as we have outlined it above, and that of communicative need depend for their usefulness upon our postulating another condition for normal language use: both require that participants are co-operative. Essentially, this means no more in the present context than that speakers make the best judgements they can manage as to present communicative needs and do the best they can to satisfy them; and listeners in their turn assume that what they hear is designed to match those needs. The point can be illustrated by another constructed example. Suppose that, on being found sitting in the friend's car, the old lady had remarked:

It's the tenth of October

What might the friend have done in the face of such an unexpected comment? One possibility would have been to conclude that the lady was not rational and take her to the police station for her own safety. But to do this would be to step outside ordinary conversational behaviour. There would be no wilful withholding of co operation here, just an abandonment of the game. Alternatively, she might have taken the remark to be an appropriate one, but one whose relevance she had failed to grasp. It may, for instance, in the old lady's perception of the matter, have been the departure point for an explanation which went something like this:

31

It's the tenth of October . . . it's my grandson's birthday . . . I had arranged to meet my daughter here and . . .

Having concluded, therefore, that the problem is her own failure to meet the old lady halfway in matching what she has been told to her present need, the friend can do either of two things: she can say that she doesn't see the relevance of the remark and ask to have it elucidated; or she can behave as if she had seen the relevance and proceed with the conversation (probably bringing it round again rather quickly to the unexplained presence of the old lady).

Dealing with mismatches

What these options demonstrate is that the parties to a verbal interaction are not bound, nor could they be bound, to co-operate all the time; nor are they necessarily successful when they try to co-operate. Misjudgements are inevitably made when one participant's behaviour is putatively related to the other participant's view of things, unless both happen to be mind-readers. But notice that the last two ways we have described of dealing with the problem exhibit further manifestations of co-operativeness. By saying something like:

I'm sorry but I don't see how that explains why you were sitting in my car

the friend behaves as though what the old lady said was intended to be pertinent, and co-operatively points out that there is a miscalculation somewhere; or, by absorbing the unexpected remark, unexplained and not yet understood, into the conversation, she tacitly accepts the good faith of the other speaker and co-operatively assumes that any relevance it may have will become apparent later.

Projecting a need

This last propensity of hearers, this willingness to accept the relevance of what is heard, in advance of the circumstances that would make its relevance apparent, is particularly important for any discussion of the kind of data we have chosen to illustrate this chapter. The teller makes clear that what he is telling is a story and by so doing he relieves himself of much of the responsibility either for tailoring what he says to a pre-existing situation or for making it responsive in a detailed way to any perceived communicative need. It is expected of listeners to stories that they will take on trust the eventual relevance of much of what they hear. To put it another way, it is for the teller to decide, in the light of a private knowledge of what happens later, what the communicative needs are at each stage in the unfolding narrative. The special circumstances that normally attend a story-telling impose a special requirement upon co-operating listeners: they are expected to acquiesce in being kept to a large extent in the dark about why they are being told one thing rather than another.

We shall proceed, then, in the expectation that the language mechanisms we are interested in will be substantially exhibited in the vast majority of cases where speakers are successfully co-operative. It should then be possible to see what additional mechanisms may be necessary for rectifying the results of non-co-operation or unsuccessful attempts to co-operate.

Existential values

To treat speech as the pursuit of purpose, co-operatively conducted by two interacting parties, is to take a very different view from that which lies behind orthodox grammatical descriptions. It may make heavy demands upon the imagination of anyone whose present thinking has been conditioned by that orthodoxy. The same is true of a fourth characteristic which we shall attribute to used speech, namely that it exploits the here-and-now values of the linguistic items that speakers make use of. Some explanation of this characteristic must be offered here, though a fuller account is better postponed until we have discussed certain aspects of the significance of intonation in Chapter 8.

Meaning and value

Any discussion of the way words and sentences carry 'meanings' that goes beyond the framing of simple pocket dictionary-like definitions turns out to be more complex than might have been expected. Indeed, the use of quotation marks for 'meaning' is necessary as an acknowledgement of the judgement of philosophers and semanticists that the significance of this word is, in itself, a considerable problem: what do we mean by 'meaning'?

33

Essentially, traditional practice provides us with two ways of approaching the problem. We may start with the idea that the word owes its meaning to a conventional relationship with some class of things or some concept that we think exists in the non-linguistic world. If we adopt this position, 'roundabout' means, for instance, a particular form of traffic control that motorists and others have decided collectively to refer to by that word; 'terrified' signifies a generally recognized condition which results from experiences like finding you may well have a disguised maniac sitting beside you in your car. Alternatively, we may think of the meaning of a word as deriving from the relationships it has with other words in the 'system'. Thus the meaning of 'friend' might be thought to be a matter of how it is related to other words in English, let us say as a synonym of 'ally' and an antonym of 'enemy'. It is a version of the second approach that provides the basis for the notion we shall call 'existential value'.

The idea of a relationship, whether of synonymy or antonymy or any other, is usually regarded as part of a set of such relationships which, taken together, embrace the entire vocabulary of the language; and it is thought of as existing more or less permanently and independently of speakers. It is then available to them for reference purposes, as a kind of grid of reliable meaning distinctions and similarities whereby to designate things and ideas. Thus, in the small section of the system into which 'friend' immediately fits, we have various words like 'enemy', 'ally', 'acquaintance', 'stranger', each of which has a 'meaning' which can be thought of as always and unquestionably excluding it. We say 'He's not a friend, he's an acquaintance/stranger', and so on. Let us, instead, consider the possibility of relationships between words existing in the present state of shared understanding between the speaker and the listener.

Existential antonyms

We will take antonymous relationships first: that is to say we will look at the way in which one word is used in order to signify exclusion of one or more alternatives. While one might easily imagine a situation in which 'my friend' could be paraphrased by 'not my enemy', there are certainly others where reference to 'friends' is intended to exclude 'relatives', and yet others where it excludes 'acquaintances'. Seen in this light, the communicative value of the word can be said to depend upon the circumstances under which it is used. Instead of thinking of meaning as a property which is inherently attached to the word, we can focus upon the way people use words—and, indeed, other linguistic items—to create oppositions, as in 'friend not relative', 'friend not merely acquaintance', which are of relevance to whatever communicative purpose is presently being pursued. We shall take it that it is this temporary, here-and-now opposition that provides the word with the value that the speaker intends and that the listener understands.

If we now examine how 'my friend' is actually used in the Little Old Lady narrative it becomes apparent, in fact, that none of the oppositions we have just considered is relevant to the telling of the tale. The difference between 'friend' and any of the possible antonyms we have proposed has no bearing upon the narrative; indeed, the narrative could be fully appreciated by anyone who happened, for some reason, not to have any of those antonyms in their vocabulary. The oppositions we need to know about in order to understand what 'my friend' stands for are oppositions that belong to the story itself. It is no more than a label for one of the people that the story is about. At the beginning, it serves to indicate that the narrator is not referring to the person sitting in the car. It is, in fact, used only sparingly thereafter, but it is possible to find or suppose occurrences, at successive stages in the narrative, when its communicative value would be 'not the little old lady', 'not the disguised maniac', and 'not a policeman', depending on which of these other members of the cast happens to be involved in the action at the time.

We shall see that appreciating the way users rely upon special here-and-now oppositions like this is crucial for an understanding of how used language works. And obviously it is of a piece with the other characteristics we have separated out for discussion in this chapter. We are suggesting, in effect, that the communicative value of any item is negotiated between participants as the discourse unfolds. If we want to know what a speaker intends to refer to we may be involved in knowing what, on this particular occasion, it is intended to exclude. And the this-not-that relationship may well be one that exists only in the world of understanding that the speaker and hearer assume they presently share.

Such a procedure can be successful, of course, only if both parties are set to take full account of the purpose and the conversational setting of the utterance. Only a co-operative willingness to perceive what communicative value is intended for a particular use of, for instance, 'my friend' would make communication possible.

It will, indeed, be apparent that we have been doing no more in this chapter than single out for separate examination, aspects of used speech that are all interrelated and interdependent, and arise from taking essentially the same view of the speech event.

Scholarly background

We have deliberately presented the ideas in this chapter as observations that derive from nothing more than a commonsense approach to our everyday experience of using language. Readers familiar with current work in the field of pragmatics will know that each of the observations has been incorporated into carefully articulated theories in some branch of that area of study. Much of what is said about purpose, for instance, invites a more formal examination in terms of the work by Austin (1962), Searle (1969), and others on speech act theory. The term 'phatic communion', used to refer to speech events which are not information-exchanging, derives from Malinowski (1923). Labov's (1970 and 1972) complementary concepts of A-event and B-event lie behind what has been said about the telling/asking distinction. There is relevant discussion of the nature of verbal interaction in Abercrombie (1964) and elsewhere. No reference to conversational co-operation can be other than indebted to the seminal work of Grice (1975). The whole area of semantics within which our brief reference to existential value ought ideally to be placed is covered by Lyons (1977).

To make anything more than passing reference to the various parts of this rapidly developing background would require a book to itself. Interested readers are referred to Levinson (1983) for a thorough coverage. There is an important sense, however, in which anything approaching a review of related literature would be out of place here, even if there were room for it. The work that scholars like those mentioned above have initiated and inspired has not, in general, been concerned with the question that engages our present interest: it has not been their aim to show how the observations they make might affect our view of the detailed organization of sentences, or—as we shall prefer to say—of purpose-oriented increments of speech. The main thrust of their work has been determined by an interest in something other than grammar: in questions raised in philosophy, anthropology, sociolinguistics, and so on. Our present interest is not in building upon their insights in terms of those knowledge-structures that they themselves have worked in. It is rather in recognizing that, taken together, they lead us to a particular perception of the nature of used speech, a perception that invites a question they themselves have not asked: if verbal communication really works like this, what does this lead us to expect the so-called 'sub-sentential' organization of discourse to be like? How do these observations, taken severally and collectively, affect our perception of how words are added to words to make useful language?

Process and product

To put the whole matter in a slightly different perspective, let us conclude this chapter by expanding upon the distinction we made in the introduction between *product* and *process*.

We suggested that Halliday's reference to this distinction is useful in that it helps to clarify a distinction we are seeking to make, between what might be described as an orthodox, sentence-based linguistic perspective, and a purpose-driven one.

When analysing a piece of language we can, if we wish, assume—and most often grammarians *do* assume—that the object we are analysing already exists in its entirety. It is assumed that there is a complete sentence or a complete text available to work on. One can therefore range backwards and forwards over the whole of the object in search of structural or other relationships among its parts. To insert the brackets or draw the tree diagram, one needs to have everything there in place beforehand. This is a style of analysis that can be described as examination after the event. What we have proposed in this book is something different. It is a method of analysis which effectively rules out an after-the-event approach to the matter. We are trying to think of discourse as something that is now-happening, bit by bit, in time, with the language being assembled as the speaker goes along. This means that we can no longer use the essentially static concept of 'constituent structure', because the function of one structure within the organization of larger structures can be explored only if everything is present simultaneously. In its place we shall use the dynamic notion of a sequence of States. In this view, each successive State is to be thought of as being replaced by a new State, as item succeeds item along the time dimension.

It has been very properly pointed out that product-oriented and process-oriented descriptions of language are not necessarily in opposition (see, for instance, Enkvist 1982: 22). A set of rules which accurately describes the organization of a product, let us say the sentence

My friend told me an amazing story the other day

might well amount, according to some grammarians at least, to a set of instructions, temporally ordered, for carrying out the various processes which will generate the desired product, a sentence. It would not be to the present point to explore the implications of this proposal. It is, however, very much to the point to recognize that the usefulness of the idea of a process as a conceptual tool is dependent upon there being some prospective output towards which the process contributes.

The purposeful increment

Let us think for a moment of the metaphorical implications of the words we are using. In the current parlance of commerce, 'products' may be as various as insurance policies or packaged holidays, but these applications are extensions of a more common practice which restricts usage to material objects like chairs and tables. A woodworker idly chipping away at a piece of wood is not normally thought of as carrying out a process. For this term to apply, some particular wooden article must be assumed to be in view. A process is recognizable as such because it contributes to the making of some recognizable object. We can say that it is the proposed outcome that defines the activity as a process. When we apply the analogy to linguistic matters, the question arises as to what outcome speakers have in mind when they carry out process after process in creating a piece of discourse.

The assumption among grammarians who adopt the generative

approach, and by many others, has generally been that what they are aiming at is some abstractly conceived entity, a sentence; and it is in some sense the apprehension of this goal that determines the performance of each successive process. We shall proceed from a different assumption: the end that speakers have in view is one which relates more directly to their common understanding of what they are about. Having said that the producers of used language are engaged in the pursuit of some communicative purpose, let us suppose that the entities they aim to produce are such as will contribute directly to the achievement of that purpose. When, for instance, the proposed purpose is to tell, let us suppose that the intended outcome is a 'telling increment'.

When we give conceptual priority to purpose in this way, we find that we have to re-examine the fundamental postulates of sentence grammar; and we arrive at the realization that, if any part of the outcome looks like a sentence, this comes about as an interesting by-product of the processes we are interested in, not as the planned outcome to which those processes owe their definition.

Our aim, then, is to discover, not how language is organized into sentences, but how it is organized in pursuit of communicative purposes. This does not, of course preclude the possibility that what we shall call a 'telling increment' or an 'asking increment' may often be indistinguishable from what a sentence grammarian calls a sentence. But neither does it rule out the likelihood that the two will not always coincide. In any case, it will be the ability of a stretch of speech to achieve a purpose that will be focal, not its possible status as a sentence.

3

Telling and asking exchanges

In this book, we shall be concerned, for the most part, with telling as a conversational purpose. It will be useful if, at this point, we establish some criteria whereby a stretch of language which is produced for this purpose can be recognized. We will do so by comparing it with one whose purpose is to ask.

If, as we said was likely to happen, the old lady in the narrative (pp 24–6) had volunteered an explanation of why she was in the friend's car, she might have said

(1) I just had to sit down somewhere

to which the friend might have replied initially, and noncommitally, 'Oh' or 'Oh dear' or 'I see'. A little later, the friend might have said something like

(2) Where does your daughter live

to which the reply would, perhaps, have been 'opposite the Rose and Crown'. In these cases, both of the participants have now contributed to the dialogue: together they have produced an exchange. To this extent they are similar. There is, however, an obvious difference between the two. In (1) the rejoinder is some kind of receipt for information received: an acknowledgement that the old lady's contribution amounted to what she presumably intended it to be—an appropriate thing to say in the circumstances. But notice that, in itself, its occurrence results in no further progress being made in the information-exchanging business that is in hand. The telling that the old lady realized was called for is actually achieved before the receipt token is issued. Indeed, if the friend had exercised the option of not acknowledging receipt of the information, as she might easily have done, this would in no way have affected the achievement of that purpose; she would not have been able truthfully to claim that she had not been told.

But if the friend's purpose in (2) is to find out something that she did not know, that purpose is not achieved until the response has been made. Once it has been made, the initiator may (or may not) produce a receipt token, 'Oh', or 'I see', effectively acknowledging achievement in a way which resembles the function of the second part in the telling exchange.

Not all the exchanges in real data are as simple as these, but we can use the two straightforward examples to provide a working characterization of exchange types:

Telling exchanges: Tellers simultaneously initiate and achieve their purpose; the hearer may (or may not) then acknowledge the achievement.

Asking exchanges: Askers initiate, but their purpose is not achieved until hearers make an appropriate contribution; initiators may then acknowledge (or not acknowledge) the achievement.

(See Figure 3.1 for a comparison of telling and asking exchanges.)

Since the possible acknowledgement in (1) is as real (if it occurs) as is the essential completion in (2), we will say that both purposes are achieved by exchanges rather than by single utterances. This practice is in line with our earlier assertion that used language is interactive, even if one party says nothing.

Initiator	Other participant	Initiator
I just had to sit down	(I see)	
Where does she live?	Opposite the Rose and Crown	(I see)

Figure 3.1

The telling increment

Sentence grammar is typically concerned with this question: what, in terms of the sentence grammarian, constitutes a satisfactorily turned out product—that is to say, a 'grammatical sentence'? So long as we remain with utterances whose purpose is to tell, we can pose a parallel question: what constitutes a satisfactory telling exchange?

Or, since a single speaker's contribution is sufficient for a satisfactory act of telling, what are the conditions that a telling increment must satisfy, if it is to achieve the purpose for which it was produced?

Our question differs in one important respect from that of the sentence grammarian: it cannot be answered in a simple way which will apply to all cases. Sentence grammars aspire to distinguish in some absolute way between all good sentences of the language and all sequences of words which are not sentences. But the exact requisites for an act of telling depend, as we have said, upon the present communicative needs of the hearer — upon what, on the particular occasion in question, needs to be told. They can never be specified in advance of a knowledge of, or at least of a reasonable supposition concerning, what that need is. At the beginning of our story

She'd been shopping

amounts to a satisfactory telling increment: it tells the hearer all that it is deemed necessary to know about the friend's recent activities, and it provides a sufficient departure point for what is to be told next, namely that she went back to the car park. But in another story, the hearer's appreciation of subsequent events may require specification of where she had been shopping, or of when, or even of both where and when. Giving this information will require a longer increment, such as:

She'd been shopping in Oxford Street
She'd been shopping the previous Friday
She'd been shopping in Oxford Street the previous Friday

These possible telling increments provide illustrations of a linear principle that we shall refer to again in the next chapter and frequently thereafter: the apprehension of the particular need that the speaker is seeking to satisfy determines how far it is necessary to go on adding word to word.

Minimum requirements for telling: syntactic

Clearly, we cannot fix on any point in a sequence of words and say 'this is the moment at which, no matter what the circumstances, a speaker's purpose of telling will be achieved'. It is, nevertheless, possible to recognize certain minimum conditions that any telling increment must satisfy. It is evident, for instance, that although we may sometimes need to add to

She'd been shopping

there is no possibility of subtracting from it and still having a possible telling increment. In an asking exchange we may find

Where had she been?   Shopping

but this kind of reduction does not occur in telling exchanges. For all practical purposes, we may take it that *She'd been shopping* represents the irreducible minimum that will occur. Quite simply, if the speaker stopped short before this much speech had been produced, nothing would be told.

We need, therefore, a way of analysing such an increment, and will provisionally do so as follows:

Nominal element (N)	Verbal element (V)
She	'd been shopping

This division into 'nominal' (N) and 'verbal' (V) elements follows a practice which is familiar enough in sentence grammar and will serve to give us a start. There are two reasons, however, why we must regard such labelling as no more than a temporary expedient. For one thing, it suggests that some of the entities we call 'elements' — in this case, the 'verbal element' — are sometimes the result of the adhesion of several words together. It looks, in fact, rather like the beginning of the kind of constituent structure treatment we are seeking to avoid. The reason for starting like this is simply that it is much easier to set up the analytical machinery we need if we think for the time being of elements which can, and frequently do, consist of more than one word. Once the machinery is in place, we shall then find that we have established some principles whereby the same sequence can be analysed word by word without our having to invoke the notion of 'structures within structures'.

For another thing, we owe the assignment of items to nominal and verbal and other classes to the work of the sentence grammarian. All grammatical categories drive from the particular theory about linguistic organization of which they are part. There can be no guarantee that the categories deriving from so widely diverging theories as a sentence-based one and a purpose-based one will be compatible. Making provisional use of traditional terms is, therefore, no more than a convenience, and one which we must be prepared to abandon if and when the need arises.

Keeping both these reservations in mind, we can say that the least syntactic requirement for a telling increment is a sequence NV.

Minimum requirements for telling: intonational

One reason for taking speech, rather than writing, for our focus of interest is that we are thereby enabled to take into account in a systematic way the effect intonation has upon the organization of language.

Our recorded data has intonation which can be transcribed and considered alongside the word-by-word transcription we provided in the last chapter. The analytical procedure and transcription conventions used are those provided in Brazil (1985). There is a brief summary of the method of analysis in the appendix. This is, of course, only one of a number of different ways of describing intonation: the reason for using it here is that its starting assumptions about the nature of used language are precisely those we examined in Chapter 2. What we have to say about intonation is fully compatible with what we have to say about the grammatical organization: in other words we are able to treat the increment of used language holistically, that is, as an event in which intonation and grammar contribute rather obviously to the same communicative end.

To begin to take intonational features into account, we will note that, in the opening of the story from which it is taken,

She'd been shopping

was spoken as a single tone unit with the tonic syllable in *shopping*

// she'd been SHOPping //

It also has a falling pitch or 'proclaiming tone':

// P she'd been SHOPping //

Had it not done so, it would not have constituted a telling increment. The alternative to a proclaiming tone, a 'referring tone' (one of the end-rising pitch movements, here designated R) would mark the content of the tone unit as expressly not presenting anything that was new to the hearer, whatever its syntactic composition might be. By saying

// R she'd been SHOPping //

the speaker would be proceeding on the assumption that this much was part of the understanding that the hearer already shared: most people do, after all, go shopping from time to time, and the fact of someone doing it on this occasion may not necessarily be newsworthy; and since to articulate that which is already understood background is not to tell in our sense, the listener will probably be left waiting until something is proclaimed. The speaker might, for instance, say

// R she'd been SHOPping // P and she went to find her CAR //

Only after the second tone unit was completed would the listener be likely to acknowledge receipt of information. Further tone units with referring tones will further delay the completion of the telling increment:

// R she'd been SHOPping // R in TOWN // R with her CAR // R and she went back to the CAR park // R where she'd LEFT it // P and she found someone SITting in it //

In this example, the end of every tone unit could be the completion of a telling increment if there were a proclaiming tone; but the speaker presents most of what she says as recognized routine among those who shop. Only the unexplained presence of someone in the car is exceptional and capable of making the whole increment worthwhile as something calculated to satisfy a need.

The function of the referring tone is to mark the tone unit as not intended to contribute directly to an act of telling. In the examples we have cited, it comes in tone units preceding others that are proclaimed, and the effect is consequently to keep the listener waiting for the completion of the increment. Consider, though, an invented example which resembles *she had been shopping* in seeming to be capable of telling in some circumstances:

My friend had been shopping

If this were spoken as

// P my FRIEND // R had been SHOPping //

the situation might be one in which several others had recounted noteworthy things that had happened while they were shopping, and with this reference as established background, the speaker introduces her friend as protagonist in another anecdote. Notice that, as far as intonational requirements are concerned, the telling could now be accomplished in the first tone unit. The waiting involved is waiting for the completion of the minimal syntactic sequence:

My friend (N)   had been shopping (V)

There is scope for an enormous range of combinations of syntactic sequencing and intonational treatment, but they all affect the telling potential of increments in ways which follow directly from what has been said above. There is not much opportunity, however, for demonstrating the truth of this statement as long as we remain with minimal syntactic sequences. In the next chapter, we shall begin to consider situations in which more than minimal requirements must be satisfied if present communicative needs are to be met. In order to make the presentation easier, we will concentrate first upon syntactic organization. This is something that we can do quite well by examining only examples that satisfy the intonational requirement by having a proclaiming tone somewhere in their presentation.

4

The simple chain

In this chapter we shall develop the idea that telling increments can be described as chains of elements occurring in time. Instead of thinking of words and other entities as occurring at places in a hierarchically arranged structure, we shall regard them as occurring one after the other in an arrangement which depends upon our recognizing:

1 the State in which they occur, and
2 the different State which, by virtue of their occurrence, they precipitate.

It should be remembered that our concern is with demonstrating a procedure: it is the details of that procedure and the principles underlying it that we are seeking to expound. Superficially, much of what we say about the examples may seem to be either self-evident or already covered in sentence grammars of the most elementary kind. This ought not, perhaps, to be surprising: we should expect different grammars to give similar accounts of very much of what we observe in linguistic behaviour. Differences lie most significantly in the mechanisms they propose for giving generalized accounts of those observations; and our present interest is in the mechanisms.

Initial, Intermediate, and Target States

When we want to refer to two or more elements arranged in sequence, like the nominal (N) and verbal (V) elements in

She'd been shopping
N   V

we will say that they constitute a chain. We concentrated in the previous chapter on the shortest chain of elements that can have a telling function; we will now give such a chain the following characterization:

Initial State $\rightarrow$ N $\rightarrow$ Intermediate State $\rightarrow$ V $\rightarrow$ Target State

This may seem like an elaborate way of representing something that is rather simple. In fact, it introduces some ideas that are central to the present approach but which are not usually part of the sentence grammarian's conceptual framework. We must, therefore, spell them out carefully before going further.

'Initial State' refers to the special set of communicative circumstances which the speaker assumes he or she is operating in before the chain begins: it embraces, among other things, the speaker's perception of what, at the present moment, the hearer needs to be told. And we have already said that, in efficiently working discourse, the hearer has, or is willing to accept, a very similar view of what those needs are.

'Target State' refers to the modified set of circumstances that comes about as a result of the listener being told what needs to be told. The whole process of telling is therefore visualized as a change from Initial State to Target State.

Our diagram recognizes, however, an 'Intermediate State', one which is brought about by the production of a nominal element, and this state is described as follows: it is one in which there is an obligation upon the speaker to go on and produce an appropriate verbal element in order to achieve the Target State that he or she had in mind when initiating the chain.

Three-element chains

We must now apply the same mode of thinking to some slightly more complicated chains. To do this, however, we need to draw upon a wider range of examples than a single retelling of our tale can provide. This larger corpus was obtained by asking nine more people to listen to the same recorded story and retell it to someone else. This provided a sizeable pool of used language in which similar, but seldom identical, assertions and assumptions were made and similar vocabulary used. Perhaps more importantly from our point of view, it was a source of examples that arose from a set of communicative circumstances with which we are now familiar, and to which we shall therefore be able to refer without having to give details of the all-important background.

We should be clear that no significance attaches to the size of the corpus in this context. It is being used only as a source of examples, and as one in which we can expect to find a fair range of the kinds of sequence that a very much larger corpus would exhibit. Neither is it important, for present purposes, that all the samples are of the same kind of discourse. Speakers engaged in other types of spoken monologue — lectures, extended contributions to discussions, oral reports, and so on — can be assumed to be making use of similar grammatical resources. The intention is not, in any case, to provide an exhaustive account of the things speakers may do grammatically but rather to demonstrate the lines along which a real-time model may be developed. If other data should prove to require modification to the descriptive mechanisms we propose, it will be possible to say what modifications can be made without contravening the principles that we shall lay down.

In the augmented corpus we find these chains; each of them has a proclaiming tone, and thus qualifies as a telling increment:

```
She  /  saw          /  this figure
She  /  was walking  /  towards her car
She  /  was feeling  /  giddy
```

Each of these involves the speaker in producing a third element in order to achieve the desired Target State. We will say that in the presentation of such chains there are two Intermediate States:

Initial State→N→Intermediate State 1→V→Intermediate State 2→?→Target State

But whereas Intermediate State 1 is a state where progress towards Target State via the verbal element (V) is demanded, Intermediate State 2 is not so easily described. It is one in which progress may be via any of three kinds of element, two of which we have not yet encountered. While the constituent *this figure* can sensibly be regarded as falling in the same category as *she* and can therefore be described provisionally as a nominal element (N), the constituents *towards her car* and *giddy* are different. We will continue to rely upon the sentence grammarian's terminology and call these an adverbial element (A) and an adjectival element (E) respectively. After V, therefore, there are four things that speakers may do. They may end the chain, having now reached the Target State; or they may go forward towards the Target State via one of the elements N, A or

E (see Figure 4.1).

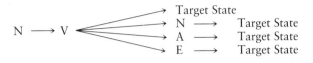

Figure 4.1

We should keep in mind that when we represent the state after V as one in which there is a possibility of choice, as we seem to do in Figure 4.1, this is not to be interpreted as meaning that a speaker will choose which way to go at this point. The diagram means no more than that a chain which follows any of the four routes will be heard as a perfectly acceptable contribution to some discourse or other. These are the routes that the operation of the language system allows. But since any real speaker will be pursuing a course from a known Initial State to a known Target State, the decision as to which route to follow must be thought of as having been taken before the chain is embarked upon.

Four- and five-element chains

Two more examples will enable us to take matters a little further:

She / piles / her / into the car
It / made / her / nervous

These two chains differ from *She saw the figure* in that production of the second N does not achieve a Target State. Instead, it precipitates a further Intermediate State in which progress towards Target State may be by way of either an A element or an E element. (See Figure 4.2.)

Figure 4.2

Finally, we find that in a chain like

This / made / my friend / suspicious / at once

a further State is introduced between Intermediate State 3 and Target

State. Instead of an NVNE chain which satisfies present communicative needs, as it does in *it made her nervous*, we have one which precipitates yet another Intermediate State and therefore demands a further element, A, before the Target State is reached:

Intermediate State 3→E→Intermediate State 4→A→Target State

A set of sequencing rules

We have considered only a handful of examples, but if we rest content with these for the time being and consider only the evidence that they provide, we can reiterate our earlier statement that the least sequence of elements that can satisfy communicative need as a telling increment is NV; all the possible routes begin in this way. But we can also see that if we are to tell anything that is to the point in many of the communicative situations we find ourselves in, it is necessary to go on and produce more than the minimal requirement. Still restricting our attention to the examples we have selected, we can say that the possible ways ahead are represented by Figure 4.3.

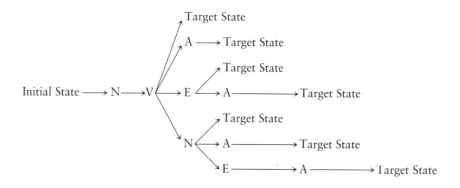

Figure 4.3

Some implications of the sequencing rules

It is obvious that, in spoken discourse at large, only a very small proportion of the sequences we find actually follow the simple rules that this diagram sets out; one needs, in fact, to search quite carefully in the story data to find a range of examples like this without getting involved in complexities that such a rule system does not allow for.

The diagram does, however, represent the kind of element-by-element finite state rule system that we set out to explore. Our concern must be eventually to see in what ways it can be modified or added to so as to take in all the other combinations of element we find in real discourse. An essential requirement, of course, will be that such modifications as we introduce do not destroy the finite state properties of the rule system. That is to say, they must not cause it to lose the condition that we have proposed as a fundamental one for a real-time model of speech, namely, that the way ahead at any point is regulated by consideration of the State which the speaker has at this moment reached in the sequence.

Before beginning this task, however, let us dwell upon some of the implications of Figure 4.3 for the kinds of chain the diagram will produce:

1 We have been at pains to insist that every chain of elements in used language occurs in the context of assumed communicative need. When we discuss the Intermediate State that exists after production of chain-initial N, we do not say simply that it is the State precipitated by that N. We say instead that it is the State that results from the modification of the (nearly always unexpressed) Initial State by the production of the N; and each subsequent Intermediate State has to be thought of as a further modification. The set of assumptions about present communicative need are carried along, as it were, from State to State until the Target State is achieved. This is an important difference between the kind of purpose-driven grammar we are concerned with and the kind that takes the unused sentence as its starting-point.

2 We have said that since the speaker is constantly aiming at a particular Target State, both the route through the network and the point of exit from it are determined by assumptions that the speaker supposes the hearer shares about what will satisfy present communicative needs. In other words, all the decisions are made on the basis of an anticipation of what the latter needs to be told. When the rules we have formulated seem to allow alternative ways of proceeding, there is not, therefore, usually any real choice for a speaker who is operating against a background of understood communicative obligation.

We may say that, by initiating a chain the speaker enters into a commitment to take the appropriate route and to continue along it just so far as a co-operative interpretation of present discourse conditions demands.

3 Something that we have not yet recognized is that, when the commitment has been fulfilled, speakers actually have two options open to them:

a. They may begin a new chain, which is (part of) a further telling increment.

I heard an amazing story   My friend told it to me
NV   N   #   N   V   N A
(# signifies end of increment)

b. Alternatively, they may use any further elements allowed by the rules for further increments. If Target State is achieved by production of *I heard an amazing story*, this State can be taken as Initial State for another increment which is realized by, perhaps, the adverbial element that the rules permit after NVN. So, if a sequence like this is presented as two tone units, each with a proclaiming tone

// P i heard an amazing STORy // P from my FRIEND //

it will constitute two telling increments even though it is a single chain.

The chain is not, therefore, to be identified with an increment in any general way. It is simply a permitted sequence of elements, syntactically defined, which may have different side-by-side relationships with increments, as the speaker's assessment of present communicative need determines.

4 In addition to operating on a strictly left-to-right basis, the rules also require that all the elements encountered on a particular route through the diagram are realized. Natural economy might suggest that some of the intermediate elements in a chain could easily be missed out since they are, to all intents and purposes, predictable. For instance, at the point in the story where this chain occurs

She piled her into the car

both participants know exactly who the pronouns *she* and *her* refer to; it would have no effect upon the interpretation that would be put upon the utterance whether these pronouns were included or not. Moreover, *into* and *the* are pretty well predictable. We shall find later that there are special circumstances under which some uninforming elements are regularly missed out. It is reasonable to ask why such omission is not possible here. The answer seems to be that, in order for the sequencing rules to work, users must know exactly what point they have reached in their progression through them. If omissions were permitted generally they would not be able to keep track of progress. Each successive element precipitates a new State, and as far as the chains we are presently examining are concerned, the sequencing rules provide a rigid framework of expectation within which it is always possible to know what the present State is, and hence what may come next.

5 The one place in the chain where the question of 'what comes next' does not arise is the last element before Target State is reached. Here, therefore, there is a certain amount of freedom to decide whether a predictable element is necessarily included or not. A case where it seems not to be is

> A friend told an amazing story the other day

The chain-final adverbial element *the other day* means little more than 'once' on this occasion, and actually tells nothing about when the story was told, even supposing that such information had any present relevance. A shortened version

> A friend told an amazing story

would probably be just as effective in satisfying communicative need and would also be in line with the requirements of the sequencing rules.

While speakers have no freedom to omit elements elsewhere in the chain, therefore, they often have the option of adding a further element after having gone as far as might be thought was strictly necessary, for instance:

> . . . and she waited (there)

where *there* is self-evidently in the car park, and

> . . . (she saw the proper exit, and) she went past (it) . . .

where *it* is self-evidently the proper exit.

A measure of uncertainty about precisely where to end chains like these is a predictable consequence of the way the rules work.

6 There are many particular elements whose occurrence is very unlikely ever to conclude a chain. Those verbal elements which are often referred to as inherently transitive are among them. There are probably few situations where, for instance:

> My friend told

would satisfy a conversational need (though this is not to say that there are none). The question of whether a verb is properly described as 'transitive' or 'intransitive' does not arise in the kind of analysis we are engaged in. We are concerned rather with what sequence of elements is appropriately produced to satisfy what needs; if we cannot find a case of need being satisfied by a chain which contains a particular verb with no N following it, then that is an interesting fact about that verb. But similar observations can be made about the probability of certain things happening after elements other than verbs. We shall regard the way the use of a particular word tends to limit what will come after it as a general one, rather than as something peculiar to verbs.

The simple chain

It will be helpful in what follows if we think of all chains that result from a progress through the diagram in Figure 4.3 as belonging to a special class. We shall refer to them as 'simple chains' to distinguish them from chains which require a further elaboration of the rules (see sample of data below). For we have now reached the point at which we must stop being so selective in our choice of examples. We must begin asking what additions it is necessary to make to our very rudimentary descriptive apparatus to take in the many utterances we find in used language, but which cannot be represented as the outcome of the rule system that produces simple chains.

Sample of data

(# signifies end of increment)

A friend . . . told this amazing story the other day . . . she
N   V   N   A   # N

'd been shopping . . . she came back to this multi-storey car
V   # N V   A

park . . . it was kind of deserted . . . she saw this figure . . .
       # NV E   # N V N   #

she walked towards the car . . . this person got out . . . it
N V   A   # N   V A # N

was a little old lady . . . she'd been sitting there . . . the
V N   # N V   A # N

daughter hadn't turned up . . . she was feeling a bit giddy . . .
       V   # N V   E   #

she sat in the car . . . she'd been trying all the door
N V A   # N V   N

handles . . . one was open . . .
    # N V E   #

5

Non-finite verbal elements

Non-finite forms

One kind of element not allowed for in the sequencing rules in Figure 4.3 occurs in the chains

The old lady sat there fumbling with her basket
We want to search your car
She found this person installed in her car

The forms *fumbling*, *to search*, and *installed* are all non-finite variants of their verbs. We shall call them '*-ing* forms', '*to* forms' and 'pp forms' (past participle forms) respectively. For the moment we will disregard the evident differences among the three and look for ways of incorporating them as a single type of element into our sequencing rules. The symbol 'V^1' will be used to represent these non-finite verbal elements.

It makes our task easier if, at the outset, we separate out two ways in which V^1 elements can be used: as 'extensions' and as 'suspensions'.

Extensions

Firstly, there are occasions when speakers, having exhausted the possibilities that progress along one of the routes the simple chain rules make available, have nevertheless not achieved the Target State required. That is to say, they have not yet fulfilled their obligation to produce a situationally appropriate telling increment. For instance, if the policeman who is reported as having said

We want to search your car

had stopped short at the end of the appropriate route NV . . . , the chain would clearly not comprise a satisfactory increment. We could, perhaps, say that he was going the right way but had not gone far enough. To discharge his obligation he must follow a longer route, in this case one that is extended by the production of a V^1:

We want . . . to search . . . etc.

An extension, then, is a further element (or, as we shall see, a sequence of elements) which is added to the sequence and has resulted from a run through one of the routes provided by the rules for the simple chain. (There are, in fact, other kinds of extension than those that are initiated by non-finite verbal elements, but we shall leave consideration of these until Chapter 11.)

Let us now make a few observations about V^1 extensions.

1 Any of the three non-finite forms we have identified can initiate an extension. The three examples used above demonstrate this in a fairly obvious way.

2 They may occur at any point later than the production of the V in a simple chain. This means, of course, that wherever Figure 4.3 allows for a Target State to have been achieved, there is another way forward via V^1. So, for instance, the State following NV may be the Target State, or it may be an Intermediate State in which the ways forward are via N, A, E, or V^1. This fragment of the sequencing rules is shown in Figure 5.1

Figure 5.1

3 The ways forward at each point of choice that the speaker reaches thereafter on the route through the diagram can similarly be augmented by the addition of V^1. Such an elaboration of the diagram highlights the similarity between the way in which V^1 is introduced into the chain and the way other elements are introduced, and gives rise to a question: Why did we not include V^1 in the sequencing rules for the simple chain? In what sense does V^1 warrant description as an extension while the other elements we have encountered do not?

There is, in fact, one important way in which V^1 affects the overall operation of the sequencing rules, and this distinguishes it from the other elements. In some cases, progress to a V^1 is sufficient to discharge present communicative obligations. It does so, for instance in

She was waiting for her daughter to arrive
N V   A   V^1

She seemed distressed
N V   V^1

In both, the V^1 leads immediately to the achievement of the Target State. Often, though, the State precipitated by V^1 is an Intermediate one. It is one in which it remains necessary for the speaker to produce one or more further elements before Target State is achieved, and we need to enquire into what possible ways forward such an Intermediate State allows.

In order to show what they are, we do not need to add anything to the sequencing rules. The Intermediate State after V^1 is exactly the same as that which we said is precipitated by V in the simple chain. That is to say, the speaker has the option after V^1 of going back to an earlier point in the route and proceeding as if V had just been produced. Thus the route following V^1 in

We want to search your car
N V   V^1 N

is the same as that followed in

They searched her car
N   V   N

The route following V^1 in

She drove off leaving the man on the pavement
N V   A   V^1 N   A

is the same as that following V in

She left the man on the pavement
N V   N   A

It is this ability to trigger a doubling back in what we are representing as a left-to-right progression, so as to start a second run through a specified part of the rule system, that distinguishes V^1 from the other kinds of element. We can think of the V^1 in such cases as these as initiating a subchain, a term we will use to signify the inability of sequences like

> to search your car

and

> leaving the man on the pavement

to stand alone as telling increments. In the case of extensions, at least, they occur only after one of the sequences we have called simple chains.

At this point we will introduce a new convention. We will use parentheses to separate off such subchains from the rest. So, the two examples we have used above will be represented as

> We want to seach your car
> N V (V^1 N   )

> She drove off leaving the man on the pavement
> N V   A (V^1 N   A   )

respectively. We have to allow, of course, for the subchain comprising no more than the single element V^1:

> She was waiting for her daughter to arrive
> N V   A   (V^1)

> She stood there shivering
> N V   A (V^1)

4 Just as V^1 can be introduced after any element after V in a simple chain, so a second V^1 can be introduced after any element in the subchain. So, in

> She found this lady waiting . . .
> N V   N   (V^1)

the subchain *waiting* sets up an Intermediate State in which another subchain can be initiated:

> She found this lady waiting to meet her daughter . . .
> N V   N   (V^1)(V^1 N   )

and after this second extension, a further extension is possible:

> She found this lady waiting to meet her daughter coming from work
> N V   N   (V^1)(V^1 N   )(V^1 A   )

Theoretically, any number of extensions can be added to earlier ones in this way. Some examples are:

She agreed to take her, worried about her
N V   (V¹   N)(V¹   A   )

She had to wait there, hoping to get some help
N V (V¹   A)(V¹   )(V¹ N   )

Chains representing more than one telling increment

Both of the above examples are spoken in the data as two consecutive telling increments. Allowing for non-finite verbal elements to initiate subchains in this way dramatically increases the possible length of a chain. It is therefore not surprising that extended chains produced in this way frequently exceed what is necessary to achieve a single Target State. We saw in Chapter 4 that, in the case of simple chains, any following elements that the sequencing rules permit, and which are not used up by the time the Target State is reached, can be utilized for further telling increments. This applies equally to chains which are augmented by extensions. Thus while

She was waiting for her daughter to arrive
N V   A   (V¹   )

can be presented as a single telling increment, it might alternatively be spoken as two proclaimed tone units, with two separate increments

// P she was WAITing // P for her DAUGHter to arrive //
  N V   # A   (V¹   )#

or — less probably, perhaps — as three

// P she was WAITing // P for her DAUGHter // P to arRIVE //,
  N V   # A   # (V¹   )

The intonational treatment of the examples given earlier was

// P she agreed to TAKE her // P WORried about her //
// P she had to WAIT there // P hoping to get some HELP //

Suspension

We have not actually redrawn Figure 4.3 (page 51) to incorporate all the possibilities of V^1 extension. To do so would leave us with a somewhat cumbersome diagram without adding anything of real significance. The important point is that, however forbidding it may look, such a diagram would not represent a departure from the kind of finite-state rule system we are seeking to establish. It would remain true that at each point in the speaker's progress through the rules the way forward was conditioned by the State they had just reached.

When we begin to look at the chains that actually occur in used language, however, we quickly find many that the rules, as they stand, will not account for. Indeed, there are many that seem expressly to refute the claim that the sequencing of elements is subject to rules of the kind that the diagram leads us to expect. Even the most superficial inspection of our story data suggests that the ordering of some elements is to some extent optional, and if the re-ordering of elements is possible, what effect does this have upon our notion of rule-governed sequences?

In one version of the story, we find

Her trick to get rid of him worked

A chain which apparently breaches the rule that a chain-initial N must be followed by V. Instead of the expected sequence

NV . . . etc.

we have

NV^1 . . . etc.

The question we must now face is whether such an apparent 'misplacement' of elements, which can evidently occur in a perfectly acceptable chain, can be accommodated in a finite state rule system. To show that it can, we shall invoke a notion we shall refer to as 'suspension'.

Suspension in simple chains

Suspension can occur even in simple chains, and it may be better to recognize the phenomenon there before tackling its use in connection with a V^1 subchain. One of our storytellers says

This woman finally asked her

instead of

This woman asked her finally

a version in which the adverbial element *finally* occurs in the final position where the sequencing rules would lead us to expect to find it. According to our expectations, the speaker produces the element in the 'wrong' place when she places it immediately after the chain-initial N.

This is less of a problem than it may seem to be. Let us maintain our assumption that there is a commitment on the part of the speaker to proceed, via a situationally appropriate route, through an ordered sequence of elements, to an already determined Target State. We will then say that anything which occurs out of sequence will suspend, but will not otherwise affect, eventual fulfilment of the commitment. For instance, since the production of chain-initial N always entails a commitment to produce a following V, anything else which happens to occur will amount only to a putting-off of the obligation to produce that V. Although in the case of

This woman finally asked her

the adverbial element *finally* occurs 'unexpectedly' after initial N, its occurrence neither cancels nor modifies the expectation of a following V that the N has set up. In other words, the Intermediate State after the intruding or suspending adverbial element is exactly the same as the State which preceded it. A simple rule can be proposed to cover such cases:

$$N \begin{cases} \to V \ldots \text{etc.} \\ \to x \to V \ldots \text{etc.} \end{cases}$$

where *x* represents any element other than the 'expected' V. We will adopt the convention of using lower case symbols to represent elements that have suspensive function; so

This woman finally asked her

will be represented as NaVN.

Characteristics of suspensions

Some distinguishing features of suspensions, then, are:

1 After any inserted element(s), the State reverts to that which existed immediately before it (them), so subsequent procedures are then fully specified by the rules, as if there had been no interruption.
2 The operation of the rules depends upon the end-point of the suspending insertion being determinable: it is necessary for users to know at what point they get back to fulfilling previously-entered-into commitments.

The requirement implicit in (2) is satisfied most obviously when the insertion is a single element, like *finally*. It is possible, however, for the suspensive element itself to set up an expectation of further situationally appropriate elements: to initiate a subchain. In such a case, suspension continues until the commitment to work through that subchain has been fulfilled. This, more complex, situation frequently arises when the element having suspensive function is a V^1.

Suspensive non-finite verbal elements

Let us examine the following example in detail:

(and) she found sitting in her car this little old lady

Here we could say that, by producing this particular NV, *she found*, the speaker would normally be regarded as having made a commitment to saying what she found. It is a characteristic of the word *found* that there are very few situations where it would be likely to terminate a telling increment, so that something like *She found . . . this old lady*, NVN, would be heard as the least chain that would achieve a Target State. But, NV is actually followed by the unexpected non-finite V^1, *sitting*. (We have, of course, said that a V^1 can initiate an extension after any element without there being any question of unexpectedness, but this one will not be heard in this way because of the obligation eventually to produce the completion of the NVN chain.) The interpolation of *sitting* will not, in itself, satisfy a communicative need: the progress of the story depends upon the listener being told where the person was sitting. The V^1 element therefore sets up its own expectations—specifically, in this

64

case, of an A element *in her car*—which must be satisfied before the speaker gets back to discharging the obligation earlier entered into to complete the original NVN chain. Symbolically, the whole is represented thus:

(and) she found sitting in her car this little old lady
    N V   (v¹   a   )N

To accommodate cases like these, the rule we represented earlier as

$$N \begin{cases} \rightarrow V \ldots \text{etc.} \\ \rightarrow x \longrightarrow V \ldots \text{etc.} \end{cases}$$

Must be amended to

$$N \begin{cases} \rightarrow V \ldots \text{etc.} \\ \rightarrow (x \ldots \text{etc.}) \longrightarrow V \ldots \text{etc.} \end{cases}$$

where (x ... etc.) represents the subchain which the production of *x* predicts in the existing discourse conditions.

Before looking at some further examples of suspension, it may be useful to summarize here the effect that this important notion has on the way the left-to-right operation of the rule system is conceptualized. The sequencing rules are not to be thought of as actually restricting choices at any point in the chain. Rather, by defining a minimally satisfying sequence of elements for each discourse context, they assign a kind of parenthetical status to anything else that occurs. But we must be clear about the way 'parenthetical' is being used here. It refers solely to the interruption of an expected ordering of elements, syntactically defined. In the two examples we have used, it may be felt that *finally* and *sitting in her car* were both parenthetical in some additional sense. In the written language, the use of commas would probably recognize this feeling that they both amounted to some kind of departure from a more normal temporal presentation of the information: using commas, they may be 'marked' for special attention. It is not always the case, however, that such a temporary departure from the simple chain pattern will be heard in this way. In an invented example:

This person sitting in her car had a shopping bag
N   (v¹   a   )V N

one would probably say that the suspensive subchain occupies its proper — indeed, its only possible — place.

We shall see, in fact, that the single process we have called suspension results in sequences which sentence grammars would regard as of very different kinds. There are some in which the disruption of ordering is conspicuous. The suspending element seems consequently to acquire some kind of emphatic or 'marked' status. But there are others where there is no feeling that it has been moved to a place where its occurrence is remarkable. This is one case, among many that we shall encounter, where our treatment of chains, simply as sequences of elements gives identical descriptions to events which are, in a very significant sense, very different. For the present, we shall content ourselves with seeing them as the outcome of the operation of the same set of sequencing rules, leaving until later the task of saying exactly where the difference lies.

Some chains in which the other forms of V^1 initiate a suspensive subchain are:

She went on wondering what to do to the next roundabout
N V   (v^1 n v^1) A

The plan to get rid of him worked perfectly
N   (v^1 n) V   A

Suspensive elements before chain-initial N

Notice that in the following examples, suspension, whether it involves A or V^1, occurs before the production of the NV that the sequencing rules require at the beginning of every chain.

Usually I meet her after work
a   NV   N A

After a bit, she started to shuffle about a bit
a   N V   (V^1 A   )

To get rid of him she asked him to help her
(v^1 n) N V   N (V^1 N)

Looking across at her, she noticed something odd
(v^1 a   ) N V   N

In all four cases, the obligation to produce an appropriate chain, which the mere act of saying something can be thought of as incurring, is held over for fulfilment until the suspensive elements are completed; the speaker then returns to meeting that obligation.

Extensions and suspensions compared

The two ways of adding to the capacity of the simple chaining rules to produce situationally appropriate increments can be compared if we consider the following examples, the second of which is invented:

(1) She decided to take the wrong exit from the roundabout
    N V   (V^I N   A   )

(2) Her decision to take the wrong exit from the roundabout was
    N   (v^I n   a   ) V

    a clever one
    N

In both of these, the composition and end-point of *to take the wrong exit from the roundabout* are determined by present communicative need. The difference between them is that in (1) the subchain arises from the need to add on elements after the end of the simple chain, and once this addition has been made listener requirements are deemed to have been satisfied; in (2), a similar communicative need results in the subchain functioning as a whole as a temporary hold-up in the continuation, and ultimate completion, of the chain *her decision . . . was a clever one.*

Sample of data

In this sample of data A elements occur as suspensions and V^I initiated subchains occur as extensions and suspensions.

she saw this figure sitting in the passenger seat . . . she
N V N   (V^I A   ) # N

walked towards the car feeling a bit scared . . . (what is) she
V   A   (V^I E   ) #   N

doing sitting in my car . . . apparently she'd been sitting
V (V^I A   ) # a   N V

there waiting for her daughter to arrive . . . it seems a
A (V^I A   ) V^I # NV   N

very strange thing to do . . . she was meant to be meeting her
            V^l   # N V V^l   V^l (V^l   N

daughter . . . finally this woman asked her . . . she
) # a   N   V   N # N

happens to look across . . . very cleverly she missed the
V   (V^l   A   ) # a   N V   N

turning . . . she pretended to be . . . a hopeless female
     # N V   (V^l   N   )

driver . . . we want to search your car
   # N V (V^l   N   )

6

The relationship between elements

The relationship among constituents

It is clearly not enough to say that elements are produced one after the other in a chain. By attending exclusively to how they occur in linearly organized sequences, we have so far made no systematic recognition of the fact that two or more of the sequences which result from taking an identical route through the rules can have widely different significances when they are viewed as meaningful utterances.

We need go no further than some of the sequences that the simple chaining rules will produce to find examples that present us with this kind of problem. Both the chains

She remembered the oddments in her car

They'd found an axe in her car

have the sequential description NVNA. But, merely to say this is to obscure a difference that is far from negligible. In the first example the adverbial element tells the hearer *which* oddments she remembered; in the second an identical element tells *where* the police found the axe.

A common procedure for dealing with this kind of difference would be to say that the meaning of each example is attributable in some way to how the various constituents of the two items are related to each other: the items can be said to be different in that they represent two different configurations of such relationships. One such relationship can be said to exist between *in her car* and *the oddments*, of such a kind that the whole phrase *the oddments in her car* works as a unified constituent inside the larger constituent — *remembered the oddments in her car*. In the second example, one might say that there were two major constituents:

(They'd found an axe) (in her car).

and that the whole of the second constituent is related to the whole of the first, rather than to any particular part of it. As we have said, we are not concerned with the merits of this way, or any of the possible alternative ways, of visualizing the 'structure'. The point that is relevant to our present concerns is that any explanation of this kind depends upon our first postulating some constituent-within-constituent arrangement. Grammarians who aim to find a way of accounting for all the possible kinds of relationship that exist in all the possible unused sentences of the language, characteristically engage in debate about how the arrangements are best represented, but there is very general agreement that a display of constituents of different 'sizes', which can be deployed in such a way that each fits inside another in some kind of Chinese box arrangement, is an essential part of the conceptual apparatus. And, as we have said, the use of such apparatus depends upon the analyst having the completed sentence, the 'product', available for inspection.

We have set ourselves a different task: that of describing the working of used speech that is now happening, not unused ready-made sentences, and of doing so without benefit of non-linear apparatus. We must, therefore, find an alternative way of describing the difference that we admit exists between our two telling increments; and it must be a way which is consistent with the linear approach that we are adopting.

Post-verbal and post-nominal functions

To begin with, we have to recognize that, in following tradition and designating one of the elements that can occur in a chain 'adverbial', we could be said to have been over-hasty, for the label has functional implications that might be misleading. While the purpose of *in her car* is indeed, on one occasion, to provide information that is related to the earlier verbal element *found* (it tells where they found something), on the other occasion the information relates rather to the nominal element *oddments* (it tells which oddments). We will recognize this difference by saying that the A element has post-verbal function in the first case, and post-nominal function in the second.

If such a proposal as this were made in connection with an unused sentence, we should have to say that the result could sometimes be ambiguous. Thus, in the invented sentence

She turned the car in the driveway

we may not know whether it meant that she turned a particular car (post-nominal function) or whether she turned it in a particular place (post-verbial function). But in the case of our two telling increments, ambiguity is not a problem. We know, for instance, that the friend was sitting in the police station and therefore could not have remembered something while *in the car*: the potential post-verbal function is therefore eliminated as far as this increment is concerned. Conversely, since there is little likelihood of 'an-axe-in-the-car' being referred to in contradistinction to any other axe, the possibility of a post-nominal function is effectively ruled out.

Indeterminacy and ambiguity

It is necessary, in fact, for our present purposes, to make a distinction which sentence grammarians do not normally make: we need to make a mental separation between two conditions which we shall call 'indeterminacy' and 'ambiguity' respectively.

Indeterminacy refers to precisely the capacity we have just noted of certain elements to be notionally related to other elements in more than one way: it is the potentiality we have attributed to *in the driveway*. Ambiguity, on the other hand, refers to the failure of an increment to make a distinction which is crucial to the successful discharge of the speaker's present obligations. If *she turned the car in the driveway* did happen to occur in a conversation and in circumstances where listeners didn't know which of two facts they needed to be told, then the indeterminacy of reference of *in the driveway* would, indeed, lead to the increment being ambiguous.

What view does our present approach require that we take of such instances of ambiguity? Firstly, we may say that they are extremely rare. If we singled them out for special attention, we should be allowing ourselves to be diverted into considerations that are, on any realistic view of the matter, peripheral. Secondly, when they do occur, they do so as a result of a failure on the part of the speaker to make that anticipation of the needs of the hearer which co-operative participation in a discourse requires. They are therefore like any other occasion when there is a mismatch between the speaker's perception of what needs to be said and the reality of the situation. The means of rectification are, as always, available to the listener: *Do you mean 'the car that is on the road' or 'he parked it on the road'?* While recognizing that a listener might sometimes need to have recourse to such a clarifying procedure, we can take it that ambiguity will not be a feature of the kind of successfully conducted co-operative discourse that we have set ourselves to describe.

But if ambiguity is rare, indeterminacy is an all-pervading feature of speech, and one which users are quite accustomed to living with. We might even argue that it is an indispensable feature of verbal communication, allowing for an economy without which language would be impossibly unwieldy. Let us examine two illustrations of this. The first comes from the conversation that was attributed to the friend and the old lady immediately after the latter had asked for a lift:

Where does your daughter live?

She lives near the Rose and Crown

Here, the reply is obviously indeterminate, as there are any number of public houses of that name, and often more than one in the same town. It creates no problems for the friend, however, because many other factors than the label, including, no doubt, her knowledge of the locality, are taken into account in identifying the place referred to. Had it been a problem, she could have asked: 'Which Rose and Crown?' The everyday use of personal names, some of which may be shared by several acquaintances of both participants, but which are nevertheless usually sufficient to identify the intended individual, provide a similar demonstration of the way indeterminacy is ignored in practice. It is worth noting in passing that, were it not for users' tolerance of indeterminacy, every pub and every person would have to be uniquely named!

For another demonstration of how users take the fact of indeterminacy in their stride, consider:

She told her to get into her car

All three items *she, her,* and *her* are indeterminate as to their reference. There is nothing in the composition of the chain to indicate whether any of these refers to the friend or to the little old lady. None of them gives rise to ambiguity, however, since our knowledge of the conversational conditions that exist at the moment the increment is spoken eliminates one potential reference in each case. We will proceed on this assumption: indeterminacy is a perfectly normal feature of used language; it is something that conversationalists find no hindrance to the achievement of their purposes, and find highly advantageous in enabling them to make economical use of their linguistic resources. It will be a fundamental claim of the present grammar that it is also an all-pervasive feature: on very many occasions when sentence grammars seek to give a formal account of the difference between two sentences, we can find an alternative explanation if we try to adopt a language user's viewpoint. We can say that decisions about the functions of the various elements — whether, for instance, a proper noun or a pronoun has one potential referent or another, or whether a particular A element has post-verbal or post-nominal function — are safely left to a listener. Operating as they do against a background which it is assumed has been substantially agreed in advance, listeners can seize upon which of any number of potential interpretations is appropriate for present purposes.

Noticing differences between unused sentences is a different matter, for in doing so one is attending primarily to differences (something that would be highly uncooperative if it were done by a user). Indeed, it is common practice to work with pairs of sentences which have been invented for the express purpose of illustrating a difference which grammarians have already decided is a potential one. There is probably no respect in which the perspective of the now-communicating user differs more radically from that of the after-the-event analyst than this one. From our present point of view, it is not necessary to assume that the causes of the differences will show up at all in an account of the organization of the used increment. They are rather differences in the conversational purposes that speakers may be pursuing, and it is sufficient if we can show how this can give rise to the phenomena that sentence grammarians notice.

Non-significant differences

Two more telling increments from the data will illustrate another aspect of the general distinction between indeterminacy and ambiguity. The example

> She took the wrong exit at the roundabout

might, if we set ourselves to look for potential differences, be held to mean either that it was 'the-wrong-exit-at-the-roundabout' that the friend took (i.e. a post-nominal use of the A element) or that 'at-the-roundabout' was where she took a wrong exit (a post-verbal use). Similarly,

> She saw a driveway on the left

might signify that it was a 'driveway-on-the-left' that she saw (post-nominal) or that she 'saw-it-on-the-left' (post-verbal). The point to be noted about both of these, probably indeterminate, examples is that neither is likely ever to give rise to ambiguity. In neither case does the indeterminacy interfere with the successful transmission of information because the rival interpretations of each amount, for all practical purposes, to one and the same thing. Indeed, even to notice the presence of indeterminacy in such cases seems to be teasing out distinctions which could have no relevance in conversation.

Indeterminacy in chains with non-finite verbal elements

Let us now return to chains which include occurrences of non-finite verbal elements and see how the notion of indeterminacy can be applied to them. In particular, let us see how the notion can be invoked to account for some of the differences in sequentially similar chains which sentence grammars have described in terms of differing kinds of constituent relationships.

Both

> She took this person to deliver her to her daughter's

and

> She told her to put her shopping bag in the car

have a linear description NVN (V^{1}NA). It might well be objected, though, that such a description overlooks a difference that users would need to be aware of. The difference can, in these cases, be said informally to have to do with who does the delivering and who was to do the putting. In the first example it is *she* (i.e. the friend), or the referent of the first N in the opening sub-sequence NVN. In the second example it is *her* (i.e. the old lady), or the referent of the second N in that sub-sequence.

To carry the discussion further, we need to borrow another term from sentence grammar. The elements that would signify who did the delivering or who was to do the putting would usually be referred to as the 'subjects' of the verbal elements *delivered* and *put* respectively. It is a consequence of the way the rules for the simple chain operate that the subject of the finite V always precedes it: all such chains begin with NV, and this N is the subject. But it follows from the way the rules for introducing non-finite verbal elements operate that there is never a separate representation of their subjects. We can extend the kind of finite state explanation we developed earlier to take in our two examples as follows. Both the NVN sequences

She took this person
She told her

precipitate a State in which two nominal elements have been introduced into the chain. The referent of either of these can now be regarded as 'in play', that is to say as available to do duty, without further representation, as the notional subject of any subsequent V^l in the chain. The V^l will therefore be indeterminate with respect to its attachment to either preceding N. The possibility of alternative attachments is very similar to that which we noted in the case of the adverbial element that followed both an available N and an available V. Once again, there is no ambiguity because of this indeterminacy. Our knowledge of the placing of each of the increments in the unfolding narrative leaves us in no doubt about which attachment is intended.

And, again, it is possible to invent a chain which might, if it were used in certain circumstances, be capable of rival interpretations. Thus,

My friend told him to make sure

could signify either that the friend wanted to make sure or that she wanted her passenger to make sure. As we have said, however, in engaging in such an exercise as this we are setting up a situation which would be unlikely to occur in practice: one which would be either avoided or rectified by co-operative interactants.

Some more examples in which it is the referent of the first N to which the V¹ can be assumed to be attached are:

She missed the turning to trick him

She was sitting in the car waiting for her daughter

She gave the old girl a lift convinced she was going to pass out or something.

Some examples of attachment to the second N are:

She asked him to get out

She left this character standing on the pavement

She found the car park deserted except for . . .

Unrestricted reference

There is one further way in which non-finite verbal elements are used which is not covered by the above. If we take it as a working assumption that the purpose of any N is to specify a referent, and that the particular role of the subject N is to specify who initiates the event signified by V or V¹, then we can easily find cases where the initiator remains unspecified. In

It's not very nice going into these places on your own

She was quite a problem to see properly

the subjects of *going* and *to see* are both unspecified: it is part of what is being told that the referent is *unrestricted* in each case. One of the things the speaker can do with a V¹ is to make a general assertion which applies to anyone.

A finite-state account

A statement of the position in finite-state terms which covers all the examples we have examined can be made, therefore, like this:

At any place in the chain where a V¹ is produced, one of the factors affecting the Intermediate State will be the participants' knowledge that one or more nominal elements has been produced already; any of these may be re-used, without further mention, for the subject of the V^1. Alternatively, a notional N that has not occurred may be so used, in which case the subchain has unrestricted reference. This last possibility means that all chains having V^1 are indeterminate in at least this respect: the notional subject may be something that has been mentioned or something that has not. It will be additionally indeterminate if there is more than one earlier N. Such indeterminacy does not, except on rare occasions, result in ambiguity.

Importantly, it is not necessary for the grammar to give separate accounts of all the potential interpretations that chains like this may permit. It is enough that speakers and listeners, working their way through the sequencing rules and coming to a V^1, are aware of which Ns are available, either explicitly in the chain or implicitly in the general background, and are able to use their knowledge of the context of the utterance to determine which is applicable in the present instance. Listeners resolve indeterminacy by making use of the background understanding they bring to the increment, not their apprehension of anything we might call its formal structure.

Non-finite verbal elements as suspensions

Two instances of the use of V^1-initiated chains as suspensions are of interest. While in an example involving extension,

> He'd found the axe hidden in the back of the car

the attachment of *hidden in the back of the car* to *he* or *the axe* is indeterminate (it depends for interpretation upon the listener's co-operative judgement as to whether it was the policeman or the axe that was hidden), there would be no such indeterminacy if the speaker said

> The axe hidden in the back of the car was enormous

This follows directly from what was said above: at the Intermediate State in which *hidden* occurs and a suspension is initiated, only one N has so far been produced. The other case is when V^1 occurs initially in the chain, that is to say before V. Invented examples are:

> Hidden in the back, they found an axe

> Hidden in the back, he was carrying an axe

We have only to recall the sense of delayed fulfilment, that we have

77

said is always associated with suspensions, to appreciate how these examples work. First, the suspensive subchain must be completed; then the promised NV must be produced; finally there will follow any further elements that present communicative need may demand. This latter requirement may result in there being any number of nominal elements, and the question arises as to which of them can be considered, prospectively rather than retrospectively now, as available to serve as subject of the suspensive V^1. This is the kind of question that it would require a vast amount of data to answer. Our examples show that either the first or second N may be so used. Both of these result from the operation of the simple chain rules, and it seems likely that this will determine the extent to which this kind of anticipatory reference is made: it is hard to find or construct examples in which the initial V^1 anticipates a subject that occurs in a subsequent extension.

Let us summarize the findings of this chapter. Some, at least, of the different interpretations that can be placed upon similar chains with non-finite verbal elements can be attributed to the several possible ways in which the non-realized subject N can be attached to a referent. By recognizing that all such chains are indeterminate, we can say that a listener's choice of one interpretation rather than another depends upon knowledge that they already have about the background to the conversation and to understandings about present conversational purposes, which are assumed to be shared. To take the matter further, we need to attend to the significance of the three non-finite forms themselves, and to the kinds of relationship they can contract with the finite V, something we shall do in the next chapter.

7

The timing of events

The two time continua

A consideration of time, a factor that we have made central to so much of our argument, necessarily enters into a speaker's use of language in two ways. On the one hand, as we have said, speech is itself a series of events which take place in time, each of which has the effect of producing a new State. This is real time, the inescapable and constantly changing now, in which all verbal interaction takes place. On the other hand, speech can be used to report events in a world outside the present conversational nexus. Our use of narrative data as a starting-point for this book makes this very clear: the various happenings that comprise the friend's alarming experience happened in a time continuum which differs from that in which any of the recorded retellings took place. In this chapter, we must begin to look at the way speech distinguishes between the two, and at the whole question of how the timing of reported events—as distinct from the timing of the utterance—is handled by a speaker.

Event time and moment of utterance

The timing of events, in the sense that those events are related to some institutionalized scale, such as is supplied by a clock, a calendar or a timetable, is normally indicated by adverbial or nominal elements:

She's usually here at four o'clock

She should have been here half an hour ago

Since it is verbal elements that usually signify events, however, it is principally through them that references to time are made. In their case, though, the point of reference is not one of those that are identified by the various conventional systems; it is the moment of utterance, whenever that may be.

We will consider first what is, perhaps, the simplest case, where the two time-scales, let us say the real time of utterance and the event time of what is reported, are not separated. The policeman in the story is quoted in one version as saying

We want to search your car

The implication here is that the act of wanting to which the policeman refers is coincident with his act of making the assertion: 'We, at this moment, when I utter these words, want to . . . etc.'. But when he says, as another version tells us he does,

We found an axe on the back seat

he assigns the act of finding to some point in time earlier than the time of speaking: 'Now, as I speak, our finding of the axe is a matter of history'. If we think of there being two times which are relevant to our present discussion, an 'event time' and an 'utterance time', then we can say that in the first example the two are represented as being identical. In the second, event time is represented as preceding utterance time.

Differentiated and undifferentiated time reference

The feature that distinguishes the two kinds of time relationship is, of course, the form of the verbs *want* (as opposed to *wanted*) and *found* (as opposed to *find*). We shall say that forms like *want* and *find* make 'undifferentiated time reference' (that is to say they treat both times as one), while forms like *wanted* and *found* make 'differentiated time reference' (they represent event time as preceding utterance time).

We have sought, in earlier chapters, to characterize the various Intermediate States that are produced by the operation of the sequencing rules on the basis of what opportunities there are at each State for further progress towards Target State. And we have said that, suspensions apart, the only way forward after chain-initial N is via V. It is tempting now to modify our sequencing rules to allow for progress after N to be via either an undifferentiated V or via a differentiated V. A fragment of the system we set out in Figure 4.3 on page 51 which incorporated this modification would look like this:

$$N \begin{cases} \longrightarrow \text{V (Undifferentiated) . . . etc.} \\ \longrightarrow \text{V (Differentiated) . . . etc.} \end{cases}$$

To represent matters in this way would not, however, be a helpful thing to do, and understanding why not is an important step towards an appreciation of how the rule system works. The essential point is this: in each case where we have said that there are alternative ways forward from a particular Intermediate State, the question of which way is taken affects the subsequent Intermediate State. For instance, if the speaker proceeds via N after V, the possible ways forward thereafter are different from what they would have been had he or she proceeded via E. But the alternatives we are now concerned with are different: a choice of, let us say, undifferentiated V instead of differentiated V will have no such effect. The State precipitated will be exactly the same, in so far as it affects the operation of the sequencing rules, whichever form is chosen. The availability of a choice between one form of the verb and another is thus importantly different from anything we have encountered so far.

Perfective and imperfective verbs

In order to make full use of this new notion, we have to take into account another distinction. It is a distinction that we could safely overlook in dealing with the two examples we chose to begin this chapter with. The working of the differentiated–undifferentiated opposition is fairly straightforward in them; but it is not always so easy to associate anything that we should normally think of as an 'event' with a verb as these examples may have made it seem to be. The concept of event time can sometimes, therefore, be more problematical.

Even in the case of *want*, we may, on the basis of our everyday experience of the use of the word, have difficulty in accepting that it qualifies as an 'event'. Part of the reason for this is that, while the *finding of an axe* is fairly obviously an outcome which we might, in principle, accurately assign to a particular moment in time, *wanting* is more likely to suggest a condition which persists over a period to time. To put it another way, *finding* is a once-for-all accomplishment, while *wanting* is not. Words which work as *found* works are often referred to as 'perfective verbs' to distinguish them from others, 'imperfective verbs', which work as *want* does, and we can once more borrow traditional terminology to recognize a difference that has relevance to our present concerns. The addition that we have to make to our original statement about differentiated and undifferentiated forms will be to this effect: when verbs are used imperfectively the opposition serves to indicate whether the event time includes the time of utterance, as it does for instance, in

My daughter lives out of town

(at the present moment, the 'living' referred to is taking place) or whether it does not, as in

The old woman sat very still in the car

(at the present moment, the 'sitting' referred to is not taking place).

Exploitation

Another fact to be kept in mind is that it is the speaker who makes the choice of one form or another. In making this choice, as in making every other one, the working expectation is that the speaker will produce a chain which fits the assumed speaker–hearer understanding of what present communicative needs are. A wrong choice could break the co-operation rule. For instance, had the old lady proffered the information

My daughter lived out of town

instead of

My daughter lives out of town

she would have been failing to say what the present situation was and therefore not helping the friend to make her decision about how to act. But in this matter as in many others, speakers often have scope for exploiting the system; proceeding in either of two possible ways that the communicative situation will allow, and thereby manipulating it in accordance with the particular conversational ends they have in mind. This occurs in at least two ways in the story data, and it is worth examining them in order to guard against a too rigidly literal interpretation of what 'event time' means.

One speaker, when recounting the original discovery of a lady in the car, says

... and she got out of the lift ... and went towards her car ... and she sees this woman in her car ...

The verbal elements in the first two increments of this extract have differentiated time reference as we should expect, since earlier events are being reported from the perspective of a subsequent utterance time. But in the third verbal element the time reference changes to undifferentiated. A common recourse in narrative is to change the perspective suddenly in this way: to act as if the event were taking place now, at the time of telling. So, in another version, we find

... the other policeman came back ... he'd looked in her car ... and he says ... what did you have in your car ...

Not surprisingly, these switches to undifferentiated time reference occur at points where particularly dramatic disclosures are made or are about to be made.

An instance of exploitation of a different kind is found in

... and they asked her for her car keys ... we wanted to look in your car ...

Here, *wanted* has differentiated time reference in spite of the evident real coincidence of event time and utterance time, a coincidence that our earlier version

We want to search your car

faithfully recognizes. A comparison of the effect of the two versions goes a long way towards explaining this departure from a time reference choice that strict logic might suggest was more appropriate. *We want to* ... sounds like a peremptory demand, and we might suppose that a thoughtful policeman would want to avoid this in the circumstances. It is softened by the use of differentiated time reference. So, too, when the old lady is represented as feeling her way towards asking for a lift, she is credited with saying

I wondered if it would be out of your way to drop me there

where 'I wonder . . . ' might have been a more truthful way of describing her situation. It is not easy to say exactly why this kind of switch occurs so commonly when people are seeking help, asking favours, and so on. We may surmise that, by locating the wanting or

83

the wondering at some time earlier than the moment of speaking they are acting as though they do not necessarily want or wonder any longer: there is a diplomatic suggestion of 'I thought (until now) that you might help me (but I can see now that perhaps it might be difficult for you)'.

What is important to recognize is that in neither of these kinds of exploitation is there any question of doing anything different grammatically. The opposition that is represented in the language by such alternations as *want/wanted, find/found, see/saw, wonder/wondered,* etc. is consistently one between undifferentiated and differentiated time reference. What we have done is notice some of the ways in which a speaker can project a certain here-and-now understanding with respect to the timing of events in evident contradiction of what both participants understand is the 'real' state of affairs. And only a pedantic, and hence uncooperative, listener would demur at the fiction.

Non-finite verbal elements

We must now move on to consider time reference in relation to what we have called the non-finite forms of the verbs—the V^1 elements with which parts of Chapters 5 and 6 were concerned.

We have recognized three of the forms that the V^1 can take, and we will begin by representing these as alternative ways of filling any of the many places where the sequencing rules allow V^1. Thus, instead of V^1, there is always, in principle, a three-way choice: the *-ing* form, *to* form, or pp form. As a set of options they resemble the differentiated–undifferentiated opposition in that the occurrence of one rather than one of the others in no way alters the possibilities of further elements being added in the resultant State. This is not to suggest, of course, that on any particular occasion in real discourse it will necessarily be possible for a speaker to choose freely from among all three ways forward. The fact that we find

I expected to meet my daughter here

in the data does not lead us to suppose that we should ever find, for instance,

I expected meeting my daughter here

or

I expected met my daughter here

As always, apprehension of one's present communicative purpose will rule out certain possibilities; and we shall have to consider later the factors that constrain what speakers actually do. For the moment, however, we will be content to say that these are the ways ahead that the sequencing rules permit, and examine the meaningful consequences of taking one of them rather than the others.

Event time with the *-ing* form

Non-finite verbal elements take the *-ing* form in

She sat there muttering

I left him standing on the pavement

In both cases, the finite V has differentiating form: the *sitting* and the *leaving* are located at some point in time earlier than the moment of utterance. But in so far as *muttering* and *standing* represent events (in the wider sense of the word we have permitted ourselves), they also have event times. It is easy to see that in both cases this is declared to be the same as that of the previous finite verbal element: the old lady's muttering coincided temporally with her sitting, and she was standing at the time the friend left. In

She finds this character sitting in her car

the V has undifferentiating form, for reasons that we discussed earlier, but it remains true that once the event time of *finds* has been fixed, that of *sitting* is tied to it in a simultaneous relationship: the finding and the sitting are represented as occurring at the same time.

Event time with the *to* form

For comparison, let us consider the significance of the *to* forms in

We want to search your car

I asked him to help me

Here, the finite verbal elements *want* and *asked* have undifferentiating and differentiating forms respectively. This fixes their

different event times. Thereafter, the event time of the subsequent V'
is represented as at some point later. Both the searching and the
helping are referred to as being 'prospective' from the event time of
want and *asked*.

Notice that, since *to* forms refer to events that are anticipated
from the time reference point of another verb, they always leave
open the possibility that, when that time comes, the event will not
actually take place. Saying 'I asked him to help me but he wouldn't'
would be perfectly normal.

This fact of potentiality, rather than actuality, together with the
communicative value that commonly resides in certain verbs, has
sometimes led people to speak of a special use of the *to* infinitive.
Thus while

I wanted to see her

probably says no more than that the wanting preceded the still
uncertain seeing,

I waited to see her

would often be interpreted as indicating that the possibility of seeing
her was the purpose of the waiting. We should be clear, however,
that these apparently different local meanings arise from the fact that
the speaker exploits the general significance of the to-form while
using a particular verbal element in a particular discourse context.
All that is contributed to the communicative value by using this form
rather than any other is that the seeing is represented as an event
whose accomplishment is viewed as prospective at the time of the
wanting or waiting.

Event time with the pp form

The temporal implications of the third non-finite form, the past
participle, are illustrated by

My friend drove on, terrified

Here, the terrifying—the event that caused the friend to be
terrified—must have preceded the event time of driving on. As far as
the event timings are concerned, therefore, that of the pp form is
fixed at some point earlier than that of the preceding finite verb.

This simple fact is, however, somewhat obscured by the way this third form is commonly used. Whereas, in the case of the -*ing* form and the *to* form, it is the event itself that is taken to be the primary focus of interest (as what needs to be communicated), in the case of the pp form it is rather the effect that the previously accomplished event has produced. Already-accomplished events can have altered the condition or quality of something or somebody at the time indicated. It is not so much the fact that the discovery of her passenger's gender *terrified* the friend that is represented as mattering now; it is rather the friend's present condition, a condition that has been brought about by that discovery.

We shall return to this matter and to the event/condition distinction later. Meanwhile, we can summarize our findings. Provided there is no suspension in the chain, the timing of events is indicated like this: the V element first fixes its own event time, and it does this by relating it in one of two possible ways to the moment of utterance. Then the event time of any subsequent V^1 is specified by relating it to that of the V. The three non-finite forms we have considered signify events whose event times

1 coincide with

2 are anticipated at

3 are already in the past at

the event time that is set by the previous V.

Linearity

It will be noticed that this view of the matter is fully in accordance with our expectations of a linear, real-time, presentation of events; the establishment of the event time of each verbal element after the first depends upon the establishment of that of an earlier one in the chain. That is to say, it depends upon the effect the earlier verbal element has had upon the progressively changing State. Thus in

She asked him to get out to help her to reverse

the time of reversing is fixed by reference to that of helping, which is itself fixed by reference to that of getting out; and the event time of *get out* has been fixed by reference to that of *asked*. 'An earlier verbal element' does not necessarily mean, however, 'the immediately preceding verbal element'. So, in the possible (but not actually recorded) chain

> She asked him to get out to get rid of him

the event time to which that of both *get out* and *get rid of* are related is that of *asked*. We might say separately: 'She asked him to get out; and she asked him to get rid of him'. We saw in the last chapter that the presence of more than one N in a chain could result in indeterminacy of relationship when further elements were added. We now see that indeterminacy can also arise when verbal elements are introduced like this in series.

The effect of suspension

All this applies when the basic linearity of the chain is undisturbed by suspensions. Let us now briefly consider a case of suspension, one involving a V^1 initiated subchain, in the light of what we have said. In

> Concentrating on the traffic, she didn't have a chance to look at her

the suspending subchain (which includes the V^1) comes earlier in sequence than the finite V. The event time of *concentrating* is not, therefore, determined until the V occurs (until it does occur, the listener has no way of knowing whether the relevant reference point will be specified by 'didn't have' or 'doesn't have'). The 'wait a moment' implications we have already associated with suspensions turn out, therefore, to have interpretative as well as formal significance.

Non-finite verbal elements with post-nominal function

In all the examples we have used in this chapter, the subchain initiated by V^1 has had post-verbal function. Let us conclude by looking briefly at two cases where it has post-nominal function. The first works in the same way as those we have examined. In

> She asked the woman sitting in the car (what she was doing there)

sitting in the car is related to *the woman*, but it is still possible to say that the asking and the sitting are simultaneous. A slight complication is introduced, however, in

The poor old dear's request to get a lift shook her a bit

What this example demonstrates is that events may be named by using a nominal element instead of being referred to by means of a verbal element. Furthermore, the event identified as a *request* has its own event time which enters into the temporal implication of the chain. For a request to have the effect of shaking someone, it is necessary for the event—let us say the requesting, or the making of the request—to have occurred. That is to say, the event time of the named event is automatically represented as having preceded the differentiated time reference point of *shook*. The *to* form of *to get* assigns the anticipated getting of a lift to some subsequent point in time, in the usual way.

It seems, then, that the generalizations we have been able to make in this chapter about how time reference is made are applicable to other elements than those we have provisionally designated V. In Chapter 9 we shall show that they have even wider application.

8

Selection and communication

Prominence and selection

It is useful at this point to interrupt our attention to verbal elements and focus for a time on intonational matters. We are told in the narrative that the friend was not able to look across at her passenger for a time because

// P the TRAFfic was bad //

The transcription of this example signifies that the tonic syllable is located in *traffic*, an intonation treatment that makes it clear what the problem was: it was not, for instance, weather conditions or road works that were engaging her attention, but traffic. The fact that, once identified as the problem, it was *bad* goes without saying. Being not bad—perhaps being light, or well disciplined—would scarcely be given as a reason for not looking across. The first thing to notice, then, is that the placing of the tonic syllable serves to match the increment to a view of what present communicative needs are.

For comparison, we can take a possible alternative version,

// P the traffic was BAD //

which would fit another situation, one in which the fact of there being *traffic*, and of its state being of present significance, could be taken for granted. Then its badness—in contradistinction, perhaps, to its usual or expected orderliness—will be newsworthy.

Now it happens that the view of present circumstances that lies behind both of these versions would be perfectly tenable in the case we are considering. The speaker appears to have the option of using either without risk of producing an inappropriate increment. This will not necesssarily apply in other cases, however. Let us put the matter in the form of a tautology: it is not possible to go through the procedure of telling someone something without behaving as though there were something they do not know. The utterance

I was giddy

for instance, when produced as a telling increment, as in one version
of our story, projects an assumption that the addressee is unaware of
the old lady's state of physical well-being: it is by seeking to make
her aware of it that the speaker hopes to explain why she is in the
car. We can, in this case, narrow down the probable area of
ignorance or uncertainty to a very clear focus: that covered by the
single word *giddy*. We might represent the hearer's state of
uncertainty before being told somewhat as follows:

$$\text{She was} \begin{cases} \text{giddy?} \\ \text{tired?} \\ \text{confused?} \end{cases}$$

She did not know which of these was the reason for the old lady's
presence in the car.

In contrast, the addressee could, in the circumstances we know to
have existed at the time when this increment was produced, have
reasonably been supposed to know that the assertion would be
about *she*, that is to say the old lady, and that the requisite verbal
element would be *was*.

Let us say that the contribution the utterance makes towards
current conversational business is to make a selection from one of
the two, three (or perhaps more) conditions that might reasonably be
regarded as an explanation of why the speaker was where she was.
By selecting *giddy* the speaker relevantly eliminates alternatives like
tired and *confused*. We will say, provisionally, that if a chain is to
constitute a satisfactory response to some assumed communicative
need, it must not only have appropriate syntactic constituency; it
must also make appropriate selections. That is to say, it must remove
uncertainties that actually have a bearing upon that need.

We can demonstrate this most clearly if we first recognize the
connection between what we have called 'selection' and the
intonational phenomenon 'prominence'. In the storyteller's
quotation of what the old lady said, it is the selective word that has
a prominent syllable. We will represent this as follows:

// i was GIddy //

It will be noticed that the property we are calling prominence is associated in the examples we have used so far with the tonic syllable, that is to say with the syllable where the speaker also makes the choice between proclaiming and referring tones. We will continue to work with examples where this simple coincidence holds for the time being.

Now, it is obvious that this chain could be spoken with the tonic syllable, and hence a prominent syllable, located elsewhere,

// i WAS giddy //

// I was giddy //

and it follows from what we have just said that such changes will result in the utterance projecting different assumptions about what uncertainties need to be removed. Thus the area of uncertainty associated with // i WAS giddy // might be

$$I \left\{ \begin{array}{l} was \\ wasn't \end{array} \right\} giddy$$

and that with // I was giddy // might be

$$\left\{ \begin{array}{l} I \\ my\ daughter \end{array} \right\} was\ giddy$$

Needless to say, neither of these versions would be appropriate in the particular situation we have in mind — though it would be possible to imagine other situations in which either one of them would be appropriate.

Existential values

Before leaving this set of examples, let us look a little more closely at the concept of selection, and its relation to communicative need. Notice first that when we tentatively gave the set of possibilities from which *giddy* was selected — *giddy/tired/confused* — we were speculating about reasons that the old lady might offer, having regard to all we know about the surrounding circumstances. The significance of this last proviso may not be immediately apparent, but it is important enough to need stressing. We have recognized that an awareness of the surrounding circumstances, which is, of course, intimately bound up with an apprehension of present communicative purpose, is the basis on which both speakers and hearers operate.

And we have said that this is one of the respects in which involvement in purposeful verbal interaction differs most markedly from what the sentence grammarian is commonly interested in — the contemplation of pieces of language as free-standing exemplifications of the working of a system. The language system would allow a vast number of possibilities at the place marked X in a specimen chain

I was X

but probably no sane person would say, for instance, 'I was distant' or 'I was remarkable' by way of explanation, when she was found sitting in someone else's car. The set of possibilities from which selection is made is not, in fact, determined by one's knowledge of what the language will allow. It depends on one's awareness of what the likely alternatives are in the present state of speaker–hearer understanding. For this reason, we will refer to the process the speaker is involved in as 'existential selection' and the set of possibilities from which selection is made as an 'existential paradigm'.

If some items in an utterance are presented as selective it follows, of course, that the remainder are presented as non-selective, and we can apply the notion of existential selection to these as well. The reason neither *I* nor *was* is prominent in the old lady's explanation is that at the places they occupy in the chain, and in the known circumstances surrounding the utterance, nothing else is likely to be selected. Let us say that at each of the places there is an existential set of one member. When we alter the prominence distribution to

// i WAS giddy //

we are, as we have said, engaging with a different set of putative conditions. But it is not only that *was/wasn't* is now identified as an existentially relevant choice; in addition, *giddy* is now presented as something for which no existential alternative need be entertained. We might say that an interest in a state of giddiness is taken to be an already established fact of the present communicative event, so in saying

// i WAS giddy //

the speaker can take it for granted that *giddy* and no other word will occupy the third place.

The way prominent syllables are distributed in speech shows that speakers constantly have in mind the distinction between items, on the one hand, whose values are presently not taken to be a matter of selection, and those, on the other hand, whose values are. Since the evidence for this assertion is of a phonological kind, it is, perhaps, not very surprising that the distinction has been overlooked by grammarians whose starting-point has been the written and 'unused' sentence. We shall see, however, that it plays an important part in determining how used language is organized.

There is one further point to notice about existential selection. In proposing the particular set *giddy/tired/confused*, we have implied that any selection from the set will constitute a different explanation, and that these three possible reasons for the person's being there are mutually exclusive. This need not be the case. Tiredness might, under some circumstances, be the already agreed cause of giddiness, so that the set of available and meaningfully different choices would not include both words: by saying *giddy* one would not then be saying *not tired*. Indeed, since it was part of the agreed background understanding that being tired amounted, in effect, to being giddy, the two could be regarded as 'existential synonyms'. If, on the other hand, the owner of the car had asked whether it was tiredness that was the cause of the old lady's odd behaviour and the latter had replied 'No, I felt giddy', we should have a situation in which the same pair of words were regarded, for present purposes, as 'existentially antonymous'.

The general point is that words—and other, longer, stretches of speech—enter existentially into here-and-now relationships, both of opposition and equivalence, which often have little to do with the way the words of the language seem systematically to be organized into permanent relationships of synonymy and antonymy in a dictionary.

We can, then, analyse some stretches of speech like this:

// at ONE point // she took her HAND out // from under her JACKet // and when she SAW it // she was TERRified //

where existential alternatives might be something like

// at anOTHer point // she took her PURSE out // from under her SHOpping // and when she exAMined it // she was SATisfied //

(The symbol // represents a tone unit boundary, and each tone unit in these examples makes a single existential selection.)

Tone units with two prominent syllables

It very often happens, however, that in the stretch of speech the speaker delivers as a tone unit, there is a need to indicate more than one selection. There may, in other words, be a need for two prominent syllables. Thus, we find

// and she TOOK the NEXT turning //

which, in the place where it occurs in the story, can be expanded into something like

and she TOOK (= did not PASS) the NEXT (= not the CORRECT) turning

and the existential paradigms represented like this:

and she $\begin{Bmatrix} \text{took} \\ \text{passed} \end{Bmatrix}$ the $\begin{Bmatrix} \text{next} \\ \text{correct} \end{Bmatrix}$ turning

Evidently, we must now abandon the simple equation of prominence with tonic syllable, for the tone unit with two prominent syllables makes only one choice of tone. In a two-prominence tone unit there is another syllable which has a similar selective function, and it is a matter of observation that this other selective syllable always precedes the tonic syllable. Since this earlier syllable is not a tonic syllable it does not, of course, have the same phonological characteristics. It is nevertheless useful to say that they are both prominent because they are both perceived as indicating a selection.

The nature of prominence

It is not easy to say exactly which phonetic characteristics enable us to recognize a prominent syllable. A number of variables like pitch level, loudness, and length are involved, and discussion of this would be a distraction here. Probably the best way of approaching the matter is by taking note of the stress patterns that dictionaries associate with the citation forms of words. When we speak a word in isolation in the way that dictionary makers usually have in mind, we have no alternative but to present it as a complete and single tone unit: the word is, in the peculiar circumstances of citation, the unit of communication. Citation forms therefore provide us with a reliable guide to what tone units sound like. The one-prominence and two-prominence patterns are heard in words like

cor'rect

un'certain

where the allocation of secondary and primary stress corresponds to our representation

// corRECT //

// UNCERtain //

This is to say that prominent syllables that are not also tonic sound like those with secondary stress in such citation forms, and those that are tonic sound like those with primary stress. When we seek to apply this to used speech, however, we have to keep two things in mind. One is that the sound which counts, in citation, as a primary stress is subject to variation and depends upon which tone is used. The other is that the actual assignment of prominence to any word depends upon whether the word is selective or not in the particular circumstance of the utterance. The presence of either kind of stress in the citation form is no guarantee that the syllable will be prominent when the word is used. In particular, words which have two prominences in their citation forms seldom have two when they are used.

Selection in two-prominence tone units

The occurrence of two prominent syllables in one tone unit can have another significance over and above that which we have just attributed to it. One such tone unit from the data is

// so she SAT in the CAR //

A reasonable account of the existential selections here might be represented as

so she SAT (= she didn't continue to STAND) in the CAR (= not in the COLD)

Here, as in the previous example, it is fairly easy to think of both prominences making separate selections (*sat/stood*, *car/cold*).

Indeed, a version which presented the same information as two separate telling increments

// P so she SAT // P in the CAR //

would have very similar communicative effect. But this is by no means true of all cases. When the friend says of her strange passenger that she

// looked REALly ILL //

we can scarcely find existentially likely alternatives to both *really* and *ill*. It seems more sensible to describe what is happening here in a slightly different way. What the speaker is doing is opposing . . . *REALly ILL* as a whole to some notional alternative like 'fine' or 'fit', or—depending on the circumstances—'a bit off colour'. In this case, we must regard the two separate and consecutive selections as working together to define what, for the purposes of the conversation, amounts to a single one.

For another example of this, we can refer to one version of the story, in which the friend was asked what she had in her car. She remembered:

// a   HANDbag //
// my   SHOPPing //
// the   TOOLS //
// the   SPARE TYRE //

We could imagine a point in the conversation at which this list constituted an existential paradigm. If, for instance, the policeman came back and said that the first three of the items were missing, the only one left would be *the spare tyre*. So, making selective reference to the missing item would involve the speaker in opposing a two-prominence tone unit to a number of other tone units, each with one prominence. In other words, the two prominences in some tone units contribute to conversational progress by jointly defining a single selection.

Often, too, even when the alternative sense—the other possibility that is excluded by implication—is best expressed by another two-prominence tone unit, we cannot say that there is a simple either/or relationship between the two first prominences or between the two last prominences. If, as it seems proper to suppose,

// i'm NOT very GOOD at this sort of thing //

is opposed, in the story, to some contrary assertion that might be expressed as

// i can reVERSE the car very SKILfully //

we certainly cannot think of *not* as being opposed to *reverse*, or *good* as being opposed to *skilfully*. Two-prominence selections demonstrate even more clearly than those with only one prominence that existential antonyms seldom correspond to the way words are supposedly related to each other in the abstract and unused system: they make it very clear that it is sense selections not word selections that parties to an interaction are engaged in making.

We are not suggesting, of course, that it is usually possible to say with any degree of certainty just which alternative is excluded by an act of selection; nor is it necessary that we should be able to do so for the argument to hold. If, as we have said, the meaning of selection is 'this rather than anything else that present circumstances make likely', there is no necessary implication that the excluded alternative could actually be specified by the speaker or supplied by a hearer. But attending to a few cases where we can say with some plausibility what we think is excluded makes it possible to see how, in a general sense, the single prominence and the double prominence configurations we have identified as tone units work in organizing spoken language into communicative events. It enables us to take the important step of viewing any stretch of speech as an end-to-end sequence of separate existential selections, each one represented by either a 'simple' (one-prominence) or an 'extended' (two-prominence) tone unit.

The way this process brings together certain stretches of language and separates then off from other stretches is quite independent of any perceptions that sentence grammars might represent by bracketing procedures. It is the consequence of the speaker's assessment of what contrasts are relevant to present communicative needs. Something of the way it affects the outcome becomes apparent if we compare how one of the storytellers began our anecdote

(1) // R this STORy // P was TOLD to me by a FRIEND //

with something he might have said instead

(2) // R THIS story was TOLD to me // P by a FRIEND //

Both these increments have two tone units. In (1) the speaker first refers selectively to what he is about to tell as a *story*. (It might have been something else, for instance, a joke.) He then declares its origin: it

// was TOLD to me by a FRIEND //

If, as might be the case, this is intended to guarantee its authenticity, we might think of excluded alternatives as, for instance, it

// is ONE that's going aROUND //

the point being that the teller did not get it from a questionable source. Alternatively, this may be intended to absolve the storyteller from any responsibility for its truth. The excluded alternative might then be

// i'm SURE it's TRUE //

The constructed example, (2), invites a different interpretation. The speaker first assumes that the telling of stories has already been acknowledged as current business: the particular story he is about to retell was told to him. He thereby excludes the possibility of its having come from some other source: from his own experience, for instance, or from a magazine he has read. He then says who, from among the possible informants, actually told it: it was not, for instance, someone he happened to be sitting opposite on the train.

There may seem to be little difference in the way these two versions of the chain will affect the communicative state we have in mind. The story will proceed along similar lines either way. The fact that we have another way of viewing the organization of increments is of considerable help, however, when we try to explain how two sequences of words which appear identical, can permit of two different interpretations.

In the next chapter we shall return to the event-timing function of verbal elements. It will be useful then to be able to take account of the concept of existential selection in our exposition.

Sample of data

This data has been transcribed to show distribution of prominent syllables and division into tone units.

// she'd been STANding in the CAR park // and it was FREEZing COLD // and she asked her to TAKE her round to her DAUGHTer's // so she aGREED to take her round // she said WHAT else could she DO // she COULDn't leave her STANDing // in this CAR park // and they GOT back in the CAR // and she STARted to drive OFF // and she was a BIT sort of conCERNED // that this woman DIDn't SAY anything // and she kept VERy very QUIet // but SHUFfled about in her SEAT a lot // and sort of SEEMED a bit NERvous // at ONE point // she TOOK her HAND out // from i DON'T KNOW // where she HAD it // in GLOVES // or under a JACKet // and when she SAW her hand // she got REALly FRIGHTened //

9

More on verbal elements

Analysis of multi-word elements

We are now in a position to look again at those parts of chains we have been calling verbal elements. It will be remembered that we took the decision in Chapter 4 to work provisionally with the unanalysed blocks we labelled nominal (N), verbal (V), adverbial (A) and adjectival (E) elements. The understanding was that, although this was seen as a useful way of simplifying our task initially, a real-time finite-state account of syntax would need ultimately to show how the smaller components that we can identify within many of these elements can themselves be accounted for in a way which was consistent with our general approach. Although it has been convenient to begin by exploring the rules which govern how element follows element, we need now to move closer to asking what determines the way word follows word. Let us re-examine some of the sequences we have called verbal elements with a view to starting on this task.

In the analyses we have undertaken, we have regularly regarded sequences like:

have searched

was waiting

had been expecting

as each comprising a single element. In doing this we have followed a well-established tradition in sentence grammar where such sequences of words are commonly referred to as constituents like 'verb phrases' or 'verbal groups'. But postulates like groups and phrases belong to the conceptual apparatus that arises from a preoccupation with the internal structure of unused sample sentences. We need now to show that, as stretches of used language, their internal arrangement can be accounted for in another way. It turns out, in fact, that we can get quite a long way towards doing so without making any substantial alterations to the sequencing rules we have set up.

We saw in Chapter 5 that the sequencing rules already allow for the possibility of a non-finite verbal element following any element in the chain. If we now take the simple step of recognizing that the first word in each of the sequences we have cited—*have, was, had*—is, in itself, a complete and finite verbal element (V) then the occurrence immediately after it of a non-finite verbal element (V¹) follows naturally from the operation of the rules. Thus, instead of analysing the policeman's assertion

We/have searched/your car

as NVA (that is to say, treating *have searched* as a single V), we already have grounds for analysing it as

We/have/searched/your car

that is to say, as NVV¹A.

This amounts, of course, to a more far-reaching change than a mere substitution of one symbolic representation for another. For one thing, it encourages us to look for similarities between the temporal implications of the VV¹ sequences that we find in chains like this and those we examined in Chapter 7. Such similarities tend to be obscured in most sentence grammars, since the alternative tense forms that are attributed to verbal phrases (*search/have searched/am searching/have been searching*, etc.), and the other various uses of non-finite verbs, are usually treated in quite separate sections of the book. Furthermore, a decision to treat each consecutive word as a separate step forward through the chain, making its own contribution to the communicative value of the utterance, deprives us of the opportunity to discuss temporal implications on the basis of a postulated 'tense paradigm'. This piece of descriptive apparatus, which represents the speaker as making choices between tense forms, some of which comprise one word and others of which comprise more, is available only if one accepts the notion of constituency structure. It follows that other means must be found in a finite-state grammar of handling the information that the paradigm representation embodies.

Selectional possibilities of auxiliary *have*

Let us compare the way existential selections are made in this invented pair:

(1) We searched your car
(2) We have searched your car

If (1) were spoken with a prominent syllable in *searched*, this
element would contribute as a sense selection to the communicative
value of the chain. When used, as it is said to have been used, by the
policeman, the most probably excluded alternative is something like
looked in: it has been no perfunctory inspection! We say this
amounts to a sense selection because it specifies which of a number
of significantly different possible events took place. The qualification
'sense' is necessary because, as we saw in Chapter 8, *searched* also
represents a primary event time selection: the speaker specifies
differentiated *searched* as opposed to undifferentiated *search*. At
least two separate selections are made in the same word. Version (2)
is different. Here, too, *searched* makes a sense selection, but the
potential event time selection is a secondary one: the pp form
excludes one of the other (non-finite) carriers of secondary time
selection. Primary event time is now selected, if at all, in *have* (as
opposed to *had*). And although this latter cannot comprise a sense
selection, it represents a further selection, that of 'polarity' — *have* as
opposed to *haven't*. The selective potential of both *searched* and
have searched are, therefore, as represented in Figure 9.1.

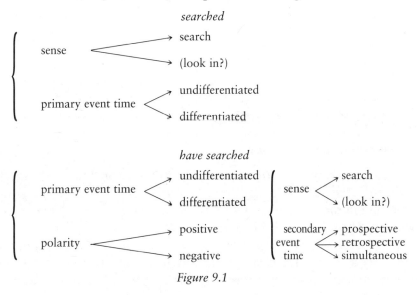

Figure 9.1

The following brief comments refer to Figure 9.1:

1 When it is used in this way, as a potential selector of only event time and polarity, *have* is commonly referred to as an 'auxiliary', and it is convenient to make use of this term.

2 There is another use of *have* in which it may make a sense selection. For instance, in [the old lady] ' . . . had a shopping bag' *had* is an existential synonym for *carried*. Although it is usually non-prominent, it can be prominent and then signifies a selection against another sense such as *lack*.

3 Figure 9.1 represents only potential for selection. Whether any particular element is actually presented as selective (by the allocation of a prominent syllable) always depends upon present communicative need.

4 If auxiliary *have* has prominence, it signifies either a polarity selection or a primary event time selection, so

> // they HAD searched it // alREADy //

might be a corrective reply to

> // have they SEARCHED your CAR //

or a polarity selection

> // WHY don't they SEARCH your car // . . . // they HAVE searched it //

5 In most cases, both event time and polarity can be taken to have been already determined, so *have* does not often have prominence. (This is often recognized in spelling by the use of such forms as 'We've searched your car'.)

Communicative deficiency

Specifying primary event time or polarity may sometimes be exactly what is necessary to satisfy communicative need. This is commonly the case in the response parts of asking exchanges, where increments like // i HAVE // serve this purpose. Usually, however, some kind of verbal sense selection is at least part of what the message is about. It follows that, in such cases, when auxiliary *have* is used, it satisfies the requirement of the sequencing rule that a V should be produced at this point, but leaves unsatisfied the need for sense selection. This latter need must be met by a further verbal element, and since this will be in the same chain it can only be a non-finite one. We will say of a chain which stops short after *have*

We have

when sense selection is called for that the chain is 'communicatively deficient', even though it has the minimal requirements, NV, for a satisfactory chain.

We can, therefore, redefine the Intermediate State precipitated by V: it is a State in which progress to Target State, either directly or via any one of the next permitted elements, can be made, but only if an appropriate selection has been made.

It is worth noting that the awareness that there is 'more to come' after the V, and that progress to the next element in the simple chain sequence is held up until it does come, once more affects our perceptions of how language is organized: it can easily give rise to a 'constituency' kind of explanation. Fulfilment of the dual requirement for formal V and for a potential sense selection depends upon both *have* and *searched* being produced, and this contributes powerfully to a feeling that the two hang together as a single entity.

Auxiliary *have* followed by non-finite forms

The rules proposed would, in principle, allow for any of the three non-finite forms to follow auxiliary *have*. Let us examine each of the possibilities in turn.

1 The communicative value of auxiliary *have* + pp form follows directly from what we have said and becomes very clear if we once more compare

We have searched your car

with

We searched your car

In the second example, *searched* both specifies the event (searching as opposed to doing something else) and specifies differentiated time reference; and since the two specifications occur in the same word they cannot be varied independently. In the first example the undifferentiating form of *have* establishes a time reference point

105

which is equated with the moment of utterance. The pp form of *searched* then has its usual effect of placing the event time of the act of searching at some point earlier than that set by the earlier verb: at the time reference point, which in this case is the moment of utterance, the act of searching is already accomplished.

2 An example which used auxiliary *have* + *-ing* form, like

We have searching your car

would be marked with an asterisk in many sentence grammars, and thus be ruled out of consideration as being 'ungrammatical'. Certainly we should not expect to hear it, and we might reasonably ask why.

An interpretation of its various components along the lines followed in the case of *we have searched* would be something like this: the event time of *searching* is equated (*-ing* form of *search*) with a time reference point, which, in this case is equated with the moment of utterance (undifferentiated form of auxiliary *have*). In other words, its communicative value would be identical with that of the undifferentiating form of the simple verb in *we search your car*. While *have searched* serves the useful purpose of separating utterance time from event time, *have searching* makes no such useful separation. We might speculate that the latter is not used because there are no conceivable circumstances in which its communicative value would differ from that of the one-word version.

3 The third possibility, having auxiliary *have* + *to* form seems to occur only rarely. More common are instances in which *have* constitutes a sense selection, as in

// we HAVE to search your CAR //

In this case, the policeman would be speaking of having to do something as opposed to, say, wanting to do it or hoping to do it. The VV^1 sequence is, therefore, similar to those we were concerned with in Chapter 7.

Although the data provide no examples, there are, however, occasional uses of *have* as an auxiliary followed by a *to* form, and when they occur their communicative value is exactly as we should predict. In

We have yet to find one

the event time of *to find* is fixed prospectively with respect to a time reference point which is, in this case, equated with the moment of speaking.

These last three paragraphs, and particularly the discussion of **have searching*, bring us to the edge of a question that we shall have to confront later. It is evident that the rule system we are describing would make possible very many chains that are unlikely ever to be encountered, or are encountered only rarely. To some extent, at least, it seems likely that this is because occasions never or seldom arise in which they would be useful. This is not the point to explore this possibility further. We shall return to it in Chapter 18.

Auxiliary *be*

Let us now consider an auxiliary verb that enters freely into VV' sequences with all three of the non-finite forms, auxiliary *be*. We find all of these:

Someone was sitting in her car

I was to meet my daughter here

My friend's car was parked in the multi-storey car park

We should, therefore, be able to see whether the same considerations apply to the communicative value of these as we found apply to the other sequences we have dealt with. Before looking for similarities, however, it is first necessary to recognize the way in which *be* differs from all the verbal elements we have met so far. We will examine its use briefly in:

My friend was parked
N   V V'

The old lady was cold
N   V E

It was a man's hand
N V N

She was in the car park
N V A

These examples make it clear that the Intermediate State precipitated by any form of *be* is one in which a speaker can take any of the ways forward that we have represented in our sequencing rules. The relevant part of those rules is repeated as Figure 9.2.

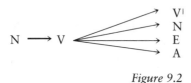

Figure 9.2

The only kind of sequence we do not normally find in telling increments is one in which the production of *be* as V is sufficient to achieve Target State (a fact that we can associate with the exceptional inability of this verb ever to be selectively sufficient).

Events and conditions

What all the above sequences have in common is that, whatever element follows *be*, it has a function that we can roughly describe as specifying the identity, condition, location, or quality of that which was referred to by the chain initial N. Even if we adopt the extended notion of what constitutes an event that we have already found necessary, it is scarcely sensible to describe the difference between, let us say, *she is cold* and *she was cold* as being a matter of event time. The addition to our terminology of the more-or-less arbitrarily chosen expression 'condition time' will make it possible to say, rather more reasonably, that the undifferentiating form *She is cold* equates the condition time with the time of utterance ('at the time I speak she is in a condition we can describe as cold') and the differentiating form *She was cold* places the condition time at some point earlier than the time of utterance ('at the time I speak the condition I refer to as cold is a matter of history').

This distinctive significance of *be* can be further clarified if we compare it with *have*. Occasionally we can find otherwise similar chains in which the two verbs can alternate. Thus the data includes:

My friend had parked in the multi-storey car park

and might equally well have included:

My friend was parked in the multi-storey car park

In the first of these the event of parking is related retrospectively to the moment of speaking. In the second it is the condition of being parked that is so related. (Notice that speakers are not bound by such literal considerations as that it was not she but her car that was in that condition.) The fact that these two versions would be interchangeable for many speakers evidently arises from the fact that the difference between having performed the act of parking somewhere and having one's car in the parked condition there is unlikely ever to be of much practical importance.

Auxiliary *be* followed by non-finite forms

There are, however, occasions when present communicative need has to be viewed as a matter of specifying condition rather than event. By electing to begin a verb sequence with a form of *be*, a speaker signifies an intention of doing just that. Let us now see how this works with each of the non-finite forms

1 *Be* is followed by a pp form in

My friend was parked in the Hurst Street car park
She was terrified

In both cases, the element was first of all fixes a condition time at some time earlier than utterance time. It simultaneously gives notice that the following element will be concerned with condition. The pp forms of *parked* and *terrified* attach an event time to each of them which has preceded the condition time: the condition is one which has resulted from an earlier act of parking or terrifying. This means that, as we saw in Chapter 7, use of the pp form entails taking a perfective view of the earlier event: the parking and the terrifying are regarded as having been completed. It is worth noting that the difference between

She was parked

and

She was giddy

resides essentially in whether the condition is viewed as the consequence of an earlier event or not. The indeterminacy of some words like *lost* in the unused sentence *It was lost* arises because the condition may be attributed to a past event of losing (when *lost* is a pp form) or not (when it is an adjectival element like *giddy*). Again, we have to note that such indeterminacy is unlikely ever to result in ambiguity.

2 Moving now to consider sequences comprising *be* followed by an *-ing* form, we can see that in

Someone is sitting in her car

She was shivering

both forms of *be* give notice that it is condition, not event, that is subsequently to be specified, though they relate the condition time to the moment of utterance in different ways. Specification of the condition occurs in *sitting* and in *shivering*, but it is now accomplished not by reference to something that has happened earlier but by reference to what is happening now: the condition of the subject is characterized by reference to what they are currently doing. The relationship between the condition time in question and the event time of the activity that produces the condition is, as we should expect with the *-ing* form, one of contemporaneity.

It also follows that, since the condition is a consequence of 'what is happening now', verbal elements that are used to specify it are used non-perfectively. We can see this if we compare

Someone sat . . .

with

Someone was sitting . . .

While *sat* is indeterminate as between perfective and non-perfective, *sitting* is not: the event is viewed as one which continues through a time span which includes the condition time already indicated.

3 Instances of the third combination, *be* followed by a *to* form, are not very common in most kinds of discourse. We do, however, find examples like

I was to meet my daughter here, but . . .

Here, the condition the old lady attributes to herself at the differentiated time reference point is one of expectation: meeting her daughter was something that had not yet occurred but which nevertheless affects the situation she has found herself in. The *to*-form therefore carries its usual implication of a potential event placed prospectively at a subsequent point in time.

Expectation in a slightly different sense can be attributed to another (invented) use of this combination:

You are to be back by ten o'clock

used, most often, to a child, such an utterance is usually thought to have some kind of imperative force. We may say, though, that simply to intimate — as this speaker can be said to do — that 'at this moment, your condition is one in which your returning at a certain time is anticipated' will usually amount to issuing an instruction, particularly if speaker and listener are in the kind of relationship where instructions are assumed to be in order. That is to say, the particular local value of such an utterance can be traced to the exploitation of the general values that accrue to this combination of verbs when it is used in certain discourse conditions. In the terms we have used earlier, we can say that the speaker 'instructs' or 'orders' by telling.

Longer verbal sequences

It remains to apply what we have said above to increments which use more than one auxiliary verb before the non-finite form. An example is

She had been waiting for half an hour
N V V^1 V^1 A

The selections made in the VV^{1}V^1 sequence are as follows: *had* selects differentiated time reference; *been* indicates that the increment will be concerned with condition, and that the condition existed at a time preceding the time reference point of *had*; *waiting* specifies the event that results in the condition, in this case one which coincides temporarily with it.

A similar account could be given of each of these invented examples, except that the temporal implications of the last V^1 would be different:

111

She had been deceived

(The act of deception preceded the condition.)

The arrangement had been to meet in the car park

(The condition was one in which the act of meeting was prospective.)

When we consider the non-occurrence of certain possible three-element verbal sequences, we can find similar explanations to the one we gave for the non-occurrence of some two element sequences. Thus, if

They had searching

can serve no conceivable communicative purpose,

She had being deceived

cannot either.

In the next chapter we shall extend our account to take in sequences that make use of another kind of verbal element and another non-finite form.

10

Modals and the plain infinitive

Modals

There are a number of frequently used verbal elements that have not been allowed for in our account so far. To begin extending our treatment to include them, let us consider the following:

She can take a look at this person's hands

My daughter may be sick or something

You'll have to turn round

I shall turn in this driveway

Each of these has, as its finite verbal element, one of the verbs that are commonly referred to as 'modals': *may, can, will, shall*. These require separate attention because they signify neither event nor condition; they serve rather to indicate the speaker's assessment of the degree of probability or certainty of the event or state that is signified thereafter. Thus, taking a look at the hands is declared to be possible but not certain; so, too, is the sickness of the daughter. The person treats having to turn round as a future certainty, and the friend treats turning round in the driveway in the same way.

Some distinguishing features of the modals are:

1 They resemble the auxiliaries *have* and *be* in that they select for time reference (*can/could may/might will/would shall/should*) and polarity (*can/can't may/may not will/won't shall/shan't*). Regarding time reference, however, we have to think of the form of the modal as relating what we will call, for convenience, a probability time (rather than an event time or a condition time) to utterance time: 'Now, as I speak, she may/will . . . ' etc.

2 They resemble event-type verbs in that they can select for sense:

$$\text{she} \quad \begin{Bmatrix} \text{can} \\ \text{will} \end{Bmatrix} \quad \text{take a look}$$

$$\text{I} \quad \begin{Bmatrix} \text{may} \\ \text{shall} \end{Bmatrix} \quad \text{turn in this driveway}$$

The elements that can be entertained as possible existential alternatives, however, belong to a very restricted class, comprising essentially other modals.

3 Since their potential for selection is always related to the 'probability' of some event or condition, they are communicatively deficient: progress towards Target State is always via a V¹ which has the selective potential for specifying what the event or condition is. Thus, for instance, we could find no occasion when it would be appropriate to say 'She can . . . ' without following it with some non-finite verbal element like 'take'.

4 The V¹ that follows them, whether it is the required sense selector or a modal, has base form instead of one of the three forms we discussed in Chapter 9.

Base form of non-finite elements

The base form is the form under which dictionaries usually organize their verb entries. With the exception of *be*, it is indistinguishable, by sight or sound, from the undifferentiated form of the finite verb (*take*, as opposed to differentiated *took*). It does not, however, represent a selection in the way that finite verbal elements do: we do not, for instance, find 'She could took a look'. Neither does it represent a time selection in the same way as other non-finite forms do, and this last fact calls for investigation.

We have seen that the auxiliaries *have* and *be* specify an event time or a condition time to which the time of a subsequently mentioned event or condition is then related. A *to* form used in these circumstances refers to that event prospectively. In a somewhat similar way, modal verbs signify a probability time for an event that has not yet happened. In both cases, therefore, there is a reference to events or conditions yet to come. We need to know why those events are referred to differently.

The explanation seems to be as follows: both *have* and *be* leave open the possibility that the time reference points of subsequent V's will be before, after, or the same as their own; that is to say, they may take the *-ing* form or the pp form as alternatives to the *to* form. There is also sometimes a possibility of a following non-verbal form. The modals by contrast, leave the speaker with no such possibility of choice. *Can + take* and *may + be* are, in effect, related as single entities, and on a once-for-all basis, to the real time of the utterance. Having settled the probability time, there is never a possibility that the event time will be other than later: the 'taking' is necessarily attached to the undifferentiated probability time of *can*, and the state specified after *be* is necessarily attached to that of *may*. To put it in another way, we can say that, by using a modal verb the speaker is irrevocably committed to producing a verbal element and also one with prospective implications, something which does not apply in a general way to other kinds of verb. The base form of V^1 is used whenever independent choice is precluded in this way.

Modals in sequence with non-finite forms

We can now add modalization to what we have to say about the sequencing rules. At the Intermediate State precipitated by the production of chain-initial N, the speaker must first decide whether specification of probability is pertinent to present communicative needs. If it is, the required V will be a modal. The modal will not, however, be communicatively sufficient, so there will be need for one or more V^1 elements: as many V^1 elements, in fact, as are needed to achieve a State at which an element capable of making an appropriate selection has been produced. For the reason we have given, the V^1 immediately following the modal will have plain infinitive form.

The example

(1) He may have hidden something in the car

will serve to show how the procedure works. Let us start with the auxiliary *have*. As a plain infinitive, this cannot make either a polarity choice, or a time reference choice: these have both been settled in the preceding modal; and because of its auxiliary function it does not make a sense choice. It is reasonable to ask, therefore, why it is included at all. The answer becomes evident if we compare this example with the invented alternative:

(2) Something may be hidden in the car

The selection that distinguishes these two increments is that between *have* and *be*, and the effect of choosing one rather than the other follows from what we have said about the two verbs: the first is an assertion about the possibility of an event, the second an assertion about the possibility of a condition. Neither the event nor the condition have so far been specified, however: the sequence therefore remains communicatively deficient until a pertinent sense selection has been made. In (1) the pp form *hidden* places the event at an earlier time than the undifferentiated reference time of *have*. In (2) the same form of the same verb indicates that the condition prefigured by *be* was one brought about by an earlier act of hiding.

Conversational use of modals

The foregoing account of modals, presented simply in terms of the way they occur in the linear presentation of speech, may seem to miss out a great deal that could be said about them. Their use is, for instance, notoriously difficult for some foreign learners to master, a fact which suggests a far more complex rule system than the one we have proposed. Some of the complexity becomes apparent only when modals are used in connection with asking increments, and in discussing them here we are unavoidably using examples whose full discussion must await the treatment of such increments in Chapter 17. We may, nevertheless, ask why their conversational use seems so much less straightforward than one might expect.

Firstly, there is the tendency we noted in Chapter 7 for speakers to use the differentiated time reference choice to make such events as requests or suggestions more acceptable socially. This applies equally to modals. 'Could you give me a lift?' or 'Might I borrow your car keys?' seems to avoid what might be regarded as inappropriate directness in the enquiry by exploiting differentiated probability time. Here the speaker tactfully proceeds as if the possibility might have existed at an earlier time but may no longer do so: 'That is what I thought of asking (but perhaps I shouldn't?)'. The same applies to the way should is often used as an alternative to *shall*: 'Should you be offended if I . . . ?' and *would* as an alternative to *will*: 'Would it be going out of your way to take me there?'. We can say of these, as we said of the special uses of verbal elements with differentiated time reference in Chapter 5, that they are instances of the exploitation of the system. The strictly fictional shift in the time perspective serves no other purpose than a diplomatic one. One fact worth noting is that it is frequently very difficult to say whether one form is a better one to use than the other; the question of whether or not to behave *as if* the request or suggestion was now a matter of history is not settled by appeal to a clear-cut grammatical rule; it depends upon a rather subtle assessment of one's relations with one's listener.

Secondly, there is the very common use of *shall* and *will* in something that has often been thought of as a future tense. The possibility of using them in this way arises naturally from what was said above. To associate certainty, the extreme end of the probability scale, with a future event amounts to saying that its subsequent occurrence is now determined, as is evident in:

We'll go and search it (i.e. the car)

Elements like this are, however, subject to a measure of indeterminacy that tends seriously to obscure the picture. Often, futurity — and, therefore the implication that the going and searching are without doubt going to happen — can be taken for granted by both speaker and hearer. The modal therefore then has no prominence:

// we'll GO and SEARCH it //

When modals are given prominence, a number of interpretations are available. This is because, as we have said, modals can represent selections in three distinct existential paradigms. In

// we WILL SEARCH it //

will may represent either of the following:

1 A selection of polarity: *will* is opposed to *will not*. There is commitment on the part of the speaker not to neglect to search it.

2 A possibility time selection: 'We will search it now, even if we haven't done so before.'

117

3 A sense selection: *will* is opposed, perhaps to *may*. 'There is positively no question about whether we will search it or not.'

When a chain like this occurs in used language, acquaintance with the communicative setting is usually sufficient to resolve any potential ambiguity. Implications of 'determination', 'compulsion', 'commitment', and so on, which can all be traced to one or more of the possible selections, are readily picked up by an engaged listener. If, for instance, the friend had said to her strange passenger

You will get out

the latter would be likely to hear it as having imperative implications simply because she was speaking of the certainty of a future event that would usually be under the passenger's control, not hers. Such an utterance resembles 'You are to be back by ten o'clock' in being used only in circumstances where peremptory control of other people's actions is deemed to be in order. And as in that case, we have to make a mental separation between how the formal presentation of the increment, in itself, affects its communicative value, and how local values accrue to it because of the situation it is used in. It is principally when one is required to propose an interpretation for one of the modals without prior knowledge of its present use that potential ambiguities become a problem.

Finally, it has to be said that some of the conventions concerning the use of specific modals seem not to be agreed among users. One storyteller attributes to the friend the request

Can you just get out and help me to reverse?

Now most attempts that have been made to describe the precise meanings of the modals would say that this was an inappropriate use of *can*: that what the speaker 'meant' was *will*. A facetious, and uncooperative, reply

I can, but I won't

would underline the 'error'. The fact seems to be that *can* and *will*, and also *can* and *may* are often used, by some speakers at least, as existential synonyms. There is also considerable difference among speakers, and often within the everyday usage of individuals, in the way *will* and *shall* are used. Much has been written, usually of a prescriptive nature, concerning such expressions as *I will/I shall*, *You will/you shall*. This is not the place to add more. The present point is that none of these matters can be regarded as affecting, or being affected by, the linear organization of the increment. In this latter respect, the use of modals is governed in the way we have described.

Verbal element *do*

We have said that polarity can be selected by the auxiliaries *have* and *be* and by modals. Thus the storyteller could negate

She had parked in Hurst Street

She was going back to her car

She could see this old lady sitting in it

by saying

She hadn't parked . . .

She wasn't going back . . .

She couldn't see . . .

Verbs which have the potentiality for making sense selections, however, do not select polarity. In order to negate

She told me this story

She went back to her car

it is necessary to use a form of the auxiliary *do*:

She didn't tell . . .

She didn't go . . .

We can think of *do* as selecting a 'negation time', either differentiated or undifferentiated, to which all subsequent time references in the chain will be related. It resembles the modals in being followed by a plain infinitive; and, as in the case of modals, we can associate this with the fact that there is no possibility of separate time reference in the second element. However, there is a difference for whereas the modals always make prospective reference to the event or condition designated by the following element, the time reference of the element following *do* is necessarily the same as that of *do* itself: *didn't tell* and *didn't go* are both once-for-all selections of differentiated time reference.

Plain infinitives following other verbal elements

Before leaving the topic of the plain infinitive, let us note some other verbal elements that are followed by the plain infinitive. Although these would not normally be regarded as modals, they resemble them in that the Intermediate State they precipitate is one in which the next time reference is fully determined. Examples are:

> She let the old lady get back in her car
> She made him get out to help her reverse

Clearly, there is no possibility of the event time of *get back* or *get out* being thought of as anything other than prospective with respect to *let* or *make*. To make someone do something or to let them do it can each be regarded as a single event and therefore as having single event time in much the same way as *may get back* or *can get* would be.

Sample of data

In this sample of data, all the VV^1 sequences are underlined. They include both the kind of sequence discussed in Chapter 7 (those in which primary and secondary time references are associated with elements that are potentially sense selectors) and the kind discussed in Chapters 9 and 10 (where primary time reference is made in an auxiliary or a modal element).

> I <u>was talking</u> to a friend . . . she'<u>d parked</u> up Hurst Street somewhere . . . this old lady <u>was sitting</u> in her car . . . she <u>was supposed to have met</u> her daughter there . . . her daughter <u>hadn't come</u> . . . she <u>was supposed to arrive</u> half an hour ago . . . something <u>had happened</u> to her daughter . . . she <u>could have had</u> an accident . . . she <u>agreed to take</u> her to her daughter's . . . she <u>couldn't leave her standing</u> there . . . she <u>started to drive</u> off . . .

120

11

More extensions and suspensions

Much of what we have said in the last six chapters has been concerned with the use of non-finite verbal elements. It will be recalled that these were introduced after we had set up a sequence of rules for the simple chain. They were presented as illustrations of the kinds of mechanism we have at our disposal for extending the power of those rules to produce more complex chains. In particular, we have shown that they can be used to initiate two kinds of lengthening of the route for getting from Initial State to Target State in order to satisfy particular communicative needs. We have distinguished two methods of lengthening, which we have called 'extension' and 'suspension'. We said at the time that there were other ways, both of extending the chain and of suspending its completion, than by using non-finite verbal elements. We must now investigate what these are, so that we can apply the method of analysis we have been using to the description of other stretches of used speech.

Reduplication

One kind of extension is easily described. It is found in

She inspected her passenger, this little old lady

She looked again at the face

In these cases, the second N or the A which is provided for by the sequencing rules is followed immediately by another element of the same kind: the chain is extended by the addition of an N after an N or of an A after an A. We shall call this kind of extension 'reduplication'.

A reduplicating element can also constitute a suspension as it does in

This old lady, this bloke, got out

where the occurrence of the reduplicative N, *this bloke*, delays the production of the expected verbal element.

The suspensive use of a reduplicating A usually requires a slightly more elaborate explanation. Since the expected place of an adverbial element is at the end of a simple chain, no second A that follows it will be suspensive unless there is also some other modification of simple-chain ordering. Consider this chain:

The old lady sat in the driver's seat in the car to keep warm

To trace the route through the rules of which this is the outcome, we need to be aware of two kinds of modification being used in conjunction with each other. The speaker's purpose is to tell why the old lady was in the car; in order to achieve the Target State, progress via *to keep warm* is ultimately necessary. The first adverbial element, *in the driver's seat*, occurs where A is provided for in the chaining rules, but the second, in the car, constitutes a suspension. In

After that, at the next roundabout, she took the wrong exit

the first A of the reduplicating pair is suspensive, as are all chain-initial adverbial elements. Then *at the next roundabout* occurs as a second suspension. There are therefore two consecutive delays in getting to the 'expected' N.

The + symbol

We will, henceforth, use the plus symbol (+) to indicate a reduplicative relationship between adjacent elements. Our two examples involving extensions will therefore be represented like this:

She inspected her passenger, the little old lady
N   V   N+   N

She looked again at the face
N   V   A+   A

When suspensions, and hence lower case symbols, are involved, we have:

This old lady, this bloke, got out
N+   n   V   A

The old lady sat in the driver's seat in the car to keep warm
N   V A+   a   (V¹   E   )

Preposition/nominal elements

There is one more kind of reduplication that we can accommodate into our rule system if we recognize a distinction that we have overlooked until now. In

> She came to a driveway, a turning on the left

it is *a driveway* that is the first N in an N+N pair. But we have so far regarded this as part of an adverbial element. By using the same symbol, A, for elements of this type and for elements like *apparently* and *again*, we have been able to keep in step with the fairly general agreement as to what constitutes adverbial status, and at the same time recognize a measure of similarity in the way both types behave with respect to the sequencing rules. We have also been able to avoid complicating our statement with a distinction that has not yet had any significance. At this point we must separate the two kinds of element, however, and use a different representation for the first kind. We will call it a 'preposition/nominal element'.

With this modification, our example will now be represented thus as having two occurrences of P/N elements:

> She came to a driveway, a turning on the left
> N V   P/N+   N   P/N

A turning is thus treated as the consequence of reduplication after *a driveway*. Similarly

> She looked at this person, this little old lady
> N V   PN+   N

Indeterminacy resulting from reduplication

The use of reduplication is, like that of non-finite predication, the source of many instances where different chains are given identical descriptions when we view them simply as sequences of elements, but where, from the sentence grammarian's point of view, there are significant differences.

To explore this, let us consider a group of examples, each of which results from a similar use of a reduplicating N:

> She offered the old woman a lift
> My friend told me an incredible story

She made him a real fool

As a preliminary step, we must examine further the way in which nominal elements function in simple chains. There are two possible occurrences of N in such chains, and we have provisionally attached the traditional term 'subject' to the first—the one that precedes V in all chains. The occurrence or non-occurrence of a second N depends upon which communicative need the speaker is seeking to satisfy; but there are some verbs which are highly likely to precipitate a state in which one is expected. It would be difficult to imagine a situation in which, for instance, *she found* or *the old lady put* would be regarded by either participant as amounting to a complete telling increment. Elements which involve the speaker in this kind of commitment are the 'transitive verbs' of traditional grammar. As we said earlier, however, we take them, for present purposes, to be simply special cases of the general way in which certain particular words precipitate Intermediate States in which the ways forward are predetermined in certain ways. To label verbs as intransitive or transitive would be, from our point of view, to obscure the essential fact that it is perceived communicative need that determines the possible ways forward. All that we can say about particular verbs—indeed, about the words that realize any of the other elements—is that situations are, or are not, likely to arise in which their production will satisfy a communicative need without further addition(s) of a particular kind.

But to say that there is often a need for a second N after certain verbal elements is to acknowledge only part of the truth. A chain which begins

She offered the old woman

has the expected N, but only under very exceptional circumstances would it achieve Target State. The reason for this is very simple: old women do not, in our usual experience, fall into the class of things that are likely to be *offered*. An alternative chain,

She offered a lift

sounds far more likely; in fact, in the context we are now familiar with, where someone had been expecting to be picked up by someone else who hadn't arrived, its occurrence could be said to be highly probable.

The obligations placed upon the speaker in cases like these can be described by making use of the notion of 'appropriate selection'. Quite simply, if *the old woman* is not among the class of things that are thought to be offerable, it cannot represent an appropriate selection from among the set of things that might, in the present circumstances, be offered. And when the item that fulfils the formal requirement for an N manifestly does not represent a suitable existential selection, the speaker has an obligation to produce another N that does. Only then can progress be made, either directly or via other necessary elements, to Target State.

Notice, it follows from this that if the formally required N does amount to an appropriate selection, as in

She offered a lift

Target State may be deemed to have been reached. Going further, as in

She offered a lift to a little old lady

is then a matter of assessing whether specifying the putative recipient of the lift is communicatively necessary. If it is, the rules provide for the necessary P/N . . . *to a little old lady* to follow.

An exactly parallel explanation can be offered for

She made him a real fool

The foreshortened chain

She made him

could, in certain not too far-fetched circumstances, constitute a telling increment; but at this point in the narrative, the friend has just got the passenger out of her car and left him on the pavement, so this is hardly such a circumstance. It is one in which the possibility of *making a . . . (?)* could reasonably be entertained, but scarcely that of *making him*. Again, therefore, the requirement of the sequencing rules that an N be produced after V is satisfied, this time by the production of *him*; but since *him* is not, in these circumstances, an appropriate selection, the further N, *fool*, is required.

Another very similar example is

My friend told me an incredible story the other day

An invented version

My friend told an incredible story (to me) the other day

would probably be existentially equivalent in any situation. But

My friend told me the other day

would require a different context—one in which the question of what had been told (a story) was already conversationally in play. Only if this were so, might we consider that *me* represented an appropriate selection.

The sequences that these examples represent can be subdivided on the basis of the group of verbs from which the verbal element is selected:

1 offering, giving, refusing, selling, etc.
2 making, appointing, calling, etc.
3 telling, asking, ordering, etc.

The point stressed here, however, is not that they differ, but that they all arise from a similar set of circumstances, namely that when the speaker has produced an element of a type prescribed by the sequencing rules for a particular Intermediate State, the requirements associated with that State may yet be such as to require production of another element of the same kind. This second requirement arises, not from the imperatives of the rule system as such, but from the specific insufficiency of a chain which employs that verb to satisfy present communicative need without a reduplicative N.

A fourth example of N reduplication appears to be different:

She inspected her passenger, the little old lady

The comma we have used in the written form can be taken to represent the fact that in the recorded version there is a tone unit boundary after *passenger*. Both tone units have proclaiming tones:

// P she inSPECted her PASsenger // P the little old LADy //

The speaker therefore presents this chain not as a single telling increment but as two. She first tells what the friend did, and then tells something about the passenger. In the context in which this is an appropriate chain, *she inspected her passenger* is not communicatively deficient, so the option of reduplication is available for an additional telling. But this use of a reduplicative nominal element, to provide a gloss upon something that has been referred to already, does not necessarily involve an extra telling increment. The element concerned is suspensive in this example, and has a referring tone:

// R the EXit // R the PROPer one // P was the FIRST one OFF //

What happens here is that the speaker first introduces *the exit* as something that is a generally understood feature of the roundabout they have reached, and then decides that such a reference may be deficient: she consequently makes a further selection, *the proper one*, before going on to the verbal element prescribed by the chaining rules. The same principles of organization underlie both of these examples as underlay the earlier ones, for all their apparent differences.

The same is true of the kind of N+N sequence we find, in what appears to be a very different case:

She went back to the car park

This represents a very common use of N reduplication. It occurs, however, within the stretch of speech we are presently regarding as a nominal element, and an examination of it is best postponed until we take a closer look at these in Chapter 14.

Same or different referent?

Given the large number of circumstances in which reduplications occur, and the consequent possibilities of indeterminacy, it might be expected that the chances of ambiguity would be considerable. It is worth noting one reason which reduces those chances considerably: an already shared understanding of what linguistic items are presently intended to refer to in the non-linguistic world is an essential part of the basis upon which successful telling depends. It is easy to see, for instance, that both the reduplicating nominal elements in

She made him a real fool

and

She inspected her passenger, the little old lady

refer to the same 'thing', but in

> My friend told me an incredible story

and

> She offered the old woman a lift

they refer to different things. Co-operative listeners could be expected to appreciate this difference, and the possibilities of their mistaking the speaker's intention are consequently reduced.

Reduplicative N as extension or suspension

In most of the examples we have used in this chapter, the reduplicative N can be thought of as a single element tacked on to the end of an otherwise fully explained chain as an extension. It can also be inserted into a chain as a suspension. In the first case, Target State is then achieved, while in the second case the speaker goes back to fulfilling whatever commitments were still outstanding before the suspension occurred. The communicative usefulness of suspension is vastly increased, however, by the possibility of another kind of extension that the rules make available, a possibility we shall call 'finite second predication'.

Finite second predication

Let us first consider

> She thought this old dear was very quiet sitting there
> The policeman said they had found an axe in the back

In each of these examples, an N is introduced in accordance with the NVN part of the sequencing rules: *this old dear* and *they*. This N, then, initiates a further run through the rules. Once again, we can see that it is communicative deficiency that necessitates the continuation. The foreshortened chains:

> She thought this old dear . . .
> The policeman said they . . .

would scarcely achieve Target State in any circumstances. The way forward taken in these two examples suggests that the Intermediate

State that results from the occurrence of a second N is the same, so far as further sequencing possibilities are concerned, as it would be if it were a chain-initial N: both *this old dear* and *they* are re-used as initial Ns of a further subchain. We must suppose that this way forward is always available in principle, but in practice occasions for making use of the facility seem to be very restricted: such extensions are found only after a limited range of verbal elements, sometimes referred to as 'reporting verbs' like *thought, said, believed, think,* etc., as in

I hope you don't mind

I don't think my daughter is coming

She pretended she wasn't very good at that kind of thing

Finite second predication is also used, however, in conjunction with N reduplication. An example is:

The police told her they had found an axe

Here, . . . *her they* . . . is an N+N pair, and it is the reduplicative N, *they*, that serves as the first N in a further run through the rules. There is no question of re-use here: the subchain has its own subject nominal element:

The police told her they had found an axe
N   V N+ N   V V^{I} N

(Indeed, with a change of intonation, such a sequence could often serve as two separate chains:

// P the police TOLD her // P they had found an AXE //)

There are probably even fewer verbs that are followed by this kind of subchain in the simple way we have described, but with two other changes we shall discuss in the next two chapters, double modifications like these turn out to be highly productive. Recognizing them enables us to give a description to many more of the chains that we find in used speech but have up to now provided no way of dealing with.

Meanwhile, we can note that this kind of extension arises from another case of communicative deficiency. Whereas

She told the police her story

is likely to meet a communicative need,

She told the police this woman

is virtually certain not to do so. The second predication

. . . this woman had begged a lift

is therefore required before an appropriate selection can be deemed to have been made.

Summary

At this point it may be helpful if we brng together for comparison the various kinds of extension and suspension we have described.

Extensions

Non-finite Second Predication

-*ing*	I saw her sitting in the car
to	She asked her to get out
pp	She went on scared by all this
plain	She let him get out

Finite Second Predication

She thought the old lady was very quiet

Reduplication

N	She gave this old lady a lift
A	She was sitting in the car in the car park

Suspensions

Non-finite Second Predication

-*ing*	The person standing there was an old lady
to	To get rid of him she said she must turn round
pp	The things found in the car included an axe

Finite Second Predication

She said she felt giddy very faintly

Reduplication

N	Her passenger, this old woman, was very quiet
A	After shopping, in the car park, she had a shock

12
Zero realization

Second mention

In our discussion of the simple chain in Chapter 4, we noted that the working of the sequencing rules depended upon all the elements prescribed for a particular route being realized. Even when words were manifestly non-selective, and therefore perhaps not strictly necessary for the telling purpose to be fulfilled, we find no instances of speakers moving on to the next Intermediate State without producing the intervening element. We now have to say that this requirement is a peculiar feature of the simple chain. Once speakers get into the additional elements that we have called 'extensions' and 'suspensions', we find occasions when they may omit elements — indeed, when they regularly do so.

The phenomenon which we shall call 'zero realization' — omission of an element that the logic of the sequencing rules might lead us to expect — is actually exhibited in all the V^I initiated subchains we have met. We have said, for instance, that the notional subject of the non-finite predicator in

She took this person to deliver her to her daughter's

She told her to put her shopping in the car

is the referent of one or other of the nominal elements that have already been introduced. The fact that there is nothing to designate that referent in the place immediately preceding the V^I can be taken to suggest a new kind of rule: notwithstanding the way the sequencing rules have been formulated, there are occasions when they are overridden by a need to avoid making second reference to any entity in the same chain. Except for cases involving an unrestricted subject, the Intermediate State in which V^I is produced is one in which one or more entities have been referred to by means of a nominal element elsewhere in the chain, and any one of these can be taken as the subject of the V^I without additional reference being made to it. *She* (the friend), and *her* (the old lady) have already been mentioned, so the place in the subchain where one or other would be represented if the speaker were producing an NV-initiated sequence is left empty.

The Ø symbol

This kind of omission has, in fact already been allowed for in the way the rule for the introduction of a V¹ has been formulated. It could be argued, therefore, that it is misleading to talk about an omission at all. Nevertheless, the absence of a second reference in the place where it might have been expected to occur is of some interest; to remind ourselves of the fact of 'zero realization' it will sometimes be helpful to make use of the symbol Ø for the 'expected' element that is 'missed out' of the chain. Thus, in each of these the examples above are represented by

She took this person to deliver her to her daughter's
N   V   N   ØV¹   N P/N

She told her to put her shopping in the car
N   V   NØ V¹ N   P/N

In these, Ø will be taken to indicate that in the place it marks there is nothing to stand for the entity that has been referred to already as *she* and *her*.

It may seem an odd thing to do, in the kind of data-based exercise we are engaged in, to take symbolic note of something that is allegedly missing. The reason for doing it is that the notional element we are concerned with is not realized just as regularly as all other elements are realized. In cases like these, zero realization of something already referred to is part of that set of listener expectations on which users rely in order to know where they have got to in the chain of elements.

Another objection might be that in chains of this particular kind the symbol Ø is entirely redundant. For there is no realization of the notional subject of any non-finite verbal element: the use of the symbol V¹ is, therefore, a sufficient reminder of the 'empty slot' that precedes it. By using both Ø and V¹ we are, in effect, saying the same thing twice. This is why we have found no need to introduce Ø until now. It turns out, however, that we can extend the range of our descriptive mechanism considerably, and so take in many more of the chains we find in used speech, if we recognize the phenomenon of zero realization in certain chains that do not include non-finite verbal elements.

Zero realization in finite second predications

Let us take as a starting-point the following:

(1) They inspected the car She'd left it outside
    N   V   N   #N V V^{I} N A

Presented like this, as two separate chains, the example satisfies the expectation we referred to earlier that all the elements encountered on the chosen route through the sequencing rules will be realized. Even though *it* in the second chain, for instance, can only refer to *the car* that is mentioned in the first, no speaker will omit it (or some alternative reference item). Notice, however, that a version which is presented as a single chain but is otherwise similar illustrates a different application of the rules:

(2) They inspected the car she'd parked outside

Up to a point, this chain is accounted for by the mechanisms we have already proposed: the NVN sequence *They inspected the car* is followed by reduplicating N *she*; and this in turn initiates a further run through the rules—a finite second predication—in the way that we have said an N, introduced by whatever means, may, in principle, do. What is missing, though, is any representation of the thing that was *left*. The element that was represented as *it* in (1) is left unrepresented when the two assertions are recast in (2) as a single chain.

A different set of conditions for zero realization seem to be operative here. Any Intermediate State that follows the production of the reduplicative N *she* will obviously be one in which the referent of the first N of the pair *the car* + *she* is in play. The rules make this referent available for use in any N slot of the subchain, without further mention. We can therefore recognize zero realization in the chain thus:

They inspected the car she'd parked outside
N   V   N+   (N VV^{I} ØA   )

where Ø stands for the unrealized second representation of *the car*.

Again, the incidence of zero realization is strictly regulated in the speaker's performance. That is to say, its occurrence is fully determined by the existing Intermediate State. Indeed, one way of describing what happens would be to say that there is no real omission: the State is itself one in which the earlier mention is a relevant factor, and the prescribed progress is then via any route that does not entail second reference. Zero realization does not, therefore, destroy, the finite state properties of the system.

Some more instances of zero realization that can be explained in the same way are:

It was about an old lady she was going to take to her daughter's
NV   P/N+   N V V^I V^I Ø P/N
(she was going to take *the old lady* to her daughter's)

She drove past the turning she wanted
N   V   P/N+   N   V   Ø
(she wanted *the turning*)

She told them about the person she'd given a lift to
N V   N   P/N+   N V V^I N   P/Ø
(she'd given a lift to *the person*)

It was about an old lady she found in her car
NV   P/N+   N   V   Ø P/N
(she found *the old lady* in her car)

All the foregoing cases involve extensions. It would be easy to find a similar list in which suspensions display the same kind of pattern, for instance:

The little old lady she found in her car turned out to be a man
N+   (n   v   Ø p/n   ) V   V^I N
(she found *the little old lady*)

The street she went along was pretty busy
N+   (n   v   p/   Ø)V E
(she went along *the street*)

Who

There is one special case where the argument we have advanced might lead us to expect zero realization but where it is not found. It is of sufficient interest to warrant attention. Let us consider:

She was waiting for her daughter who hadn't turned up

Here, *her daughter* has just been mentioned in the simple chain, and the second reference considerations alone might lead us to expect that she will not be represented in the organization of the subchain: we might expect a Ø at the place in the subchain where realization might otherwise be obligatory. In fact, that place is occupied by *who*: *who* turned up means *her daughter* turned up.

This is not, in fact, a breach of the rule we have proposed. For it is built into the formulation of that rule that the Intermediate States which permit zero realization are those which follow a reduplicative pair of Ns. Omission of a second reference to *her daughter* would result in that necessary condition not being met. We could say that *her daughter* + *who* is produced in order to meet it.

This simple statement of the facts is sufficient to describe what users do when confronted with a communicative need that has to be responded to by the use of such a chain. It is worth noting, however, that the requirement for N+N is not just an arbitrary constraint built into the rule system: it is a predictable consequence of the way the system works.

Let us recall Figure 4.3 on page 51, which represents the possible routes through the simple chain, keeping in mind the various modifications we have since described. In all the chains we have looked at in this chapter, the speaker has completed one such route, and our interest has been focused upon what happens thereafter. In each case, we can represent the speaker's subsequent course as resulting from a return to the beginning of the diagram. The speaker follows a second run through the rules by whatever route and for however far present conversational demands indicate. Thus, in this sentence the subchain that is actually realized follows the route:

She told them about the person she'd given a lift to
$\quad$ N $\quad$ V V^i $\quad$ N $\quad$ P

In this sentence it follows the route:

She went past the exit she should have taken
$\quad\quad$ N $\quad$ V $\quad\quad$ V^i $\quad$ V^i

The important point is that in each of these cases the rules do make a route available to produce such a subchain. In each case, it is possible to say that the speaker follows a legitimate route which satisfies present communicative needs, having first taken into account that those needs do not now require re-specification of one of the nominal elements. But in the case of the exception, there is no such route available. All chains which have a finite V are initiated by an N, and to omit second reference to *her daughter* in

She was waiting for her daughter (who) hadn't turned up

would be to fail to produce such an N. We can say, provisionally, that *who* is included to ensure that a crucial place in the left-to-right sequence is not left unoccupied.

Optional elements

Two questions arise from the foregoing account of zero realization. The first concerns the fact that for each of those examples we have cited as illustrations of the phenomenon there is an alternative version which makes use of one of the words which are generally regarded as belonging to the same class as *who*. We might find

It was about an old lady who(m) she was going to take

instead of

It was about an old lady she was going to take

or

She drove past the turning that she wanted

instead of

She drove past the turning she wanted

Notice, firstly, that these alternative versions are entirely in line with the operation of the rule system as we have represented it. Nominal element reduplication may occur anywhere, and the insertion of *who/whom* or *that* results only in there being three Ns instead of two.

Although this extra element is often optional, there seem to be occasions when it is nearly always included, and it is proper to ask what they are. The most likely answer seems to be that they are produced whenever the subchain is spoken as a separate tone unit. This means that when a chain is made to represent two separate telling increments, as in

// P she WENt past an EXit // P that she SHOULD have TAken //

the subchain is likely to have the form which includes a *who*-type word (*that* in the present case). It should be stressed that this is not a breach of the zero realization rule. In every case it remains true that second mention in the expected place (i.e. after *taken*) in . . . *she should have taken* is avoided. All that has happened is that an element which is redundant, both as a filler of a slot and as a carrier of information, has been inserted at the beginning of the subchain.

In dealing with such alternative forms as these, we are brought face to face with a consideration that we have so far been able to avoid. At least some of the examples of the use of 'extra' *who*-type elements tend to occur in the very careful performance of educated speakers who are operating in the light of a learned standard of 'accuracy' or 'elegance'. It is a matter for speculation to what extent they represent a carry-over from the written language or result simply from the influence of prescriptive grammarians who have succeeded in investing one of the possibilities with preferred status. In this connection, it is interesting to notice that both versions are equally consistent with the working of the sequencing rules.

The second question concerns the special nature of *who*, *that* and other words used in a similar way. What property fits them both for the 'place-filling' function we noted in

. . . her daughter who hadn't turned up

and for use as 'extra' reduplicative Ns? We shall have to address this question at some length in the next chapter.

Uses of zero realization compared

Meanwhile, we will conclude this chapter with a summary statement of the two sets of circumstances in which we have found zero realization occurs.

1 In the case of non-finite second predications, the referent of any preceding N may be the unrealized notional subject of the V^1.

2 In the case of finite second predications, any N in the subchain after the subject N has zero realization if realization would amount to a second mention of the first N of a reduplicating pair.

13

Open selectors

The pertinence of selection

In our earlier discussion of the concept of selectivity (Chapter 8), we confined our attention to words which, depending upon the existing state of speaker–hearer understanding, might either represent or not represent an existential sense selection. This applies, in fact, to most words. In moving now to a consideration of words like *who*, which we encountered in the last chapter, we have to take into account items for which this choice of status is not available. The existence of these items has a very considerable impact upon the way the sequencing rules are exploited in speech and they need to be examined in some detail.

Let us first consider the role of *who* in a different context. Compare:

// P my FRIEND told me //

// P WHO told you //

This comparison actually involves us in going beyond the telling situations on which we are presently concentrating, for *who told you* would usually have interrogative function. Although new considerations are introduced by this widening of our area of interest, we need not be too concerned with them for the moment. We will simply say of these two utterances that the first fits a situation in which one of several people might have 'told me', and the speaker says which. *My friend* therefore represents an existential selection. Other members of the set from which it is selected are those other people who are recognized by both participants as potential tellers. The second utterance is similar to the first in one respect: the matter of which of the possible candidates 'told' is represented as existentially pertinent. By this we mean that the selection we think of as needing to be made at the place occupied by *who* is an important part of what the communication is all about. Its making is seen as a crucial requirement of the communicative need that the speaker is presently addressing. But it is different in that the selection is not actually made. Indeed, the whole point of such a question-like utterance is usually that the speaker wants the other participant to make it.

We have a situation, then, where an element:

1 indicates that some meaningful choice is necessary if progress is to be made in the present interaction; but
2 leaves the making of that choice until later.

Who belongs to a class of items which are regularly used as what we will call 'open selectors': they signify the pertinence of selection, but leave the actual choice unmade. Their use contrasts with that of *my friend* above, and with that of most elements having prominent syllables, which simultaneously tell that a selection needs to be made and also make it.

The working of chains which contain open selectors can be described by invoking yet again the notion of speaker commitment: they are, in a special sense, anticipatory. They amount to an appropriate step in the syntactic chain in the purely formal sense: that is, they serve as fillers of the slot that the sequencing rules forbid us to leave empty; but, by indicating the present need for a selection and stopping short of actually making one, they set up an expectation of more to come. Whether that expectation is subsequently to be satisfied by the same speaker, as in a telling exchange, or by another, as in an asking exchange, is a question we shall have to address later.

Open selectors in telling increments

For an example of the use of an open selector in a telling increment, compare:

// P she USually comes at FOUR //

// P she COMES when she's finished WORK //

In the first example, *at four* is selective. The existential paradigm would comprise all of the times at which the old lady might reasonably expect her daughter to turn up. In the narrative, the simple chain NVP/N satisfies present communicative needs. But if the second example stopped at the same point in the sequence, we should have

She comes when . . .

Now, although an NV chain *She comes* just might possibly have the capacity to meet communicative requirements in certain telling situations, the chain that is lengthened by the addition of an open selector manifestly does not. By going on to produce *when*, the speaker arrives at a new Intermediate State. It is one in which the specification of a time has been raised as pertinent to present needs. Or, to put it another way, the sequence, as now extended, projects a situation in which the anticipated selection is recognized to be communicatively necessary. As it is an open selector, however, it does not, in itself, specify the time. Only after the commitment to do this has been fulfilled will the Target State have been reached.

Functional indeterminacy of open selectors

Before looking in detail at how the deferred selection is made, we must recognize another complication which this example introduces. In the earlier case of *who told you*, it would be possible to think of *who* as an alternative manifestation of the nominal element that the normal working of the sequencing rules demands: to represent the sequence as NVN. But in the case of *she comes when* . . . the open selector seems like a replacement for what we have become accustomed to calling an adverbial element, suggesting the representation NVA. There are reasons for not doing this, but for using a separate symbol W for the open selector in both examples: WV and NVW.

Essentially, the reason is that the distinction we have tacitly assumed exists between N elements and A elements is not always clear cut. We have to recall the warning given in Chapter 4 that the traditional categories of sentence grammar may not always provide a satisfactory basis for our kind of description. We have now recognized the central importance to the speaker of the need for making appropriate existential sense selections, and it is very easy to show that elements we might want to classify differently—as nominal elements, adverbial elements and P/N elements with adverbial function—can all represent situationally relevant alternatives at some particular point in a conversation. An existential paradigm might well be represented as, for instance:

$$\text{He left} \begin{cases} \text{the next day} \\ \text{immediately} \\ \text{on Friday} \end{cases}$$

To put it another way, the set of options from which the utterance derives its existential value is not necessarily expressed as an opposition between two examples of the same part of speech, as we have tended to assume. And, since we started with the proposition that speakers are engaged in making choices relevant to present communicative need, rather than manipulating formal items of grammar, we should not be surprised that the similarity between what can be done with nouns and what can be done with adverbs, leads to a certain amount of indeterminacy as between classes.

The recognition of this kind of indeterminacy has far-reaching implications for the kind of description we are proposing. We have, of course, been able to fend off the problem up to now—and shall need to give it only occasional attention in what follows—because of a general tendency for items which traditional procedures lead us to classify as nominal elements to be in existential contrast with each other, and for those that are recognizable as adverbial elements on the same basis to be similarly used. It is hard to imagine a situation in which, for instance, an opposition between *the car* and *finally* would play a part in the accomplishment of communicative purpose. This makes it possible largely to ignore the fact that when we classify elements it is, in reality, existential senses that we are classifying and not the formal tokens that realize them. But one area of the grammar in which the fact of interchangeability certainly does need to be accommodated is that in which open selectors are involved. We shall therefore use the symbol W to mean neither an 'N replacement' nor an 'A replacement', but rather as a step in the progression through the sequencing rules which might, if replaced by a selector, take the form of one or other of these. The unfinished sequence *she comes when* (NVW) can therefore be thought of as having some such interpretation as: she comes at some unspecified time, which might be indicated either by a selective N or by a selective A.

Selection by equation

The next thing to attend to is how the obligation to go on and specify that time is discharged. We can conveniently recognize two stages in the explanation. Firstly, because of the ambivalent status of the W item, *when*, as either N or A, we can regard it as the first of a reduplicating pair W+N (. . . *when + she* . . .). Next, notice that the subchain initiated by the reduplicative N will, when it is produced in a situation where time has been said to be pertinent, lack the element that would specify it.

. . . she has finished work . . .

does not actually have an adverbial element to specify a time. We have a situation similar to that which we recognized in our discussion of zero realization in the last chapter. Time has already been referred to, however equivocally, in the first element of the reduplicating pair, as *when*: there is therefore no second mention in the subchain. If we represent the complete chain as NVW+NVV'NØ, using Ø to represent the unrealized second reference to a time, we have a basis for the interpretation which is regularly placed upon such increments. Paraphrase is often awkward, but will serve to make the point. The purport of

She comes when she has finished work

can be expressed, for present purposes as:

She comes at a particular time # She has finished work at that time

Or, alternatively, we might say:

She comes at time x # She has finished at time x

where x is the expression of an unknown in a sense which closely resembles its algebraic usage.

An interesting point to note about the example, and about many others following a similar pattern, is that both references to time are actually uninforming in so far as their information content is concerned: nothing is told about when either the coming or the finishing work occurs except that they occur at the same time. Neither the open selector W nor the unrealized Ø amounts to the kind of selection that would, in itself, enable conversational progress to be made. Present communicative need is satisfied by telling how the (unspecified) timing of one event is related to the (unspecified) timing of another.

A similar account can be given of examples like

I can't think where she is

I can't think where (NVV'W) would, in many situations, stop short of satisfying present demands: the open selector *where* indicates that a selection of some location is pertinent, and therefore sets up an expectation that one will be made. The subchain . . . *she is* (NVØ), predictably does not realize the potential second mention of the location. Again, a paraphrase will help to show how the two elements, W and Ø, work together to take care of the pertinent location, without specifying it in any geographical sense:

I don't know (or can't think) W # She is Ø

Once more the required communicative progress is made, not by referring to a specific place, but by equating one unknown with another.

Prominent and non-prominent W

A comparison of the two examples we have just examined will enable us to say something more about the two open selectors concerned. *When* makes it clear that it is time that is at issue and *where* makes it clear that it is place. In neither case is there likely to be any doubt about this when the two increments occur in the narrative: nothing would be lost in the way of communicative value if some neutral open selector—one that was not marked for time or place—were available for use. There is no likelihood of the speaker intending 'She comes where she has finished' or 'I can't think when she is', so the distinction that the *when/where* opposition makes is already implicit in the situation. Occasionally, though, we find instances where this is not the case. Sometimes the point of the communication may be precisely this distinction between time and place. We sometimes hear things like:

I know where the meeting is, but not when it is

We evidently over-stated the case earlier when we said that open selectors are not selective: they can operate as terms in an existential paradigm in which they are opposed to each other; and when this happens they have prominence in accordance with what we have said about the relation between this feature and selectivity:

// i know WHERE the meeting is // but not WHEN //

Similar paradigms can comprise other pairs of open selectors which can be thought of, in the present situation, as comprising a relevant opposition, and when this happens prominence is assigned in the same way. In the more common cases, the question of whether the selection is from among various expressions of place or various expressions of time can be taken to be already determined, and the fact is reflected in the absence of prominence in the open selector:

// i CAN'T think where she IS //

Selection by predication

The kind of specification by equation we described above is only one of the ways in which open selectors can be used. Other cases require slightly different interpretations, but nothing that is new needs to be added to the descriptive apparatus. Consider, for instance:

She gave her a lift because she was worried about her daughter

Here, we can think of *because* as having an existential value equivalent to 'for a reason'. The deficient sequence *she gave her a lift because . . .* therefore indicates that the reason for giving the lady a lift is pertinent to present concerns. It therefore sets up an expectation that the reason will be forthcoming, and the subsequent subchain will be heard in the light of that expectation.

This time, however, we cannot resort to the paraphrase:

She gave her a lift for an unspecified reason # She was worried about her for that reason

It may be impossible, in fact, to insert a single element in the promised subchain that would count as a second mention of *because*. A reason, unlike a time or a place, generally requires more than one element to specify it. There is, therefore, no unrealized element, or Ø, in *. . . she was worried about her daughter*. This chain clearly does not work by relating one unstated selection to another unstated one. Rather, the whole of the subchain +(NVEP/N) is to be understood as making the promised selection:

> She was worried for reason x #
> [x = (the fact that) she was worried about her daughter]

As the second element in the reduplicating pair W+N, *she* incurs a commitment to go on with a further predication.

A similar example is:

> The friend agreed although she didn't like giving lifts to strangers

Here *the friend agreed although* (NVW) signifies that the friend agreed in spite of some fact as yet unspecified. Reference to the fact by means of an open selector signifies that it is pertinent, so the subsequent subchain will be heard as saying what it is: . . . *she didn't like giving lifts to strangers*. Similar, too, is:

> I'll take you if it isn't too far

which means something like: 'I'll take you on a certain unspecified but pertinent condition'. The condition is that *it isn't too far*.

Suspensions

Each of the foregoing examples involves the use of a subchain as an extension. Little that is new needs to be added to account for the use of similar subchains as suspensions. Consider, for instance, an example which is like the last one except that the subchain comes first:

> If it isn't too far, I'll take you

The effect of the ordering of elements in this chain can be viewed as follows: the open selector *if* sets up expectations of two kinds:

1 Simply as an open selector it indicates that the presentation of a condition is pertinent, but leaves unsatisfied the obligation to specify that condition. Specification follows immediately: *If . . . it isn't too far* (w+nve).

2 Merely to say that there is a pertinent condition, and then go on and say what that condition is, is not usually, in itself, to do anything that would advance communication. It remains to say what depends upon fulfilment of that condition, that is to say, to

146

go on and produce the expected NV and anything else that present conversational conditions may demand. The whole of the subchain *If it isn't too far* suspends, but does not otherwise affect, eventual completion of the chain: (w+nve)NVV'N.

A slightly different staged explanation can be offered for

What she was doing in the car was a mystery

1 *What* (i.e. something pertinent but unspecified) is said to be *a mystery*.

2 By producing a chain initial open selector in this way, the speaker incurs an obligation to make the selection that it anticipates. This is done in: *She was doing (something) in the car* (Nvv'Øp/n, where the element we have represented by *something* would amount to a second mention of whatever *what* stands for and therefore has zero realization).

3 If we regard *what* as doing duty for chain-initial N, its production commits the speaker eventually to going on and producing the obligatory V. Thereafter will follow any further elements that present communicative needs require. After fulfilment of the selection-making subchain *she was doing in the car*, the remaining elements fulfil this last commitment. Notice that, since the two representations of notional 'something' in this chain are as W and Ø, we have another case where it is identified only in the sense that what she was doing is existentially equivalent to what is a mystery.

Slot-filling *who*

The notion of an open selector provides us with a single way of giving a generalized explanation to a wide range of 'sentence types' that would feature in quite different parts of a sentence grammar. For instance,

What she was doing in the car was a mystery

I can't think what has happened to her

If it isn't too far, I'll take you

would usually be taken to exemplify structures in which there were three quite different sets of relationships among the constituent parts. The present proposal is that they all result from following essentially similar sequencing rules.

For yet another sentence type, let us return to the use of *who* that we left only partly explained in the last chapter in

She looked at the person who was sitting there

We said there that *who* occurs to satisfy a particular requirement of the sequencing rules, namely, that there should be an N to initiate the subchain, N *lives there*. To this extent, therefore, we know why it is there. What we did not explain is what there is about this particular item which makes it suitable for this kind of 'dummy' slot-filling function.

The need for slot-filling is a fairly general feature of chain-making. We have already seen that in

She decided to give her a lift

both *she* and *her* occur only to satisfy the requirement of the sequencing rules that the place they occupy should not be left empty. In the circumstances in which this telling increment occurs, the speaker assumes that there is no need to specify who does the deciding or who is offered the lift, and the non-selective status of the two items is reflected in their lack of prominence accordingly. But this depends upon the listener having heard the two items in the light of an awareness of both the Initial State and of the putative Target State of the increment. At the point in time at which *she* occurs, there could, in other circumstances, have been mention of someone else, as, for instance, in

She decided to give the police a call

We will say that, although the speaker is safe in treating *her* as non-selective in the known context, there is a potentiality for selection at the place in sequence it occupies:

$$\text{She decided to give} \begin{Bmatrix} \text{her} \ldots \\ \text{the police} \ldots \end{Bmatrix}$$

Consider now the—admittedly not very probable—two-chain sequence

She looked at the man # He was sitting there

The element *he*, like *she* and *her* in the other example, occupies a potential selection slot. After the completion of the first chain, the speaker could refer to almost anyone or anything with the initial N of the next one. It is only an assumed understanding that *the man* is still the topic of the interest that makes *he* non-selective. But in

She looked at the person who was sitting there

the use of the open selector *who* is appropriate for a situation in which there is no possibility of a new selection being made. It projects an understanding that the two elements of the reduplicating pair N+W necessarily refer to the same thing.

Futhermore, the anticipatory implications which we have associated with open selectors like *who* are very clear here. The word indicates that there is more to be said about the person. While

She looked at the person
N   V   P/N

just could, in some circumstances, achieve an appropriate Target State, the lengthened sequence

She looked at the person who
N   V   P/NW

would never do so. As the second element in a reduplicating pair, *who* initiates a further predication WVV'A which provides the promised additional information.

Open selectors, then, being incapable of making sense selections, can be used when no selection is assumed to be possible. We can take it that this is the property which results in their occurring where no element is strictly necessary: that is, on those occasions when, as we have seen, speakers seem to have a free choice between using a chain with such an element or using an otherwise identical chain without one. Thus, the similarity in communicative value between

She said that she was feeling giddy

and

She said she was feeling giddy

or between

She was looking for the place she'd left the car

and

    She was looking for the place where she'd left the car

depends upon there being no possibility of reselection by *that* and
where.

Sample of data

This sample of data includes open selectors.

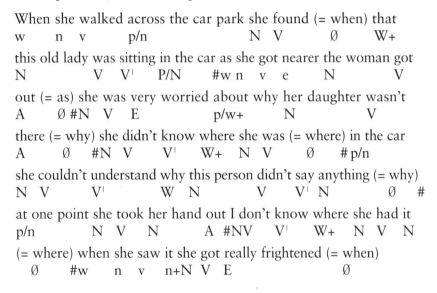

When she walked across the car park she found (= when) that
w   n   v   p/n   N   V   Ø   W+

this old lady was sitting in the car as she got nearer the woman got
N   V   V¹   P/N   #w n   v   e   N   V

out (= as) she was very worried about why her daughter wasn't
A   Ø #N V   E   p/w+   N   V

there (= why) she didn't know where she was (= where) in the car
A   Ø   #N V   V¹   W+   N V   Ø   # p/n

she couldn't understand why this person didn't say anything (= why)
N   V   V¹   W N   V   V¹ N   Ø   #

at one point she took her hand out I don't know where she had it
p/n   N   V   N   A #NV   V¹   W+   N V   N

(= where) when she saw it she got really frightened (= when)
  Ø   #w   n   v   n+N V   E   Ø

14
Nominal elements

Events and things

Most of those parts of a chain that we have referred to as 'nominal elements' can, like those we started out calling 'verbal elements', be analysed as sequences of smaller, word-like parts. To extend our analysis to take in this kind of detail, we will begin with the commonsense observation that nominal elements are used to refer to the thing or things that an act of communication is about. We can say, further, that communicative progress, as we have conceptualized it, will be achieved only if a speaker makes situationally appropriate reference to certain 'things'.

This way of stating the matter can never be more satisfactory, of course, than is the use of a term like 'event' to represent what verbs refer to. It can only be made to cover all cases if we agree to extend the use of 'things' to include 'people', and 'places'. There are, in addition, substances and qualities which we have to think about as existing in mass rather than as discrete entities; and there are also the countless abstractions to which we customarily assign substantive status, simply by referring to them as if they were 'things'. While the act of disagreeing is more or less obviously an 'event', it is probably only because of the way our language is organized that we can regard a disagreement as a 'thing'. We shall assume this extended, and somewhat amorphous range of reference in what follows and provisionally apply 'thing' to everything that is traditionally thought of as being designated by a noun.

Characterizing and identifying

Language provides us with two ways of specifying a thing: we can 'characterize' it or we can 'identify' it. On some occasions, communicative progress depends only upon the listener knowing what kind of thing is intended. Thus, in

They reached a roundabout

151

it is enough to know that the thing they reached had the characteristics that the participants jointly associated with the word. In another case, however, like:

Someone was sitting in the car

appropriate interpretation depends upon the hearer appreciating which car the speaker has in mind. The fact that someone was sitting in *a car* when the friend reached the car park would have considerably less significance.

In straightforward examples like these, we can regard the articles *a/an* and *the* as advance warnings to the hearer that the subsequent noun is to be regarded as either a characterizer or an identifier. But since the articles are, in themselves, incapable of either characterizing or identifying anything, they commit the speaker to going on to produce something that will do so. They function, in part, in a way which resembles the suspensions we have already encountered: an Intermediate State has been reached in which a following noun is the least contribution that will satisfy the need for characterization or identification. They differ from those suspensions, however, in that they have no other use: their occurrence does not amount to anything like a displacement of an element which the chaining rules would, if suspension were not called for, have the speaker put elsewhere.

The simple alternation of *a/an* and *the* is obscured somewhat by a convention which applies when the thing(s) characterized are plural. It is then the absence of an article that gives advance warning of characterization:

I don't give lifts to stangers

The same applies when we characterize something that is thought of as not capable of being counted:

The hands had hair on them

Let us now make more restrictive use of the symbol N, and reserve it for the 'thing-word' whose ocurrence the article delays; and let us use 'd' for articles, and 'd°' for articles which have zero realization. We can then represent some of our earlier examples as follows:

They reached a roundabout
N   V   d N

A lady was sitting in the car
d N   V   V¹   P   d   N

I don't give lifts to strangers usually
NV   V¹   d°NP   d°N   A

The hands had hair on them
d   N   V   d°N P   N

Advance advice to the hearer that a coming noun should be interpreted in one of the two ways, either as a characterizer or as an identifier, may often be sufficient to facilitate communicative progress. When we are told that *the hands had hair on them* we have no difficulty in identifying *the hands* as those of the passenger; nor do we need to know more about the character of the *hair* for present purposes. When we are told that *they reached a roundabout* we can assume that the thing reached is sufficiently well characterized in this way. Elsewhere, however, the N, when it is reached, may not in itself make the selection that present conversational needs require: that is to say, co-operative behaviour may involve the speaker in supplying more detail: hearers may need to know which hands (for instance, the passenger's), whether the hair was black or red, straight or curly; or what kind of roundabout (for instance, a large one). The rest of what we have to say about the nominal element will be largely concerned with how the communicative deficiencies of a simple dN (or d°N) sequence are made good: how specification appropriate to the present situation, whether by characterization or by identification, can be achieved.

Speaker's choice

The following two examples will enable us to bring into focus the two ways in which communicative sufficiency may be achieved, and also to acknowledge a problem that arises whenever we invoke such a notion. Consider:

She went past the exit from a roundabout

She looked for a wide opening

In the first of these, the speaker achieves sufficiency by post specification: by going on to say *from a roundabout* after the deficient N. In the second, it is achieved by pre-specification: by producing *wide* before the N. Seen in the light of our real-time model, this posits a distinction which might, under some circumstances, be significant: in the second example the deficiency of *opening* is anticipated; in the first, the deficiency of *exit* may not be appreciated by the speaker until after it has been said, a circumstance which could result in its being spoken as two separate telling increments:

// P she looked for an EXit // P from the ROUNDabout //

The problem arises from the fact that it is the speaker alone who determines what is said and how it is said. Although we can have no access to his reasons for doing one thing or the other, we have to ask on what grounds *the exit* and *an opening* could be treated as deficient here. Identifying something as *the exit* (not the entrance) or characterizing something as *an opening* (not a side road?) might easily be thought to be sufficient in the narrative under consideration. But, the speaker's assessment of the situation is evidently different. He acts on the assumption that the listener needs to be told whether it was the exit *from a roundabout* or from, let us say, the car park; and perhaps because it is relevant to the coming reference to the pretended difficulty of reversing the car, that it was a *wide* opening. There is, of course, no way of saying objectively whether these assumptions are justified or not. We have to accept what is done and seek to analyse it on its own terms.

The matter is shown in slightly different light in

You know the one in Hounslow

She looked at the person in the other seat

Both *the one* and *the person* are deemed by the speaker to be communicatively deficient. In the first example, the deficiency may, indeed, be regarded almost as an inherent feature of the N that has been used. There are probably no circumstances in which *the one* would be in existential contrast with anything else. The case of *the person* is less clear cut. Taking a logical view of the situation, there was only one person present apart from the friend, so there is strictly no need for selection at all.

// she LOOKED at the person //

or

// she LOOKED at her //

would have been sufficient to make the meaning clear. It is not unusual for speakers to be more explicit than necessary, as in this case. It is worth noticing that, although over-explicitness might sometimes be tiresome for the listener, it is not uncooperative in the way that under-explicitness might be. We can reasonably think of speakers as erring on the safe side.

Post-nominal specification

A chain, the deficiency of which would be in little doubt, is:

She looked down at the old lady's feet and saw she was wearing a pair

In the recorded example, post-specification is achieved by the addition of

. . . of boots

No new mechanisms are needed in order to incorporate this into our description: it is simply an instance of the use of a P/N element after N, as is allowed for in the simple chaining rules, where the P/N has what we have called post-nominal function.

This is only one of several ways whereby post-specification can be achieved. There are, however, some observations that we can usefully make about it which will be found to apply equally to examples in which it is achieved by other means.

1 The P/N element has post-nominal function, but we saw in Chapter 6 that similar elements are also potentially post-verbal, so that all examples like this are indeterminate.

   She went past the exit on purpose

   results from taking the same route through the rule system as

   She went past the exit from the roundabout

The vocabulary used, however, and the conclusions we could

draw from that vocabulary about probable contexts, even if we had no access to the actual context, would leave us in no doubt about which function the P/N has in each case.

2 Because the N and the P/N serve existentially as a single act of selection, the organization into tone units very often reflects this fact, as for instance, in

... // the EXit from a ROUNdabout //

where *exit*, though selective, is not sufficient to make the necessary identification. This can be compared with likely intonational treatments of the examples having post-verbal P/Ns:

// she WENT past the EXit//on PURpose //

rather than

... // an EXit on PURpose //

We must be clear, however, that other factors can affect the intonation of both kinds of chain. Although the treatments we have suggested would probably serve to remove ambiguity if they were read aloud as sentences, we cannot say that, when one of the patterns occurs in used speech, it is a straightforward indicator of which function the P/N has.

3 We have said that once Target State has been reached, further elements allowed for by the rules can be used to reach a further target. So, if *driveway* happened to be an appropriate and sufficient selection in some conversation, then it could terminate a telling increment, provided there was a proclaiming tone present:

// P she was LOOKing for a DRIVEway //

and the P/N element could then be used as another telling increment:

// p on the LEFT //

Similarly, though, if communicative sufficiency has been achieved without producing the P/N element, a post-verbal addition can be used in the same way:

// P she was LOOKing for a DRIVEway // P with GREAT CARE //

156

The fact that the same option is available whether the P/N has post-nominal or post-verbal function, is another reason why we cannot regard intonation as an infallible indicator of function on any particular occasion.

4 In the examples we have used, the post-nominal P/N elements occur as extensions. Very similar considerations apply to their use as suspensions:

The door of the car was open

But, since the need for this kind of post-specification arises, by definition, only after a deficient N, it does not occur initially in chains, as post-verbal P/Ns do. And since Target State cannot be reached until after V has been produced, P/Ns that follow the subject N are never presented as separate telling increments.

5 When post-selection is necessary, the sense of 'having to wait' until the listener has all the information necessary to know what is being characterized or identified encourages a similar judgement to the one we noted in connection with verbal elements: that the deficient element and the post-specifying element together seem to comprise some recognizable constituent—the noun phrase or nominal group of sentence grammars.

Other kinds of post-specifiers

All three of the types of subchain that we have discussed as possible extensions, or as possible suspensions, can be used to make up for communicative deficiency in the N in ways which exactly parallel the use of P/Ns.

Examples of finite second predications so used are:

The person who was driving looked across

The car park she'd left her car in was nearly empty

The officer who had asked for her keys came back

The exit she wanted was the first

She missed the turn she should have taken

Examples of non-finite second predications are:

The person sitting in the car got out

She needed a place to turn the car

It was a strange thing to do

They looked at the things left in the car

An example in which a reduplicative nominal element serves a post-specifying purpose is:

Her daughter lived in Blackmoor Avenue

Clearly, to live in Blackmoor is not necessarily the same thing as to live in Blackmoor Avenue, and an increment which stopped short after the first N of the pair would be deficient as a response to the communicative need that the longer increment was intended to satisfy. One important fact about *Blackmoor Avenue* is that, although it arises from the process of N reduplication, and is therefore an instance of N+N, it does not contribute to communicative value as two separate parts: it identifies the daughter's place of residence as a single entity. The two-prominence tone unit of the recording,

// . . . BLACKmoor AVenue //

represents, as a whole, an existential selection from among the roads she might have been thought to live in. Sufficiency means going far enough to identify the selection, and here this involves producing both the nominal elements.

But other potential addresses might have included, let us say,

// CHESter street //

a presentation which arises from the convention of treating *street* as a non-selective item in such cases. Even here, though, both Ns are produced: termination at 'Chester' would result in a deficient chain. There are many reduplicative Ns which follow this pattern:

// she was sitting in the PASSenger seat //

// she tried all the DOOR handles //

// they wanted to borrow her CAR keys //

// she THEN drives to a poLICE station //

In each case, the N+N comprises a single selection which requires only one prominence: once *passenger* has been produced, the speaker can assume that nothing other than *seat* will follow. Both words are nevertheless necessary, and for reasons that we recognized in the case of other reduplicative Ns in Chapter 11. Just as the foreshortened chain

She offered the old woman

would have inappropriate value in the context in which it occurred, so too would

They wanted to borrow her car

In some kinds of talk (and even more in some kinds of written language) several reduplicative Ns may occur in succession. When this happens it can be explained in the same way. In each of these cases:

the car

the car park

the car park attendant

the relief car park attendant

communicative sufficiency is achieved only after the last N has been produced, even though the formal requirement for an N could be said to be satisfied at any point after the first. A newspaper headline over a report of the friend's experience might read

Car park axe man police warning

where the same would be true.

Pre-nominal specification

Two sequences that have a superficial similarity are

your car keys

her big hands

It is possible to argue that *car* and *big* have the same function: both 'modify' the following word and work together as a single constituent in analogous ways. They arise, however, from different uses of the sequencing rules. In both cases, *her* and *your* resemble *the* in precipitating an Intermediate State in which identification is expected. We have seen that the inadequacy of *car* to fulfil this expectation results in the addition of the reduplicative N, *park*: there is no disruption of simple chain ordering. *Big* fails to satisfy a different kind of expectation: it is an adjectival element and so leaves undischarged the formal commitment to produce an N which strict adherence to the simple chain rules would require. After V, a chain which followed those rules without suspension would be

Her hands were big

As we said in Chapter 5, suspension refers only to the way in which formal elements occur in relation to each other, and does not imply that the speakers are in any other sense 'breaking off' in the middle of what they are saying. A suspensive E and a following N are often presented as a single selection:

// this COLD BUILDing //

// the BUSy TRAFfic //

This applies also, and in a rather special way, to

It was a little old lady with a shopping bag

Here, the expression // a LITtle old LAdy // (or, elsewhere, // LITtle old DEAR //) does not characterize the person concerned as 'a lady who was little and old', so much as serve as a composite label for a kind of character who is often encountered in stories, particularly nursery stories. Existential selection tends to be from such paradigms as // the LIttle old LAdy //, // the BIG bad WOLF //, // LITtle red RIDing hood //, and so on. There is a similar deliberate reference to stereotypes in

// with her FUNny little HAT on //

// a HOPEless female DRIver //

Examples in which we can think of the speaker making independently selective choices of e and N are:

her big hands

the next turning

hairy hands

a strange thing

It is possible to see that the things concerned may have been other than *big*, *next*, *hairy*, or *strange*, and that had they been so this might have had consequences for the further development of the story.

Ordering of adjectival elements

The formal difference which we noted between *car keys* (N+N) and *big hands* (eN) may seem to be one of those hair-splitting distinctions that have more to do with the descriptive mechanisms we are using than with anything that will have interest for users. It does, in fact, have one important consequence for something users do regularly. Reduplication involves producing two elements of the same kind immediately after each other, so *car* and *keys* are not separated. This means that if specification requires both a suspensive E and an N, they occur in that order:

an empty car park
d e   N+ N

This is only one of the ways in which ordering restrictions seem to be operative when there is more than one specifying element before an N. Examples which illustrate these restrictions are rare in the data, and may very well be rare in spoken language at large. The piecemeal way in which speech is assembled probably favours the use of successive post-nominal specifiers rather than a string of pre-nominal Es. One example in which two Es are used is

She had big hairy hands

and an interesting feature of this chain is that an alternative version seems to be equally likely in the context

She had hairy big hands

We can compare this with the stereotyping sequence which involves N reduplication:

She pretended to be a hopeless female driver

Where a rearranged ordering

a female hopeless driver

seems very unlikely indeed.

The ordering of suspensive adjectival elements is evidently not, in general, free, however, and a grammar must have something to say about what limits the speaker's freedom. One factor can be seen in

a spare tyre

Here, the selective function of *spare* places the tyre concerned in a well-recognized class of such objects: motorists and garage mechanics inhabit a world in which tyres are notionally recognized as either 'spare' or 'not spare'. For contrast, consider the invented example:

a new tyre

Here, 'newness' is not so much a matter of classification as of quality. While a clear-cut distinction might be made between 'spare' and 'not spare', mechanics or others could well be in dispute about the comparative 'newness' of two tyres. *New* might be opposed, on a particular occasion of use, to a range of alternatives like 'nearly-new, part-worn, illegal', etc.; and while we should seldom, if ever, say that one was 'more spare' than the other, we could easily say that one was 'newer' than the other. In other words, classifying adjectives owe their value to an existential paradigm which is taken to be absolute and permanent by users; those which attribute a quality to the object concerned derive their value from a paradigm which is debatable and understood to be valid only for the present situation.

In this respect, *spare* more closely resembles the N *female* in

a hopeless female driver

because drivers can be classified on the basis of a universally recognized supposed distinction between 'female' and 'male'. We can connect this similarity with the fact that, like these nominal elements, they occur after any qualitative adjective there may be in the sequence. We probably expect

a new spare tyre

rather than

a spare new tyre

The convention seems to be first to supply qualitative information, and then to supply classifying information—assuming, of course, that both are necessary. If an N is also needed, this occurs next to the N with which it is in a reduplicative relationship, as can be seen in another invented example:

She went back to the empty public car park

Two observations are necessary here. The first is that many words cannot be placed definitively in groups on the basis of whether they do or do not represent selections in a 'permanent' and generally accepted paradigm. We have used *new* to exemplify the kind of word that does not, but this clearly depends upon the situation in which it is used. For a garage hand sorting tyres which happen to have got mixed up into a pile that are new and a pile that are not, the relevant existential paradigm is one that is definitively given in the context. We may then want to say that 'a spare new tyre' is somewhat less improbable than 'a public empty car park'. In making such a judgement, however, we are really commenting upon the relative likelihood of particular communicative needs arising in readily imaginable situations. What we have is another illustration of the fact, referred to in Chapter 13, that the relevant classification is not of word-tokens, as such, but of the existential senses that they realize in specific contexts. If we take adjectives to be words rather than realizations of senses, a discussion of their ordering can never be more than approximate, and exceptions are likely to be found to any rule we may promulgate.

The second observation follows on from this. Successful attempts to describe such ordering have been based upon computational evidence and are therefore statements of probability (for instance Sinclair *et al.* 1990). They are, moreover, based upon the analysis of written text. No such study has been attempted of spoken English. We can only surmise that when it is it will reveal, for reasons we have already given, that there will be few of the lengthy accumulations of pre-specifying elements that are theoretically possible.

For three other possibilities of elaboration before N, we will confine ourselves to what can be found in the data. Firstly, consider the following examples:

(1) This story . . . My daughter . . . . . . your car key . . . the old lady's hands

We said earlier that the article *the* gave notice that identification was pertinent, but did not itself contribute to it. Items like *this, my, your* can simultaneously do both. In a situation where *the story* is deficient, *this story* might be a sufficient identifier. The Intermediate State following production of *the old lady's* is similar to that following the production of *my*.

(2) Policemen . . . Two policemen . . . The policeman . . . The two policemen . . .

Quantifiers like *two* occur immediately after the article. This is obvious in the case of *the two policemen*. It may be less so in the case of *two policemen* because this is a situation in which the article has zero realization. Whereas *the two policemen* = d quantifier N, *two policemen* = d° quantifier N.

(3) My friend told me this amazing story

She went across the deserted car park

The non-finite *-ing* and pp forms can be used suspensively as if they were adjectives. As verbal elements they make event time reference, and in this respect are related to the V in the way we are now familiar with: the amazing and the telling are simultaneous, but the act of deserting the car park had been completed before she went across it. Interestingly, *to* forms are not used in this way, presumably because to pre-identify something by making reference to an event that had not yet taken place would not be very helpful.

Intonation of pre-specified nominal elements

Intonation interacts with the circumstances we have discussed above in ways which can be somewhat complicated to describe but which are straightforward enough in the way the forms of increments derive from the operation of general principles. To illustrate this, we will conclude this chapter by contrasting the intonation treatment of two nominal elements each of which is preceded by two pre-specifying elements. In one of them, the whole sequence up to the N is spoken as a single tone unit:

// a HOPEless female DRIver //

In the other, the speaker assigns prominence (and, indeed, a tonic

164

syllable) to each of the adjectival elements as well as to the N:

// She had BIG // HAIRy // HANDS //

In the first, the whole sequence is presented as one selection: a single characterization of the kind of person she was. Within this sequence, *female* is treated as non-selective. In one way, this is transparently justified in the story, for it has already been established that the friend is not male. We can, however, take the wider currency of the expression into consideration. We know that this kind of disparaging description is used only in relation to women. The assumption is that if one is a hopeless driver the fact that one is female can be taken for granted: in the classificatory framework within which the expression generally occurs, // a HOPEless DRIver // would effectively say the same thing.

It is also known, of course, that the person was a driver, so

// a HOPEless (female) driver //

would make the only selection that was strictly necessary. The reason this presentation is not found is that it is not the separate selective functions of *hopeless* and *driver* that are relevant here. It is rather that the two combine to define a 'two-prominence' selection, opposing a kind of person who is recognizable as a 'hopeless driver' to, perhaps, a 'skilful reverser of cars'. Another version, which made the only selection in *driver*,

// a hopeless female DRIVer //

would be communicatively deficient in another way. If it could be assumed that listeners knew that the person in question was hopeless and female, to say simply that she was a *driver* as opposed to, say, a passenger would manifestly not meet the communicative needs of the occasion.

For comparison, notice that *big*, *hairy*, and *hands* are all presented as separately selective. The things referred to are characterized by the N as *hands* as distinct from any other part of the passenger's person that may have been visible. But simply referring to hands would scarcely amount to a pertinent selection. The deficiency is made good by pre-characterizing them both as *big* (not woman-sized?) and as *hairy* (not feminine?). By presenting the two selections separately in this way, the speaker invites listeners to respond successively to the one observation and then the other, something we can appreciate if we compare an alternative version:

// she had BIG and HAIRy // HANDS //

which opposes the composite characterization *big* and *hairy* to some other possibility.

Notice that a different ordering of elements:

// she had HAIRy // BIG // HANDS //

would be equally probable in the one-selection-per-tone-unit version. This is because both the properties referred to are regarded as matters of quality rather than classification. If, however, either the size or the hairiness of the hands had already been referred to, a version like this might be expected:

// she had BIG hairy HANDS //

// she had HAIRy big HANDS //

In either case, the word which designates a characteristic that is taken to be already established occurs after the other. This can be attributed to the fact that once a property has been incorporated into the shared background it can be regarded as a basis for classification.

One thing that the above examinations re-emphasize is the essential significance of here-and-now understandings in interpreting what takes place. Existing conversational conditions impinge upon our account of our two examples and the variants we have suggested for them in two ways: they are the only basis we have for explaining which words are selective and which are not; and in many cases they affect the ordering of pre-nominal elements by determining which elements are to be treated as classifiers and which are not.

15
Talk about talk

Every grammar must set limits to what will be considered to come within its purview. We have said that we shall generally limit our attention to considerations that affect, or are affected by, the ordering of elements in the chain. In this chapter, we shall take one step beyond this limit and consider matters that sometimes affect relationships *between* chains: that is to say, we shall begin to move 'upward' in the sense that we are looking at the organization of larger stretches of discourse than can necessarily be accounted for by reference to the sequencing rules we have proposed.

What does the discourse count as?

Let us re-examine the opening of the version of the anecdote that appeared in Chapter 2. The analytical tools we have developed so far enable us to represent this as two telling increments that result, respectively, from taking two different routes through the same set of sequencing rules:

My friend told me this amazing story the other day
N   V   N+N   A   #
she'd been shopping
N   V   V¹

It is fairly easy to see, however, that this account overlooks a significant difference between the communicative values of the two. *She'd been shopping* contributes as one increment towards the total telling event on which the speaker is presently embarking, in other words towards an account of the friend's experience. But *my friend told me this amazing story the other day* has a different purpose: it tells the listener what that account will be, namely a story. Notice that in recognizing this difference we are not influenced by the formal organization of the chains concerned. We know the first serves only a preparatory purpose because simply reporting that your friend had told you a story would be a very odd thing to do.

167

It is part of everyone's understanding of verbal activity that there are various kinds of discourse, and we are probably all accustomed to listening to each kind in a different way: the explanation that the old lady offered for her presence in the car, the description of the stranger that the friend would doubtless have been asked to give to the duty officer at the police station, the advice that the officer might have offered later about who not to give lifts to in the future, would probably each be received and responded to differently. For instance, the friend might thank the officer for the advice, but would scarcely thank the old lady for her explanation (except, perhaps, ironically). The question of what (a part of) a discourse is intended to count as can often be an important part of a participant's perception of what is going on in a conversation. The fact that we have names like *story*, *explanation*, *description*, etc. for the different things that a piece of discourse can count as is a clear indication that it matters, and we sometimes hear such names used in a preliminary labelling:

Let me explain . . .

I'll try to describe what happened . . .

I should like to offer you some advice . . .

The increment that precedes the beginning of the story serves a similar purpose. We shall call it a 'preliminary increment'.

A preliminary increment of the 'I'm going to tell you a story . . . ' kind provides various sorts of information for listeners. For instance, they are forewarned to interpret everything that follows in the light of the fact that it is a story. It is intended to be responded to in its completeness: to be heard through to the end without anyone else seeking to take speaker role. Attribution to *a friend* might also, as we have already said, serve to limit the storyteller's responsibility for its truth, but at the same time give assurance that its source is a reliable one. The usefulness of information like this is hardly in doubt; but such usefulness depends entirely upon there actually being a story to follow: the function of the increment is solely a preparatory one.

This last fact is made very evident if we imagine the hearer responding to it in the way we have said that telling increments are often responded to:

Teller: My friend told me this amazing story the other day
Hearer: Oh

Such a response would usually represent conspicuously unco-operative behaviour on the part of the listener because it would treat the information as something that was being conveyed for its own sake—and was therefore to be reacted to immediately—and not as the precursor of things to come that it is so evidently intended to be.

Notice, too, that if this increment were produced and not followed fairly soon by something that made a start on fulfilling the promise of *a story* it would be the teller who was failing to co-operate. 'Fairly soon', however, does not necessarily mean immediately: for several telling increments, each with a purely preparatory function, may precede the matter that is promised:

> I've got a story for you # It's one my friend told me # She says it's absolutely true # It happened to a neighbour of hers # she'd been shopping . . .

While such preliminary increments occur in co-operative talk only if there is something to prepare for, the last chain in our earlier example would usually constitute a perfectly acceptable opening to the story if there were no preliminary statement(s) about what it was meant to count as: the teller could quite well launch into the narrative without such preparation:

> She (or my friend) had been shopping

The preparatory matter is evidently included at the speaker's discretion. Situations will occur where it will be deemed proper to include it and others where it will not.

We can, then, clarify the distinction we have made between the two kinds of increment we have treated together as 'telling'. There are those whose purpose it is to make progress relative to whatever is currently of concern to the participants. In the case of the story this can be said to be what happened. We might think of these as the essential parts of the interaction, in the sense that without them there would be no cause for the other kind to occur. The latter, by contrast, are incidental: by producing them, the speaker is not referring to those events or other matters that the talk is intended to be about; that which is referred to is (some part of) the discourse itself. They are talk about talk.

Retrospective labelling

Similar references to the status of what has been said can be added at the end of an event. Several people who heard this anecdote said, sceptically, something to the effect that it was 'a good story', making it fairly clear that they didn't regard it as entirely true; and it would be possible for the storyteller to conclude with a disclaimer like 'Well, that's what she said!' that had a similar effect. We can add to the observed fact of preliminary increments the possibility of retrospective increments.

We might note in passing that neither is likely to occur when the purpose of the discourse is social bridge-building. We do not say anything like 'What follows will not be a genuine enquiry about your health but an indication of goodwill'. It seems to be part of the convention within which such enquiries occur that we do not make explicit what we are doing. Phatic exchanges, themselves, undoubtedly can serve a preparatory purpose in another sense: we often go through social rituals to pave the way for what we should describe as the 'real' conversation. An adequate account of the macro-organization of some kinds of two-party discourse would want to recognize this, but from our present point of view the fact that they are not 'talk about talk' is sufficient reason for regarding them as different phenomena.

Recognizing the distinction within the totality of non-phatic exchanges causes us to re-examine what we said about telling increments in Chapter 3. We said there that the least requirements for a successful telling were that the appropriate route should be taken through the sequencing rules to achieve the desired Target State; and that some part of the chain should be proclaimed. Once these requirements have been met, there occurs a point at which, under appropriate conditions, the listener may acknowledge receipt. Now

// R my FRIEND // P told me an aMAZing STOry // R the OTHer DAY //

satisfies both requirements. But, as we have said, it would not usually be acknowledged as the carrier of now-relevant information. Because it tells only about discourse yet to come, the listener is still waiting to be told something further. We can extend the notion of speaker commitment that we introduced when discussing the telling increment and say that by producing a preliminary increment the speaker is committed to going just as far as is necessary for the listener to feel that the story has been completed.

We must therefore reconsider the idea of a Target State that we have been working with, for although the short-term target is the completion of a single telling increment which satisfies present communicative need, the long-term target may be the completion of a story, an explanation, a description or some other recognizable stretch of speech. To achieve the latter will require at least one, but very often many more telling increments, the number depending upon the exact nature of what has been promised.

Unlabelled intentions

We have said that labelling may be done explicitly in a preliminary increment or it may not. When there is no anticipatory labelling of what is to come next, it will nevertheless often be the case that the long-term need for a particular kind of discourse will be jointly recognized by speaker and listener. The knowledge that anecdotes are currently being exchanged around the bar or over the dinner table will be enough, without there being a special label, to establish that what is to come will be one; and the circumstances of the encounter in the car park would be enough for the friend to hear that what the old lady was embarking on was an explanation. In such cases, the commitment to go on until the tale or the explanation is complete will be equally binding.

Essential and incidental items

When we say that preliminary or retrospective increments occur only in association with those that carry the essential information of the talk, we recognize a situation that has been described in terms of 'dependency' in sentence grammars. A representation like this:

(preliminary) main . . . (retrospective)

where the brackets indicate optional constituents that may precede a compulsory 'head' or follow it, is reminiscent of, for instance, the way a nominal group may be represented in systemic grammars:

(modifier) head (qualifier)

We do not, however, have to begin thinking at this point in terms of the kind of hierarchical arrangement that systemic grammars postulate. No descriptive apparatus is needed beyond saying what is possible at successive States in a linear progression. Beginnings and endings are points that are identified by reference to time. We are still dealing with phenomena that can be accommodated in a finite-state model.

Secondary purposes of increments

When we decided to regard telling and asking as the primary purposes upon which our description would concentrate, we recognized that a speaker's perception of what he or she was doing on any particular occasion might well be expressed in terms other than these. We can do things by telling and by asking, and storytellers might, as we said, think of themselves as warning, entertaining, or trying to outshine their listeners. We can rephrase this slightly and say that they can intend what they are about to say to count as a warning, an entertainment, or an entry in the anecdote-swapping competition they happen to be a party to. Such declarations of intent are very similar to that which we said above told listeners that what was to follow counted as a story, an explanation, or a piece of advice.

It would probably be unusual for a speaker actually to name one of these intentions in a preliminary increment. We do not often say 'I am about to give you a warning' or 'I am now going to entertain you'; but we might well say 'My friend gave me some excellent advice the other day', a fairly certain indication that what was to follow was a passing on of the advice to our listener. Some invented examples of ways in which we give advance information about the secondary purposes we intend our messages to serve are:

You'd better be careful. A friend of mine had been shopping . . .

How about this one then. A friend of mine had been shopping . . .

That's not as amazing as something I heard. A friend of mine had been shopping . . .

Here, as in the other cases, the preliminary increment is produced at the speaker's discretion. It will not normally affect the status of what follows if it is omitted, because usually the placing of the story in the particular ongoing interaction will make it clear what it is intended to count as. In this respect, the advance labelling or non-labelling of warnings, entertainments, entries in a competition, and so on, affect the organization of talk in very similar ways to the labelling or non-labelling of stories, descriptions, and explanations. And retrospective increments could be imagined in each case. For instance, the teller could finish with 'So just you remember that, the next time someone asks you for a lift'; or a listener could say 'I'll remember that . . .' etc. In either case, the cautionary implications would be made explicit.

Illocutionary force

There are many thing that a stretch of speech can count as. Something one says might, for instance, be considered by one's listener to amount to a promise, an order, or a challenge. Readers who are familiar with the work of the philosophers, J. L. Austin and J. R. Searle will recognize that we are here extending the range of application of our informal description 'what the discourse counts as' to include what they have called 'illocutionary force'. Their insistence that many of the things people say are said in order to 'do' something, rather than to 'mean' something, has at least a superficial resemblance to our present claim that speech is purposeful.

Speech act theory has tended, however, to concern itself with the non-linguistic conditions that must exist before a particular speech act can be 'felicitous'. For instance, Searle's rules, whereby an act of promising may be judged non-defective, require, among other things, that:

a speaker cannot promise to do something he (would be expected) to do anyway;

the speaker must intend to perform the action. (Searle 1969: 64)

Our present concern, in formulating a real-time grammar, is rather with what linguistic events may precede and what follow the essential increment we are concerned with. In saying that something may be pre- or post-labelled a 'promise', we are concerned only with what the speaker presents it as, or the listener understands it to be: felicitousness may not be an issue. We may recall the frequent practice of 'going through the motions' that we referred to in Chapter 2: many people make assertions that pass for promises knowing full well they cannot or do not intend to carry them out. And many listeners are well aware that this is the case. Neither the assertions nor the responses to them necessarily differ in their linguistic composition from those in a similar exchange which is, and is known to be, sincere.

The difference in perspective becomes very clear if we consider Austin's (1962: 5) first demonstration of the way performatives work by citing instances like 'I name this ship . . .' or 'I do' (as part of a marriage ceremony).

Utterances like these occur at a pre-arranged stage in a public ceremony, where nothing else could be said. They cannot be said to be responsive to the communicative needs that participants associate with a particular stage in the progress of conversational business. Neither is there any question of their being responded to in the way we should expect in a conversation: it would be breaking the peculiar rules of the ritual for anyone to reply 'Oh' or 'I see' or 'Thanks'. Speech act theory characterizes such events as these without reference to a conversational setting because the setting is agreed beforehand to be not of that kind; and when the same principles are extended to acts like promising and warning, no mention is made of what they may follow or what may be followed by them in the linear presentation of speech. It is no part of the philosophically formulated concerns of these writers to be interested in such matters.

We have taken the position that telling and asking can be distinguished on the basis of what sequence of events is necessary to bring each of them to a successful conclusion; but when we come to consider those instances of each which serve particular secondary purposes, we find they have only optional labelling, either before or after the event, to distinguish them. When labels are used, they serve to indicate what an increment counts as; but such labelling is possible with many stretches of speech, some of which would normally be thought of as performing speech acts and others not. To put the matter in another way, 'What does the discourse count as?' has wider application than 'What speech act does the discourse perform?'. Although the attempt to isolate, identify, and describe the total set of speech acts is of importance in the world of philosophical enquiry in which it is made, it has no special interest for someone trying to discover how utterances are assembled in real time.

Explicit and implicit purposes

We will proceed, then, on these bases:

1 A very large number of secondary purposes including, but not exclusively, those that are associated with speech acts, can be achieved by pursuing one of a much smaller number of primary purposes like asking and telling.
2 The fact that a stretch of speech has a secondary purpose is often not indicated in the language: the listener's appreciation of what the telling or the asking counts as depends as often upon what is already known about the situation as upon what is said.
3 When the speaker judges it necessary, by preliminary increment or by retrospective increment, to make a secondary intention known, this can be accommodated within the framework of the grammar as it now stands; there is no need to recognize grammatical devices that are not already in use, so to speak, in describing the essential increments.

In connection with (2) above, we can note that when the secondary purpose of an increment is labelled, it is often not simply to give information about what it counts as, but for some other local reason, a reason that is often known only to the participants. It is quite likely that the old lady—assuming, of course, that she had really been as she represented herself—could have told the friend, quite truthfully, that her daughter had promised to meet her in the car park. This does not mean necessarily, or even probably, that the daughter had at any time said anything like:

I make you a promise. I will meet you in the car park

Very special local conditions would be necessary for this to sound right. An awareness of the daughter's customary unreliability might, for instance, be an important factor. Instead of making explicit reference to the status of the utterance as a promise, it would be more usual for both speaker and hearer simply to assume that that was what a telling increment like:

I'll see you in the car park

counted as.

The daughter could, of course, say what she meant it to be taken to count as retrospectively:

175

I'll see you in the car park. That's a promise

or the old lady might make explicit her view of the matter in a similar way:

I'll see you in the car park. Right. That's a promise.

It is still clear, however, that there would have to be some other factor in the situation than the simple undertaking to be there for such insistence to be justified. Usually, if we tell someone we will be there, the fact that we have made a promise is taken for granted.

What is the discourse about?

Another process which works in exactly the same way as the labelling we have just described is exemplified in:

You know what these places are like when it's getting late

which is spoken as

// P you KNOW // R what these places are LIKE // R when it's getting LATE //

Syntactically and intonationally this increment could serve a telling purpose. There would, however, be something rather odd about telling someone that they knew something. If we know something, we usually know we know it, so the distribution-of-knowledge conditions for telling seem not to exist. Neither do the conditions for asking. The usual conversational purpose of this kind of chain is, in fact, to intimate that you are about to be told! We can take its communicative value to be something like 'I am going to tell you what it was like when she got there'. This is, therefore, another piece of information about what is to come, but this time the preliminary information concerns not what the discourse is to count as so much as what it is going to be about.

When the friend realized that the person she had picked up was not what she seemed, one narrator said:

What was she going to do now

Clearly, this chain does not have an asking function in spite of appearances. No response is expected; indeed much of the interest of the tale depends upon the fact that the listener doesn't know! It will be heard as an indication that the narrator is about to tell what the friend did next. In another version, at approximately the same point in the story, we get:

So she decided to play a trick on him

Again, we can see that the increment serves the preliminary purpose of telling what the ensuing discourse will be about: it will give details of the *trick*. In neither of these cases does the chain we have quoted further the development of the narrative except as a precursor of what is to come. And in both cases, failure on the speaker's part to go on and provide the promised details would probably be regarded as a breach of an undertaking just entered into.

Retrospective increments which tell what preceding discourse has been about seem likely to be infrequent in the kind of speech event we are examining. Storytellers do not often provide backward-looking summaries before proceeding to the next stage though, as Sinclair and Coulthard (1975: 38–9) show, teachers frequently do so in pursuit of their classroom purposes. One of our oral narratives does, however, include:

// P so he got OUT // P he stepped onto the PAVEment //

These two chains would both qualify as telling increments on the basis of the criteria we have proposed; but given the background understanding against which they are produced, we cannot say that the second amounts to a significant presentation of information. Both participants know that 'getting out' and 'stepping onto the pavement' amount to the same thing: they are existentially synonymous. The second increment is, in effect, a restatement of the burden of the first expressed in other words. Paraphrases and reiterations like this resemble the preparatory increments we have examined above in that, in a rather special sense, they say what another part of the discourse is about: they are talk about talk. In another version, after describing in detail the means whereby the friend persuaded her passenger to get out, the narrator says:

That's how she got rid of him

a succinct restatement that captures the drift of quite a lot of preceding talk without taking matters any further.

Discrete labelling

As we intimated at the beginning of this chapter, it has been concerned with matters that might be said to be on the borderline of grammar as we have defined it. Attention has been directed towards the way chains realize events in the larger organization of the discourse rather than towards the organization of the chains themselves. The labels we have identified consist, grammatically speaking, of increments which result from following an appropriate route through the sequencing rules in exactly the same way as other increments. They are 'discrete' in the sense that they represent a complete run through those rules and are therefore not grammatically attached to those other increments.

One reason for introducing them here is that they provide us with a way in to another kind of labelling procedure which does affect the organization of those chains which carry what we have called the 'essential' information. 'Non-discrete' labelling will be the subject of our next chapter.

16

More talk about talk

Non-discrete labelling

Let us first recognize that the kinds of labelling we have associated with separate increments, inserted expressly for the purpose, so to speak, can also be achieved within the chain that the speaker wants to label. For instance, had the daughter thought that explicit labelling of her promise was necessary, she could have said:

I promise to meet you in the car park

a rather more probable way of putting it, perhaps, but not different in communicative value from:

I make you a promise # I'll meet you in the car park

The new version, unlike the earlier one, results from a single run through the sequencing rule NVV'NP/N. In this chapter we shall be concerned with cases like this, where both the labelling and the presentation of essential information are achieved in the same chain.

We will begin with two examples from the data where the function of the labels is to indicate what the remainder of the increment is intended to count as:

// R aPPARently // R this POOR old WOman // P had been SITting there WAITing //

// R PROBably // P it WASn't a burglar //

The intonation of these two increments is typical of those displaying this kind of suspension in so far as the suspensive A element is spoken as a separate tone unit. We shall return to this later. Meanwhile, we will ask in what sense those elements can be said to provide preliminary information about what is to follow.

The assertion that *this poor old woman had been sitting . . .* etc. is based upon such evidence as the speaker had available; but he didn't claim to know what she had been doing. He makes clear at the outset that, although he is going on to tell something, what he tells will fall short of a categorical statement of fact. Similarly, before saying *it wasn't a burglar* the speaker indicates that what he is about to say will be no more than a statement about probability. Paraphrases which worked in a similar way but had discrete preliminary labelling would be:

> I'll tell you what appeared to be the case # the poor old woman had been sitting . . . etc.
>
> One thing was probable # it wasn't a burglar.

In cases like these, we have no readily available vocabulary item like 'story' or 'promise' to help us in making the point, but this should not be allowed to obscure the essential similarity between these and those to which such items can be applied. One might argue, of course, that from a sentence grammarian's point of view, 'I promise' on the one hand and 'apparently' and 'probably' on the other affect the meaning of their sentences in very different ways. We will here point up their similarities rather than their differences: they mark the assertion that will follow is something other than a simple act of telling. They give preliminary notice of what that assertion will count as.

Another point of similarity is that the preliminary element can often be dispensed with. The listener, who knew how limited the background knowledge of the narrator of this story was, would be likely to regard

> This poor old woman had been sitting there waiting

as nothing more positive than what appeared to be the case, and

> She wasn't a burglar

as only a statement about probability, even without their being marked as such. We frequently state probabilities, opinions, secondhand observations, and so on as if they were established truths, and do so quite innocently, knowing that our listeners will take them at their intended, rather than their face value.

Pre-empting the purpose

The other purpose we have attributed to preliminary labels, that of indicating what the discourse is to be about, is illustrated by

Finally, this woman asked her for a lift

In the end, she agreed to take her

The two assertions, that the woman asked her for a lift and the friend agreed to take her, are material contributions to the exchange of information that the speaker judges it necessary to impart: they are the essential parts of the story. To appreciate how the suspensive elements work, let us recall the contexts. Before actually asking for a lift, the woman had made it fairly clear that she would like to be taken to her daughter's; and before agreeing, the friend had debated with herself whether she should do it. A listener to the narrative could be assumed to have an interest, both in the outcome of the 'softening-up' process and in the conclusion of the subsequent debate. The communicative value of the adverbial element in both cases is something very similar to

What I am going to tell you about (or what I assume you will want to know) is what the outcome was

or

I assume you will want to know what the friend did and shall now tell you

There are good reasons, connected with the effective presentation of the tale, for setting out in advance the parameters of the ensuing information, but if we discount these, an increment without the chain-initial A would provide the same information:

This woman asked for a lift

She agreed to take her

Much the same is true when a subchain, rather than a single element, is used suspensively before N. In

When they came back they asked her what is in the car

the preliminary subchain *when they came back* indicates what the speaker is going to talk about next: the coming discourse will begin to satisfy an interest in what the police found when they went out to search the car. Similarly, the suspensive subchain of

To get rid of him she played this trick on him

indicates that the following information will be about how she got rid of him. (As we have already said, in this case the information that is thereby labelled is itself a preliminary increment: there will be a further expectation that the trick will be described.)

Preliminary information of a slightly different kind is provided in

// R VEry CLEVerly // P she MISSED the TURNing //

Here, *very cleverly* is an indication that the speaker is about to say something about the friend's actions that will be seen to demonstrate her cleverness: what follows will be about a clever move. Notice that the preparatory item amounts to an advance assessment of the friend's action at this point in the story. Although there are occasions when missing a turning might be adjudged 'very foolish' or 'very careless', this is an occasion when the speaker confidently expects that the listener will go along with her favourable judgement; and in so doing, she actually anticipates not just the missing of the turning but the eventual happy outcome of the subterfuge: 'You will agree with me when you hear the result that this was a clever thing to do'.

Tone choice

All the suspensive elements and subchains we have examined above resemble the first in that they are presented as complete tone units. They are thus discrete intonationally, if not syntactically. They represent separate selections. We can go a little further in explaining their function, if we now take note of the tone that is used.

The particular account we have given above of *very cleverly* works only if it is assumed that both speaker and listener will ultimately be in agreement about the cleverness of what the friend does. In the context of the story, such agreement can reasonably be taken for granted, and the fact that the teller does take it for granted is reflected in her use of referring tone. This tone is not the only possible choice, however. We could imagine a situation in which a listener, judging the offering of a lift to a total stranger a foolish thing to do, would be predisposed to think of everything she did as foolish. It would then be necessary to tell that listener that what is now to be described is a clever act. A speaker who was sensitive to this might then use a proclaiming tone

// P VERy CLEverly // she . . . //

But since preliminary labels of this kind serve to indicate what interest the speaker is about to address, it is not surprising, perhaps, that the interest concerned will often be taken to be one that has been already negotiated or can be taken for granted: they will usually have referring tones.

For a further illustration of this, there is the case of what happened at the police station. To say that the policemen 'went outside' is, in the circumstances of our story at least, to leave listeners with a strong expectation, almost amounting to certainty, that they will come back. There is also little room for doubt about what they went outside for. Consequently

// R when they came BACK //

The referring tone reflects the fact that both things belong to the area of shared understanding. A possible paraphrase which captured its preliminary function would be: 'You know, of course, that they came back and will want to know what they told her. Well, I am about to tell you . . .'. Something similar applies to the other examples of suspension we have just examined. The suspensive material has coincided with a complete tone unit with referring tone:

// R apPARently // // R PROBably // // R FINally // R in the END //

The assumption in each of these cases is that what the ensuing increment counts as, or what it will be about, is something that can be treated as if it had already been settled between participants: 'You know, of course, that what I am about to say . . . amounts only to a statement of probability' or '. . . concerns what the outcome of her deliberations were' or '. . . will be about what happened at the end of her deliberations'.

Suspensions at the beginning of the chain

One thing for which we earlier offered no general explanation is the practice of producing elements or subchains of elements suspensively before chain-initial N. We merely said that the process of suspension made this practice possible without destroying the finite-state properties of the rule system. We can now add to this. Such suspensive matter serves to pre-characterize what follows, either as what it counts as or as what it is about, in a way which exactly parallels the use of syntactically discrete increments.

It remains to see how listeners can be given preliminary intimation of this kind when there are no suspensive elements before NV: that is to say, when chains begin in the way the simple chaining rules lead us to expect them to begin. Examples are:

This old lady told her about her daughter

The traffic was bad

There is, of course, a well-recognized sense in which these two increments can be said to be about *this little old lady* and *the traffic* respectively. Very often, when introducing the categories of a sentence grammar in the classroom or elsewhere we say that 'the subject stands for that which the sentence is about'. But this would lead us to the conclusion that

// FINally // she aGREED to TAKE her //

was about she (= the friend); and we have made the seemingly contradictory assertion that it is about what happened *finally*. The problem arises, of course, because the expression 'what something is about' can be used in two different ways.

The confusion is reduced if we expand one meaning of 'what it is about' to 'what the listener wants to know about'. The preliminary element *finally* serves to focus a particular interest that is attributed to the listener, an interest that we might capture by ascribing to him an (unspoken) question 'What happened finally?'; it is the answer to this question that the rest of the chain provides. We can then say that, in the other sense, the answer to this unspoken question is a statement about someone referred to as *she*. Let us say that the listener's interest is taken to be what happened *finally*, and when it comes to satisfying that interest it is necessary to say something about *she*.

If either of our examples that begin with N were spoken as single tone units:

// THIS old lady told her about her DAUGHter //

// the TRAffic was BAD //

we need say no more than that they were statements about *this old lady* and *the traffic* respectively: no particular interest is attributed to the listener apart from an interest in the whole assertion. But when it is spoken like this:

// R THIS old LADy // P TOLD her about her DAUGHTer //

the first example does more than this. It gives preliminary notice that it is *the old lady* about whom something is about to be told. It then goes on, without the interpolation of a new subject, to tell something about her. That is to say, the two different meanings of 'what it is about' attach to one and the same reference. It happens that the old lady had, in fact, just been spoken of as the strange occupant of the car, so the two-stage presentation can be made clearer in an alternative version:

// R SPEAking of this old LAdy // P she TOLD her about her DAUGHTer //.

Here, the assumed focus of interest and the subject of the assertion about her are given separate realizations as *this old lady* and *she* respectively. The earlier, shorter, version simply brings them together in the same N.

The two tone unit version of the second example works slightly differently, but only because the first tone unit has a proclaiming, not a referring tone:

// P the TRAFfic // P was BAD //

Here, preliminary mention of *the traffic* introduces something that has not yet been considered. The listener's attention has up to now been directed towards the person in the car and what should be done to solve her problems. It is not until the friend's slowness in taking a close look at her needs to be explained that this other relevant factor is mentioned. A paraphrase will make this clear:

// P and there was ALso the matter of the TRAFfic // P it was BAD //

In both the extended version and the concise one, the first tone unit tells the listener firstly that there is a so-far unconsidered factor to be taken into account—*the traffic*. The assertion that follows then has this same N as its subject. The thing singled out for preliminary mention and the thing about which the promised assertion is made are, once more, one and the same.

185

The general effect of presenting the initial element in the chain as a separate tone unit is, therefore, to give preliminary notice of what interest the increment will address, whether it is suspensive of the expected N or not. The use of this intonation treatment enables the speaker first to indicate what interest the increment will address, and then to go on and make an assertion which addresses it. In the case of the N-initiated chains we have examined, the following assertion concerns the same N as has been used to identify the interest. It may, however, concern the reference of an N that has not yet been produced.

This last possibility is exemplified by

> . . . her hands were like man's hands . . . and her arms . . . they were hairy

In the second chain of this extract

> // P her ARMS // P they were HAIRy //

it is the second N of a reduplicative pair, *her arms + they*, that is the essential N of the NV etc. sequence. The first N, which is spoken as a separate tone unit, has preliminary function: 'I will tell you about her arms . . . '. Proclaiming tone is used, as it is not assumed that listeners will necessarily expect to be told at this point about her arms. They are told, in effect, that it was not only her hands but her arms that were remarkable. The subsequent assertion happens also to have as its N a reference to the same thing, *they*. But this need not be the case; we could easily imagine a version like

> . . . her arms . . . the hair on them was thick and curly . . .

One further use of preliminary labelling can be noted here, although no examples are found in the data. A chain like

> // R THAT exit // P she DROVE PAST //
>   n   +N V

exploits the process of N reduplication to present an increment which might otherwise have its elements ordered thus:

> She drove past that exit
> N V   N

This results in the two nominal elements being differentially represented, *that exit* as the assumed focus of interest and *she* as that about which the assertion which follows is made.

Theme

Once more, those familiar with existing descriptions will recognize in all this a re-examination, in terms of linear now-coding mechanisms, of matters that have been treated differently elsewhere. Much of this chapter has been concerned with a speaker's reasons for giving temporal precedence to certain elements in the chain—for beginning the chain with a suspensive A, for instance. It therefore covers much the same ground as discussions of 'thematization'. The concept of 'theme' as a functional division of the sentence or a clause derives from the work of the Prague linguists, notably Mathesius, and is perhaps most influentially adopted by Halliday (see especially 1985).

Like the concept of the speech act, that we referred to in the previous chapter, that of theme belongs to an approach which builds upon a quite different set of assumptions from those that are made in this book. Importantly, also, the two approaches differ fundamentally from each other in respect of their starting-points: it may, indeed, seem odd to be suggesting that the two have anything to do with each other. As we have said, we are seeking here to restrict ourselves to considerations which affect, and are affected by, the syntactic and intonational organization of the increments of speech. In this respect, the explicit marking of speech acts and thematization, and also of various other phenomena that would not be considered to be cases of either, appear to operate in an analogous way: to declare what an assertion is to count as or what focus of interest it will address, we can make use either of the first element(s) of the chain, separated off intonationally from what follows, or a separate chain. In the latter case, the chain results from taking a route through the chaining rules in the same way as we do when we are presenting essential information. Both involve use of language about language; neither requires any modification of the way the sequencing rules work.

Temporal precedence

We have concentrated in this chapter upon preliminary labelling. It seems likely that in most kinds of discourse—and certainly in the narrative data—this is more common than retrospective labelling. The giving of advance warning about how to interpret an assertion, or about what the present focus of interest is assumed to be, is more obviously useful than doing either of these things after the assertion has been made.

It is nevertheless easy to show that adverbial elements of the kind that signify the status of the assertion can occur as retrospective labels as well as preliminary ones. In these invented (but not improbable) examples, the elements *apparently* and *probably*, which we found in chain-initial position, occur where the simple chaining rules would lead us to expect them:

> // R the POOR old WOMan // P had a been SITting there WAIting
> // R apPARently //
>
> // P it WASn't a burglar // R PRObably //

The intonation treatment suggested, which presents the final A as a separate tone unit, seems the most likely one. It resembles the way such elements were treated at the beginning of the chain. The difference between these examples and those discussed earlier is that the characterization of essential information now comes after it rather than before it. Possible two-chain paraphrases would be

> The poor old woman had been sitting there waiting # That is what appears to have been the case
>
> It wasn't a burglar # I have said what was probably the case

Notice, also, that the labelling element can be introduced suspensively within the essential part of the chain:

> // R the POOR old WOMan // R apPARently // P had been SITting there WAITing //

something that would require a very conspicuous use of suspension if it were done with a complete chain:

> The poor old woman . . . I tell you what appeared to be the case . . . had been sitting there waiting

188

The following are some chains found in the data in which the first element or a first subchain is spoken as a separate tone unit:

// R AS she was walking towards her CAR // P she saw this FIGure . . . //

// R WHEN she got out of the LIFT // P she thought she saw someone sitting in her CAR //

// R apPARently // P she'd been TRYing all the DOOR handles . . . //

// R i HOPE you don't MIND // P but i arRANGED to meet my DAUGHter here // and . . .

// R and THIS old LAdy // P looked REALly ILL //

// R at ONE POINT // P she took her HAND out . . . //

// R AS they are driving aLONG // P she just HAPpens to look ACROSS . . . //

// R i was TRULy // P in a situATion . . . //

// P deLIBerately // P she WENT past the EXit //

// R VEry CLEverly // P she MISSED the TURNing . . . //

// R the MOment he's out of the CAR // P she SLAMS the DOOR . . . //

17
Asking exchanges

The choice of data on which to base this book has resulted in its giving priority to the description of telling increments. It was a deliberate choice, motivated by the expectation that a technique for description that worked for these could be adapted fairly easily for application to speech which was produced for other purposes. Our aim now is to indicate in a very general way how this can be done in relation to asking exchanges.

We shall inevitably have to make much freer use of the recorded material. Apart from occasional bits of dramatized conversation and impersonation, asking occurs in the narratives only when one or other of the subjects reports a question–response sequence between the friend and one of the other participants. We have therefore to rely more upon invented examples in this chapter than in earlier ones. The procedure will be largely a matter of extrapolating from earlier findings rather than of working upon the corpus. We shall still need to refer to the likely communicative needs that arise from a recognized set of circumstances, however, and shall therefore find it convenient to keep the narrative in mind. It will provide a ready-made background of speaker–listener understanding within which our task of analysis can be pursued without our having to have recourse to consideration of uncontextualized items.

Who knows what?

In Chapter 3 we proposed a working definition of an asking exchange as one which requires contribution from both participants before Target State can be reached. It is therefore necessary that we maintain a clear mental distinction between the exchange, which is the jointly constructed, purpose-achieving, stretch of speech, and increments, which are those stretches produced by contributing speakers. Asking exchanges require both an initiating increment and a responding increment. The Intermediate State precipitated by the initiating increment is one in which there is an obligation upon the co-operating listener to continue until the understood Target State has been reached. Although asking exchanges, like telling exchanges, can serve a multitude of secondary purposes other than the transmission of information or knowledge, we shall continue to explore the mechanisms on the assumption that speakers must nevertheless go through the motions as if the transfer of information were the intention: they achieve other purposes by asking. For instance, we pursue what are purely social ends by asking about someone's state of health as if we were really trying to find out how they are, and respondents normally co-operate in the game. And although asking initiations may sometimes fail in their purposes, we shall concern ourselves for the present with successful ones.

One of the simplest types of asking exchange, and one which shows how little needs to be added to the mechanisms we have postulated, occurs in one report of the conversation in the car park:

> and she (the old lady) said 'I was going to meet my daughter' so she (the friend) said 'You were going to meet her where?' and she said 'Here, in the car park'

Here, the initiating increment

> You were going to meet her where

closely resembles the start of a telling move

> I was going to meet her where (I usually do)

In both these cases *where* indicates the pertinence of a selection which will identify a place. The difference, of course, is that it is the initiator (the 'I') of the second example who knows where the meeting was supposed to take place and who consequently goes on to make the selection, while the one who doesn't know in the first example stops short at *where* and leaves it to the other participant to make it.

This kind of asking increment can, therefore, be accounted for by what we have already said about the operation of the sequencing rules. The only new factor is that the contributions of the two participants are needed to complete it. Before looking at other, slightly less straightforward, examples, let us use this one to illustrate some more facts about asking exchanges in general.

Firstly, as initiators of such exchanges we rely, not on any formal distinction — not upon how the chains are organized as sequences of elements — but upon our apprehension of the state of the speaker–hearer understanding within which the exchange is functioning. The crucial question is this: who has responsibility for going on to make the expected selection? In the kind of situation where interaction proceeds smoothly, this will already have been tacitly settled before the exchange is embarked upon: there will be a presumed understanding as to which of the two participants has the requisite knowledge for making the selection. There will be no question of the second speaker waiting to see whether the other goes on after where before deciding whether the latter's purpose is to tell or to ask. In all but the occasional — and repairable — cases, where participants are at odds about who knows what, this will have been decided already. We can say that the minimum prerequisite for the production of an asking increment (as, indeed, for a telling increment) is a certain presumed distribution of knowledge among the participants.

Initiating increments

Sentence grammars often state that the distinction between an interrogative function and a declarative function depends upon the sentence having a particular arrangement of constituents or following a particular intonation pattern: this is to say, it is represented as a formal distinction. This kind of assertion depends, of course, upon the assumption that it is items like sentences or clauses we have to classify. If, however, we accept the alternative proposal — the stretches of speech thus described are usually the initiating increments of exchanges — it becomes fairly evident that no formal arrangement can make an increment into a successful act of telling or asking unless the appropriate distribution of knowledge is first understood to exist. The examples used above suggest an alternative approach: let us suppose that all initiating increments are indeterminate as between telling and asking, whatever their forms may be. They are normally prevented from being ambiguous by the mutual understandings participants bring to the interaction. This means, of course, that those special grammatical arrangements and intonation patterns commonly associated with questions actually serve other communicative purposes.

Finding out or making sure?

We can best expand upon this last proposal by looking more closely at intonation. Essentially, we shall want to examine the widely held belief that there is such a thing as 'questioning intonation'.

The initiating increment attributed to the friend above actually occurs in a passage of impersonization with a proclaiming tone:

//P you were meeting her WHERE//

This fits in with our earlier assertion that proclaiming tones are used where there is assumed to be a difference between the participants' present states of knowledge. We can make a general statement with regard to asking increments: the use of a proclaiming tone indicates that the speaker is not yet in possession of information which the listener is assumed to have; the friend's proclaimed enquiry has the purpose of finding out where the unsuccessful meeting was to have taken place.

But it is not difficult to imagine a conversation in which a referring tone would be used. Let us suppose that it had gone something like this:

and she said, 'I was expecting to meet my daughter, she told me to meet her in the municipal car park'. So she (the friend) said, 'She told you to meet her where?', and she said, 'In the municipal car park'. 'But', my friend said, 'this is the Hurst Street car park'.

In this version, it cannot be the case that the friend's purpose in asking is to find out, for she has just been told where the proposed venue was. There could be a simple explanation of the daughter's non-appearance. Of course it could be that the old lady has just got the name of the car park wrong; it could also be that she has been waiting in the wrong place. It is better to make sure that she really means what she has said before telling her to go and look somewhere else. We can predict that, in a 'making sure' enquiry like this, the speaker will use a referring tone:

// R she told you to meet her WHERE //

A referring tone marks the content of the tone unit as shared understanding, and in asking situations this means that the speaker is seeking confirmation of what she thinks is the case.

One slight difficulty with this explanation is that local implications that derive from the specific context may come to mind more readily than the general one we have identified. One might feel, for instance, that the friend's request for confirmation arose from surprise, disbelief, or perhaps sympathy for someone who had been waiting for so long in the wrong place. Our present interest, however, is in finding a way of distinguishing between the effects of alternating proclaiming tones with referring tones, and in doing so in such a way that it will apply to all asking increments. Following a precedent we set earlier, we will say that one may express surprise, disbelief, sympathy, indignation, and countless other feelings by 'making sure'. It is the last-named purpose—in our terms the primary purpose that can be said to reside in all cases—that we want to focus on.

Notice that the opposition between 'finding out' and 'making sure' can be related, in a very direct way, to the use of proclaiming and referring tones in telling situations. For while, in the latter, referring tone is an indication that the speaker regards the information concerned as already negotiated, and expects the listener to go along with this assessment, in an asking situation, matter presumed to be already negotiated is treated as still subject to confirmation. We can paraphrase finding out as saying 'This is what I don't know, please tell me'; making sure is then paraphrased as 'This is what I have reason to believe we are agreed about, please tell me whether I am right'. In other words, nothing new needs to be added to what we have said about tone choice in telling exchanges to make it applicable to asking exchanges.

To see the effect of the finding out/making sure opposition in other circumstances, let us imagine a third conversation between the old lady and the friend:

> and she said 'I was expecting to meet my daughter' and my friend said 'You were expecting to meet her here?' and she said 'Yes'

Notice that the asking increment in this version has the same sequence of elements as a telling increment that the old lady might possibly have produced: 'I was going to meet her here'. That is to say, it is heard and responded to as an asking increment only because of the participants' awareness of who knows what. Moreover, the choice of either a proclaiming tone or a referring tone will affect the communicative value in the same way as it did in the earlier example:

// P you were going to meet her HERE //

will serve to find out whether this really was the case; but

// R you were going to meet her HERE //

will have the purpose of making sure that she has heard correctly, or that the interpretation she has placed upon what the old lady has said is a correct one — 'Is that what you are telling me?' (perhaps, but not necessarily, because she finds it surprising that people arrange to meet in car parks). Thus far, the parallel between this example and the earlier one is close; and this in spite of an obvious difference between them, one that is often made fairly central to the treatment of questions in sentence grammars: a major distinction — either an explicit or an implicit part of the explanatory mechanism — is that between the 'information question' and the 'polar question'.

Question types

Taking the way into grammar that the sentence-based treatment prescribes tends to make the formal representation of interrogative sentences the starting-point for most of what is said about questions. The distinction between 'information' types and 'polar' types is then treated as a second stage in the analysis. We have already said that asking increments serve asking functions quite independently of their formal properties, and we shall be saying later that the kind of response asked for — whether of the information kind or of the yes/no kind — is also a matter of speaker–listener understanding rather than of the syntax of the increment. Nevertheless, it is helpful to go along with the traditional distinction for the time being in order to explore the syntactic possibilities.

Increments which resemble the examples cited above, but which have their asking purposes made formally explicit, are:

Where were you going to meet her?

Were you going to meet her here?

Notice first that both of these chains could be used with either a proclaiming or referring tone, and with results that correspond to what we have said above. Proclaimed, they both seek to find out where; with referring tones they both serve to check on the truth of a construction that the speaker places upon what she has just heard: 'Am I right in believing that... etc.'.

Another observation applying to both of them is that the NV ordering, which we have regarded as the starting-point for every run through the sequencing rules, is changed to VN. This looks, at first sight, like a major disruption of the finite-state system we have postulated. It does not, in reality, disrupt it at all. Opportunities for selecting alternative routes do not become available until the speaker has reached the Intermediate State after the first two elements. We can restate the rule which applies to Initial State as 'produce an N and a V in whichever order present discourse conditions require'. This means, of course, it is the first verbal element that is affected in this way. It is also necessary for it to be an auxiliary or a modal, the word in which the polarity choice is made.

It is not easy to say precisely how the V/N reversal affects communicative value. The examples we have discussed above make it obvious that it is not a necessary marker of asking. Both

> You know this area well

and

> Do you known this area well

can, under certain conditions, be used to ask, as can

> You left him where

and

> Where did you leave him

As we have said, increments like the first in each of these pairs are best thought of as being indeterminate with regard to whether they present something as certain or uncertain, but not normally ambiguous in this respect. Those like the second make the uncertainty explicit. We can assume that participants in many kinds of conversation can rely to a high degree upon shared understandings and are, therefore, in this connection as in so many others, highly tolerant of indeterminacy. The extent to which uncertainty is actually marked in asking increments is probably exaggerated in sentence grammars. Working as they do with

196

uncontextualized sentences, they take little note of those factors which, in used language, make the communicative purposes of unmarked ones clear.

We must not, however, associate uncertainty too closely with asking. V/N reversal occurs with similar effect in increments which do not have an asking function. The increments

So could she get rid of him in any way

and

What was she going to do now

produced in the course of the narrative, would be understood by listeners as examples of those preliminary labels of the ensuing discourse we encountered in Chapter 16. Uncertainty is indicated in both, but the distribution of knowledge conditions places the onus for resolving it upon the speaker rather than the listener.

There remains the feature that distinguishes the so-called 'information' type of question: the suspensive use of the open selector in chain-initial position. Rather than

You were going to meet her where

we usually expect

Where were you going to meet her

An explanation of this arises from what we said in the last chapter about giving temporal precedence to particular elements. As in the examples we discussed there, the chain-initial element indicates what the increment will be about: in this case it will be about specifying the place that the open selector *where* anticipates. We can compare this with

Did she say she'd meet you here

where the first element is the one in which polarity choice is made. It therefore pre-labels the increment as one about polarity.

Responses

In asking exchanges, the response can be regarded as the increment that is required to reach the Target State. Its success in doing so might be acknowledged by the production of a receipt token by the initiator, recognizing that the sought-for information has been provided. Thus, any of the following could, in appropriate circumstances, be followed by 'Oh, I see', 'Really', or one of the other items that are available for this purpose:

Why were you sitting in my car?	I felt giddy
Who were you waiting for?	My daughter
Where were you going to meet her?	In the car park
How do you feel?	Giddy
Were you going to meet her here?	Yes
And didn't she come?	No

Such minimal responses are related to the initiating increment in an obvious way. *Yes* or *no* follows an asking increment which is concerned with polarity; and increments which indicate the pertinence of a selection by means of an open selector are followed by single-element responses which make the selections.

There are a number of ways in which this simple account needs to be modified. In some circumstances, minimal responses of the latter kind may be deficient unless there are pre-specifying or post-specifying additions of the kind we described in Chapter 14, for instance: 'my eldest daughter', 'in the large car park in Hurst Street', 'very giddy indeed', etc. On other occasions, it may not be possible to make the required selection with anything less than a complete chain:

Why did you give her a lift?

I felt sorry for her

In each of these examples there is a more or less mechanical matching of form with form. The form of the response could be largely determined by paying attention to the form of the initiation. The situation is rather more complicated, however, in a case like:

Were you going to meet her here?

Yes

The responsive *yes*, which would result from the kind of formal matching that we have just mentioned, might well be judged to complete the purpose of this exchange, and perhaps elicit 'I see' or a similar receipt token from the first speaker. But

Were you going to meet her here?

No

would be a different matter, at least in the context of the car park conversation with the old lady. It would be a surprising response because it would almost certainly have failed to complete the purpose that the exchange was initiated for, namely to find out what arrangements had been made about where the meeting was to take place. Minimal 'yes' would achieve such a purpose; but minimal 'no' would not, and a co-operative response would need to be elaborated so that it did. We might expect, for instance:

Were you going to meet her here?

(No) We always meet outside Woolworths.

What we have in this example is a fairly typical instance of a polar question being used to elicit non-polar information. Probably, there is little, if any, difference between the information-seeking purposes of

Were you going to meet her here?

and

What arrangements did you make about where to meet?

It is of a piece with all that we have said in this book that apprehension of present communicative need takes precedence over perception of grammatical form in determining what a speaker does. A co-operative respondent who knows that the present need is for non-polar information will give that information, whatever type of question they are responding to. It is worth noting that the *No* given in brackets above is included optionally; the initiator's purpose is fully achieved by what comes after it.

It would, perhaps, be unusual for even the informationally adequate 'yes' to be left unelaborated. A more typical response to the enquiry we cited above might be

Were you going to meet her here?

Yes, she said she'd see me in the car park

Elaboration like this results, however, from a different use of the mechanism that we have described. *She said she'd see me in the car park* is an existential synonym of *yes*. It is, in the terms we used in the last chapter, 'talk about talk', serving as a retrospective label to indicate what 'yes' means in the present situation. Such re-wordings of information already given are a common way of avoiding the minimal agreeing 'yes'. They differ from the elaboration that we noted in the case of disagreeing 'no', however, in that, as steps in the process of information exchange, they are often redundant.

Extended responses

There are some increments, which are formally indistinguishable from asking initiations, but which set up expectations that cannot usually be satisfied in any of the ways we have mentioned. An example would be the demand that the friend might reasonably have made:

What are you doing there (i.e. in my car)

It is hard to imagine either a single-element or single-chain response which would suffice here. Nothing less than an account of the daughter's failure to turn up, the old lady's long wait in the cold, and her giddiness and need to sit down, would satisfy the needs of the moment. The friend's utterance is, in fact, less an asking initiation which requires a response than a demand for an explanation. It is best explained, not in terms of the asking exchange but in terms of what we have called preliminary labelling. If the old lady had volunteered 'let me explain . . .' we could have said this pre-characterized what followed as an explanation. We can equally well say that by producing something which amounts to 'explain yourself . . .' the friend does the same thing. The imperative force that attaches to her utterance is easily accounted for: saying that another's discourse will be characterized as an explanation is tantamount to demanding that she give one. The 'talk about talk' description applies to an event like this in that *what are you doing there* indicates in advance what the ensuing talk will count as; or what, in this particular case, the speaker is predisposed to regard it as.

Increments which have the appearance of asking initiations are often used in some kinds of discourse to set events going by pre-characterizing them in this way. The most likely purpose of any of these

> Have you heard the one about the old lady in the car park
> Why don't you tell us about it
> What would you have done in the circumstances
> Can you describe him
> How do you think she got rid of him

would be to pre-empt the character of the ensuing talk in some way: to say in advance either what it was to count as or what it was to be about (or both), and in so doing restrict the freedom to choose of one or other of the participants.

Since the talk that is so characterized is likely to comprise any number of telling increments, we are dealing here with phenomena that cannot be described in terms of single exchanges. As we saw in the last chapter, preliminary labelling is a feature of the 'higher' organization of speech, and to pursue it further would take us beyond what we have taken to be the limits of grammar. We should not normally expect to hear a sequence like

> Why were you waiting here?
> I'd been shopping
> Oh

because such a bald assertion is unlikely to be regarded as an appropriate explanation of the old lady's presence, and since obtaining such an explanation was the likely purpose of the question, the friend will not acknowledge receipt until she judges it to be complete. We must therefore confine the notion of an asking exchange to cases where minimal responses are assumed to be adequate by both parties.

For a further example that does not satisfy this condition let us imagine a different beginning for our story. Another member of the party has just told of a frightening experience she has had. Someone else says:

> That reminds me of what my friend told me

and someone takes up the offer with

> Why, what happened to her?

What followed this could be very similar to the entire narrative reproduced in Chapter 1, a narrative which we have analysed as an extended sequence of increments mainly of the telling kind. Similarly, in recognizing that the unelaborated denial in

Were you going to meet her here? No, . . .

would probably be a less than adequate response, we may have been recognizing only part of the truth. Even an extended response like 'No, in Sainsbury's' would probably leave too much unsaid to be regarded as co-operative. The necessary extended explanation could, once again, be of considerable length, and its endpoint—the point at which the friend could have been expected to acknowledge receipt of sought-after information—would depend upon the complexity of the case.

It is necessary, therefore, to see the utterances we have examined in this chapter as potentially serving one of two different purposes:

1 to elicit a response, as asking increments;
2 to pre-characterize that follows in terms of what it will count as or what it will be about

It is only in the case of (1) that we can speak of minimal syntactic or intonational requirements. The telling that (2) requires depends upon the participants' shared apprehension of what, in the present circumstances, needs to be said.

We will make one final observation about (2). We have said that the story could have been triggered by some such increment as 'What happened?' and that if that were the case its telling would not differ significantly from any of the versions we have been working on. It is possible to see such a trigger as making explicit that communicative need to which we have said all tellers address themselves. And just as speakers can be thought of as responding to an invitation that has just been articulated, so any telling increment (or sequence of telling increments) can be thought of as answering unasked questions. It is the terms in which those question might be couched, if they were asked, that we have been referring to when we have spoken of the assumed communicative need that telling increments seek to satisfy.

18

What can go wrong?

Chains that do not occur

A grammar which aspires, as this one does, to account for what speakers do on the assumption that they are engaged in a linear, real-time, process of assembly must, if it is to be successful, demonstrate three things:

1 that the seemingly considerable freedom that speakers have to vary the order of elements within a chain can be accounted for by a rule system which operates on finite-state principles;
2 that the different communicative values which can accrue to sequences of elements which are similar when regarded simply as linear sequences can be accounted for in ways which do not postulate constituent-within-constituent relationships among elements;
3 why certain sequences of elements—those which a sentence grammar would probably label as either ungrammatical or of doubtful grammaticality—are not usually found.

Our account so far has been concerned with (1) and (2). We have shown that the device we have called 'suspension' permits the occurrence of elements at places other than those appointed for them by the simple chain rules; and, as long as the framework of expectation that is provided by those rules remains inviolate, it does so without destroying the finite-state properties of the grammar.

We have also shown that differences which sentence grammars have attributed to the existence of different kinds of relationship among constituents can be explained, not by demanding that ambiguities in sentences are capable of being resolved within the grammar, but by regarding indeterminacy as something that users expect and deal with without difficulty as long as they are operating in the awareness of a present communicative need. As a consequence, very many of the differences that sentence grammars regard as matters of grammatical constituency can be seen, from the point of view of the user, as differences that reside in the situation in which the language is used. Two increments are different because they satisfy different communicative needs.

With regard to (3) it has to be said to begin with, that the method we have adopted is not well suited to saying what will not happen. By adopting a corpus-based approach, in however informal and limited a manner, we inevitably commit ourselves to explaining the utterances we find rather than to finding reasons for excluding other, hypothetical, ones. We are, of course, prevented from using the idea of grammaticality, as this is commonly understood, by our rejection, at the outset, of the sentence as our object of study. For the intuitions that sentence grammarians attribute to us about what is and what is not 'well formed' are all related to the object in question. Grammaticality has generally been conceived of as a property of the unused product rather than of the purposeful process upon which we have sought to concentrate. Nevertheless, it is necessary to try to find reasons, both for the likely non-occurrence of certain sequences of elements, and for the strong feeling we may confess to having that some of them would be wrong if they did occur.

In attempting this, we shall appeal, not to some set of general and consolidated criteria that are inherent in the abstract system, but to certain specific limitations upon what we can do, or are likely to do, that are implicit in the way we have represented the real-time mechanisms.

Categories of constraint

As a way in, let us tentatively propose three different categories of constraint that might limit a speaker's freedom when the purpose of the increment is to tell. The assumption will be that if the speaker ignores these constraints, he or she will produce something that is recognizably wrong. All three categories can be exemplified without going beyond what we said in Chapter 4 about the simple chain:

1 Constraints built into the sequencing rules.

Although the permissiveness of these rules is perhaps more apparent than their constraining effect, there are things they do not allow. For instance, while both the route through the rule system and the 'distance' the speaker must proceed to are fixed by what presently needs to be told, sequences which do not satisfy the requirement for an initial NV will not achieve Target State whatever the communicative need may be.

2 Constraints associated with the use of particular items.

If a speaker used the verbal element 'agree' in a minimal chain:

She agreed
N   V

it is possible that Target State will be achieved. If the V that is used is 'found':

She found

it is unlikely that Target State will be achieved without production of a second N, for instance:

She found the old lady

And if the chain begins

She piled

a usable telling increment will probably depend upon there being both a second N and an A:

She piled the old lady into the car

3 Constraints arising from the use of particular words in the course of satisfying particular communicative needs.

If the friend were asked to tell the police what had happened and began by saying

I saw someone

without continuing with an adverbial element which specified where, for instance 'in my car', she would probably be regarded as not addressing present needs, although the item would be judged to be perfectly satisfactory as a sentence.

There seem, then, to be three ways in which a chain may be rendered unsatisfactory when it is considered as a possible contribution to a discourse. It is necessary, however, to make two comments about the distinctions that this preliminary analysis makes. The first is that only those examples that are covered by categories 1 and 2 would be rejected as ill-formed sentences of the language by a sentence grammar. The reference to a perceived communicative need in category 3 introduces a factor of which such grammars normally take no account. The dividing line between what is relevant and what is not in a sentence-based discussion of grammaticality thus falls between categories 2 and 3.

The second point, however, is that it is often difficult in practice to make a clear distinction between the effects of categories 2 and 3. When we say confidently that *found* will almost certainly be followed by a second N and that *piled* will almost certainly be followed by an N and an A, we may simply be recognizing that there are probably no conceivable communicative needs that would be satisfied by increments in which these verbs were used unless they were continued in the way we have described. What this suggests is that putative communicative need is really the decisive factor in admitting or ruling out particular sequences in both categories. We can usefully recall that a speaker's commitment is always to producing a situationally appropriate chain. If, therefore, we say that verbal element X, by virtue of its own value, commits the speaker to going on to produce an element of type Y, and possibly other elements thereafter, we are saying in effect that we can visualize no communicative need that would be satisfied if that continuation were not made.

It follows, then, that the distinction we have made between categories 2 and 3 is a rather artificial one, and this has consequences for what we are attempting in this chapter. We set out to investigate what there was about certain potential chains which would militate against their ever occurring, or lead to their being perceived as unsatisfactory if they did occur. The kind of constraint dealt with under category 1 does enable us to say confidently that some chains would fail a clear-cut test. Thus far, we are on firm ground. But more nebulous notions about what conversational needs are likely to arise enter into our judgements concerning both categories 2 and 3. To separate them clearly we should need to be able to say of cases that fall under category 2 that they could never, under any circumstances, be deemed satisfactory. This may be impossible to do. As sentence grammarians know, it is often possible to invent circumstances in which the most unlikely sentence would be acceptable. Similarly, although, for instance, the production of some verbs will nearly always precipitate a State which requires a further element, we cannot say unequivocally that there will never be a situation in which they will achieve Target State. The most we can safely do is to say what we have to say about such cases in terms of probability; and this, of course, means the probability of certain communicative needs arising.

There follow a few examples of the kinds of absolute constraint that fall within our category 1, and of the kinds of probable constraint that seem to fall within category 2, some of the latter being closer to the 'most probable' end of the scale than others. It is important to be clear that they are not presented as a list of rules of grammar — the rules have been described already. They are more or less random illustrations, drawn mainly from earlier chapters of this book, of the impact those rules have upon our notions of what is, and what is not likely to happen in used language, of how obedience to the set of general principles that underlie the rules limits the speaker's freedom of action in assembling chains.

Absolute constraints

1 When a speaker begins a chain with a suspensive element, or a suspensive subchain, there is an absolute obligation to go on to produce the expected NV.

2 When a suspensive element is produced after chain-initial N, there is an absolute obligation to produce the V which completes the obligatory NV sequence.

3 When open selectors are used, there is an obligation eventually to produce a subchain which makes the selection that has been signalled as pertinent, unless it is understood either that the onus is upon the other participant to do this or that the increment is a preliminary label.

4 Zero realization of the subject nominal elements of non-finite predicators is obligatory.

5 Second mention of the referent of the first N of a reduplicative pair necessarily has zero realization in a following finite second predication.

6 When an article is produced, there is an absolute obligation to

produce an N before going on towards Target State via any further elements that may be needed. Note that this requirement precludes the possibility of Nd ordering such as *'person a'.

7 If modal verbs are used, they must be produced before other verbal elements in the sequence. (Since modals do not have non-finite forms, they can occur only as the initial V in such sequences—the place at which primary time reference is always made.)

8 Certain sequences of auxiliaries are not available for use, e.g. *'(she) has sitting'. The value of such a form would, if it were produced, be exactly the same as the simpler '(she) sits'.

Probable constraints associated with particular words

1 When a verbal element which has implications of futurity is followed by a non-finite V^1, the latter will have the *to* form. We expect

> She wanted to go . . .
>
> She expected to meet . . .
>
> She decided to get rid of him . . .

2 When speakers make use of elements which are communicatively deficient, they must produce an element which makes good the deficiency before going on to the Target State via any further elements that may be required. The probable deficiency of *her* in

> She gave her . . .

makes necessary the production of a reduplicative N such as *a lift* before the Target State can be reached or progress towards it can be continued via another element.

3 Subchains are not used suspensively if the reason for using them is to make good the deficiency of another element. Thus, while

> To let the heavy goods vehicle go by, she waited

might occur,

> To reverse into the drive, she wanted

would not. Similarly, if the deficient element is an N, as in

The person sitting beside her was a man

there is no alternative version in which the V^1 is suspensive:

Sitting beside her, the person was a man

4 If a sequence of elements which is less than the chain is communicatively sufficient, the chain may be presented as two successive increments:

// P she WAITed // P to let the HEAVy GOODS vehicle go by //

But, if it is deficient, this option is not available. We do not expect to find

// P she WANTed // P to reVERSE //

divided into two proclaimed tone units in this way.

5 Adverbial elements which are unlikely to have a preliminary labelling function are not used suspensively before NV etc. In

// R MOST days // P she GOT there on TIME //

the suspensive A plausibly gives notice of what the increment will be about—what usually happens.

// R ON TIME // P she GOT there //

would make the improbable assumption that it might be helpful to say in advance that the present increment was going to be about what happened *on time*.

Category 3 constraints

We do not attempt to provide a list of circumstances in which this kind of constraint operates because all such constraints, taken together, amount to the general obligation that co-operating participants must try to fulfil: that is to say, always to produce increments which satisfy present communication needs. The choice of particular words and an awareness of their existential values—a consideration which recognizes the prevailing circumstances—are among the factors that speakers must take into account. One further illustration of how this works will help to substantiate the point, and also enable us to give another illustration of how difficult it is to distinguish clearly between category 2 and category 3 situations — to further emphasize, that is, the dependence of our judgements about what increments are usable upon our assessment of the present state of speaker–listener understanding.

The communicative sufficiency of all nominal elements depends upon the present state of conversational play. On any occasion during the presentation of the story, 'the woman' would probably be sufficient to identify the stranger: a tacitly accepted existential paradigm which opposed 'the woman' to 'the friend' would be quite normal. Situations could nevertheless be imagined in which pre-identification, 'the old woman', or post-identification, 'the woman in the car' would be necessary. Some of the storytellers do, in fact, avail themselves of the option of doing this. It is a matter of fine judgement as to whether the extra identifying information is necessary. If it is not, supplying it will be heard as nothing worse than somewhat tedious over-explicitness. But if it is necessary, failure to supply it will evidently result in an unsatisfactory increment.

Some nominal elements like 'person / one / thing', are very unlikely to be communicatively sufficient, and will therefore usually require pre- or post-specification. We used 'the person' in a category 2 element above as an element which seemed self-evidently to be deficient, and in many circumstances this would certainly be the case. The participants in our story are all *persons* so that here, and on the vast majority of occasions on which the word might be used, merely to identify someone as one of these would be insufficient. The selective potential of the word is virtually restricted to excluding alternatives like 'place / thing / animal', etc., and it would only be on rare occasions when satisfying communicative need required that one should exclude one or more of these that something like

I saw the person

would be sufficient.

We can summarize the position with regard to nominal elements as follows. Some of them, like personal names, are highly likely to be communicatively sufficient in any situation where they are actually used. There are others, like 'person', which are unlikely to be sufficient, and therefore likely to need pre- or post-identification. Neither of these assertions can be absolute, however. They have to be thought of as occupying the extreme ends of a scale of probability, a scale on which other nominal elements occupy various intermediate positions. And what applies to this particular requirement of nominal element identification applies to all the syntactic requirements that we might associate with all the elements except where category 1 constraints apply.

On-line amendments

We have looked upon unsatisfactory increments hypothetically: as arising from a putative failure to obey the imperatives of the system or meet the requirements of present communicative need. There is another kind, of which all the recorded versions of the narrative provide examples. They are, moreover, cases that can be discussed on the basis of evidence that the speakers themselves provide and are therefore more firmly based.

For a variety of reasons, speakers sometimes appear, in mid-increment, to realize that they are heading for an inappropriate Target State and change tack accordingly. We will conclude this chapter with a brief examination of the procedures they adopt to rectify the situation.

The need for such on-line amendments can be taken to arise, in a rather obvious way, from the fact that speakers are, as we have supposed throughout this book, assembling language in real time and in response to a moment-by-moment assessment of what present communicative needs are. It would be surprising if such a task did not result in some increments for which the necessary pre-planning has been less than adequate. An interesting feature of the narrative data we have been examining, however, is that, although speakers sometimes set out with incomplete plans, or with plans that have to be discarded as inappropriate, they nearly always make changes *en route* which ensure that an appropriate Target State is reached.

We can separate out a number of different ways in which this is done:

1 Second thoughts about what needs to be told can lead to a chain being abandoned and a new one begun.

> Somebody I know . . .   you know one of the big multi-storey car parks

It's like the one in . . .   you remember the one in Hounslow by the supermarket

2 One (or sometimes more than one) element can be repeated before continuing. This practice seems to arise, not so much from having planned the wrong chain as having not planned a complete chain at all.

the friend . . . the friend didn't know where it was exactly

you know how it is quite dirty and . . . quite dirty and dark at the end of a day's . . . end of a day's work

she thought this is a . . . this could be really . . . this could be really heavy

she pulled up just beside the driveway in order to . . . to . . . to turn round

she asked the little old lady to get out to guide . . . to guide her back

3 Speakers can break off and backtrack to insert or alter material that they think should have been included earlier.

after all the . . . about half an hour after all the supermarkets have shut

she hadn't locked the car . . . presumably she hadn't

it wasn't really . . . it definitely wasn't a little old lady

anyway so she offered to drive because the old lady's daughter came and showed . . . because it was about an hour after the time

as soon as the old lady got out of the car . . . the man got out of the car she drove off as fast as she could . . .

4 Speakers can substitute one element for another.

she didn't know . . . didn't say where it was

so she went up to the car and said . . . opened the door and said sorry but this is my car

the old lady was guiding . . . would tell her where to go

We cannot attach any significance to the differences that this procedure reveals, though a large-scale investigation might well enable us to do so. Probably the most important thing to recognize at present is that all such instances of what we might think of as self-correction can be explained on the basis of a real-time model: we suppose that speakers are in some way monitoring their progress towards a Target State and realizing in mid-increment, either that they are not going to get there if they continue on their present course, or that the Target State they have provisionally identified is not the appropriate one. The fact that the monitoring and on-line amendments are not conducted at the level of consciousness does not prevent our using this as a model for what is actually done. The very strong necessity that speakers appear to feel themselves to be under to make corrections is, moreover, in line with our contention that the achievement of a mutually acceptable Target State, within the constraints of the rule system, is the aim they have in mind.

19

A version of the story analysed

The extracts that have been used in this book to exemplify the various parts of the sequencing apparatus have been selected so as to make the general principles of the method of analysis as clear as possible. We have now reached the point where those principles have been described and the necessary conceptual apparatus set up. To a very large extent, describing whatever else we may find in used language is a matter of re-applying the same set of principles. It must be admitted, however, that doing this is not always so straightforward a task as it has been in the more or less carefully selected cases on which our exposition has rested. Much of the used speech we should want to be able to account for occurs, of course, outside the range of our minuscule corpus: it is obviously not possible to anticipate every problem we should encounter if we tried to do this. We can, however, demonstrate the general procedures for tackling unforeseen complications while still restricting our attention to the material that was recorded as a pool of examples.

Let us now examine a linear analysis of the syntax of one complete telling of the Little Old Lady narrative. It is, in fact, the same version as the unmarked transcript in Chapter 2. Much of the analysis follows in an obvious way from what we have said in this book. There are occasions, however, when the language may seem less straightforwardly amenable to description in the terms we have proposed. In these cases, brief notes are provided to show how the use of our apparatus can be extended to take in phenomena that have not yet been specifically discussed. Conspicuous among these are:

1 The various uses of the linking elements *and*, *but*, and *so*.
2 The use of miscellaneous elements like *well*, *anyway*, and *I mean* in circumstances where they cannot be said to represent sense

selections or enter into the organization of chains.

3 The use of set expressions like *kind of deserted* and *turned up* in which a sequence of items which could be described as a product of the linear grammar are regularly used as a single entity realizing a single sense selection.

The notes which follow the analysis will also serve to indicate some additional points of interest.

A linear analysis

1 a friend of mine told me this amazing story the other day she was a
  d N   p n   V   N+ d v¹   N   N   #N V . . .

2 she'd been shopping and she came back to this multi-storey car park
  N V V¹ V¹   #& N V   A+ P d e   N+ N

3 that she's been in and it was kind of deserted . . . erm . . . and as
  W+ N VV¹ P Ø& NV V¹   #   & w

4 she was walking towards her car she saw this figure sitting in the
  n v v¹   p   d n N V d N   ØV¹ P d

5 passenger seat . . . she thought what's that I've been burgled and as she
  N+   N   # N V   N   VN #NV V¹ V¹   #& w n

6 walked towards the car feeling a bit scared this person got out of the
  v   p   d n v¹   v¹   d N   V A P d

7 car and it was a little old lady . . . so she thought (oh well)
  N Ø#& NV d e   e N   # & N V

8 probably it's not a burglar and . . . er . . . (anyway) she asked her and the
  a   NVd N   #&   N V   N #& d

9 woman said . . . er . . . apparently she'd been sitting there waiting for her
  N   V . . .   a   N V V¹ V¹   A V¹   P d

10 daughter to arrive and the daughter hadn't turned up and she was
  N   V¹   #& d N   V   V¹ A #& N V

11 feeling a bit giddy and faint and so she went and sat in the car . . .
  V¹   E   & E   #&   N V   & V P d N #

12 it seems a very strange thing to do . . . (I mean) . . . apparently she'd been
  NV   d e   N   V¹ #   a   N V V¹

13 trying all the door handles one was open so she sat in it (so anyway)
  V¹   N+d N+ N   #N V   A #& N V P N#

14 this friend of mine . . . erm . . . said . . . (you know) . . . what are you going
  d N   P N   V   w   V N V¹

15 to do now . . . when are you meant to be meeting your daughter and the
   V'   A   # w   V N V'   V'   V'   d   N   #& d

16 woman said half an hour ago   so she said well what are you going to do
   N   V   A   #&N   V   w   V N V'   V'

17 now and (anyway) . . . finally this woman asked her if er she could possibly
   A   &   a   d   N   V   N+ W N V   a

18 give her a lift home because it was freezing and this old lady looked
   V'   N+d N A   W   NV   V'   #&   d   e   N   V

19 really ill and my friend thought . . . (oh) . . . I'd better be nice
   E   #&   d   N   V   NV   V' E

20 and it was a bit out of her way but she thought she'd better do
   &   NV   d N P   d   N   #&   N V   N V   V'

21 the . . . do the right thing so she piles her in the car and they go
   d   V' d   e   N   #& N V   N P d N #&   N V

22 off . . . and as they're driving along she just happens to look across
   A   # &   w n   v v'   a   N V   V'   A   Ø#

23 and sees her hands . . . and they weren't woman's hands at all . . . they
   &   V   d   N   Ø# &   N   V   e   N   P N # N

24 were man's hands . . . it's got hairy big hairy hands . . . the little old
   V   d   N   NVV' e   e   e   N   d   e   e

25 dear's clothes on . . . a funny little hat and everything . . . but these big
   e   N   A   d e   e   N & N   & d   e

26 man's hands ... (God) ... what am I going to do now and she looked down
   e   N   #   w   V NV'   V'   A   #& N V   A   ##

27 and she'd got men's shoes on . . . and she looked again at the face
   &   N VV' e   N   A   #   & N V   A+   P d N   #

28 and it was a man's face and she thought (God) he's a maniac what
   &   NV   d e   N   #& N V   N V d N   #w

29 am I going to do so very cleverly she got to this roundabout and she
   V NV'   V'   #& a   N V P d   N   #& N

30 missed the turning that she should have gone off   and she went down
   V   d N+   W+ N V   V'   V'   P Ø#& N V   P

31 the next turning and the little old lady said where are you going
   d   e   N   #& d   e   e N V   w   V N V'

32 (dear) we've missed my turning so this friend of mine said
      #N V V'   d N   #& d N   p n   V #

33 (well) I'm sorry I'm . . . I don't know this area very well . . . I'd better
   N   VE E #NV . . . NV N d N A   # NV

34 turn round so she went up to . . . found a driveway and it was dark by
   V¹ A #& N V A P   V   d N+ N #& NV E   P

35 this time and so she said . . . she pretended to be . . . (you know) a
   d N #&   N V   N V   V¹   d

36 hopeless female driver and said (oh) I'm terribly sorry I'm not very
   e   N+   N #& V   NV E   #NV   E

37 good at this sort of thing would you mind getting out of the car and
      P d N P N #V   N V¹ V¹   A P d N &

38 directing me at the back so this bloke . . . the little old lady
   V¹   N P d N #& d N+   d e   e N

39 gets out of the car and the moment he's out of the car she
   V A P d N #& w+   n v a p d n N

40 slams the door and shoots straight off and leaves her behind . . . so . . .
   V   d N Ø& V   A+   A Ø& V   N A   Ø# &

41 (anyway) . . . this isn't the end of the story she then drives to a police
          N V d N P d N #N a V   P d N+

42 station and reports the whole thing tells them all about it and the
   N   & V   d e   N #V N+ N P N#& d

43 police sort of nod to each other and look a bit knowing . . . (you know)
   N   V   P N   #& V E   #

44 would you mind if I just borrowed your car keys as we'd like to search
   V   N V¹ W+NV V   d N+ N W+NV V¹   V¹

45 your car they went outside and when they came back a quarter of an hour
   d N#N V A   #& w+ n   v   a   d n   p d n

46 later they asked her what is in the car she says (oh) a handbag . . .
   a #N V   N W   VP d N#N V   d N

47 and my shopping . . . and this and that so he says anything else she says
   & d N   & N & N #& N V N   #N V

48 (no . . . no) . . . there's the tools . . . and the spare tyre . . . and she goes
          N Vd N   & d e   N # & N V

49 through everything she can think of in the car and they said
   V   W+   N V V¹   P Ø P d N#& N V

50 anything else and she said no and it's then they tell her
   N+   #& N V   #& NVA N V N

51 do you know what's in the back seat of the car ... underneath the back
   V N V^1 W VP d N+ N P d N   P   d N+

52 seat of the car ... an axe.
   N P d N # d N

Comments

(The numbers refer to the numbered lines in the linear analysis.)

1   *of mine* This is strictly an unnecessary post-identification since *a friend* is sufficient as a characterizer of the referent of the first N. The sequence *friend of mine*, serving here as a composite label for one of the participants, is commonly used as a set expression in this way, signifying nothing much more informing than 'someone'. It is used again in a similar way in 11, 14 and 32.

    the other day is coded as an N. This is one of those cases where N elements and A elements (e.g. *on Friday*) are in existential opposition to each other as specifiers of time. See also *half an hour ago* in line 16, and many open selectors.

2   *and* (represented by &) has not been mentioned before. It serves here to link two chains. Its being non-prominent accords with the fact that it does not represent a selection against anything else. Indeed, there would be no difference in the communicative value of the two chains if it were not present. There are other instances of this use of *and* in lines 3 (2 examples), 5, 7, 8 (2 examples), 10 (2 examples), 15, and elsewhere. See also Note 13.

3   *she's been in* There is a change from differentiated to undifferentiated event time here.

    Ø represents unrealized second reference to *the car park*

    kind of deserted is here treated as a set phrase—the elements *kind of* which precedes the pp form of *desert* has no more effect upon the communicative value than does *of mine* in line 1. See also line 6 *a bit scared*, line 11 *a bit giddy*, line 19 *really ill*, line 43 *sort of nod*.

4   *this figure* The use of *this* as an identifier of the following N is common at the beginning of narratives. Strictly speaking, it is both uninterpretable and unnecessary. There is nothing in the context to enable the listener to know which figure is being referred to, and there is only one figure it could refer to anyway: *the figure* would be sufficient.

Ø represents an unrealized second reference to the referent of *as* = *while*: the time of seeing is equated with the time of walking. There is a similar instance in line 6 where the timing of *got out* is specified by reference to the timing of *walked*.

6 *got out* represents a single sense selection, and in this sense resembles *friend of mine* and *kind of deserted*. Notice, though, that they all result from the same use of the sequencing rules as they would if they were not set phrases. See also line 10 *turned up*.

7 *so* Note that there would be no difference in the communicative value if *and* were substituted here. See the note on line 13 for further discussion of this.

   oh well is not coded here. It is one of a number of items which
   (a) do not occur in sequences in the way that N, V, A, and E elements do, but are syntactically 'detached';
   (b) do not represent sense selections: in this use, *well* is not in opposition with *ill* or with anything else.

   See also lines 16, and 33, and also the uses of *anyway* in lines 8, 13, and 17, *I mean* in line 12, and *you know* in lines 14 and 35.

9 *apparently* An uncompleted increment is abandoned here in favour of a new one which begins with a preparatory A. Subsequent information is thus hedged about with the proviso that it is what appeared to be the only case. This reservation would not necessarily have been made if it had simply been quoted as what the woman said.

11 *and* is used differently in this line. In neither of the two occurrences is it followed by a new chain. Instead, the speaker re-uses some earlier part of the chain and continues it in a different way

   feeling a bit giddy and faint

   she went and sat in the car . . .

The first of these two is, in fact, indeterminate: reversion could be back to Intermediate State precipitated by *went* or that produced by *a bit*.

   and so See note on line 13.

13 *one was open so she sat in it* If this were presented as two syntactically unrelated chains, *One was open # She sat in it*, the co-operative listener would recognize that the second increment was intended to be heard as the natural outcome of the first. The

219

same would be true of *one was open and she sat in it*. Neither *so* nor *and*, therefore, has any effect upon the communicative value.

The difference between *and* and *so* is that the latter explicitly attributes an expectation to the hearer, namely that one event follows naturally as a consequence of another. The expectation can still be there if *and* is used. And since it is assumed to be part of shared understanding, it will still be there if no connecting element is used.

14 *going to do* This common use of *going*, signifying futurity, has the same implications as to the timing of events as it does in 'where are you going now?'. The difference is that it does not represent a sense selection. Like all cases of indeterminacy, it is seldom if ever ambiguous.

17 *finally* is another preparatory A at the beginning of the chain. It pre-classifies what follows as the outcome of the preceding discussion.

The open selector *if* can be taken as prefiguring a pertinent question concerning polarity and is existentially equivalent to a question concerning polarity. The following subchain then specifies the question.

18 The open selector *because* is indeterminate. It could be regarded as an A substitute in either *this woman asked her . . . because* (dNVNW) or *. . . give her a lift because* (V'N+N+W). The two linked subchains that follow could be interpreted as the reason for either. This is one of those cases where determining which is intended would be irrelevant—there is no significant difference between the two interpretations.

19 *and* in this line links the chain beginning *my friend thought . . .* with the chain beginning *this woman asked . . .* in line 17.

'd better This has the kind of existential value we have associated with modals like *must* and *will*, and operates in the sequencing rule in this way rather than as two separate elements: the plain infinitive of *be* follows.

22 The use of *as* and Ø here is similar to that in lines 3 and 5. The two linked subchains *she just happens to look across*, and *sees her hands* (line 23) both have their timing determined by that of earlier *was*. Both, therefore have Ø in lines 4 and 7 respectively.

30 *she missed the turning that she should have gone off* This looks like an error. We should usually expect . . . *off at* Ø (= off at the turning) The fact that *off* can be used both as an A element (as we take it to be here) and as a P in a P/N sequence may be reason for the confusion.

32 The 'vocative' *dear* resembles *well* in line 33 in that it is does not function as part of a chain.

34 *went up to . . . found a driveway* is an example of abandoning the chain and resuming it again as if after *she*.

35 *she pretended* Replanning here involves starting a new chain.

39 *the moment* can be regarded as an open selector, as can alternatives like 'as soon as', and some uses of 'immediately'. They are all A substitutes, in spite of their heterogeneous appearance: there is zero realization of the time in each of the three *and*-linked subchains that follow: the timing of each of these events is equated with the condition time of *he was out*.

41 *this isn't the end of the story* A preliminary increment which gives notice that what follows will get us to the end.

43 *look* is used here as a 'condition' verb, like *be*, and the condition is specified by the set phrase *a bit knowing* serving as an E.

44 *as* is here an open selector signifying the pertinence of a reason similar to 'because'. The following subchain states the reason.

49 *everything* is here an open selector.

51 *Do you know what's in the back seat of the car*. A preliminary increment telling what subsequent discourse will be about.

20

Uses of a linear account of grammar

There is a sense in which this book is unavoidably open-ended. By confining our attention to small samples of used language, and to a few invented chains that could be derived from them, we may have seemed to leave unanswered many questions that will arise when we try to apply the descriptive procedures to used language at large. Although the last chapter suggests that such wider application will need a certain amount of special attention to the way the system is used on particular occasions, it nevertheless encourages us to believe that if we obey the set of principles that underpin our model, we shall be able to use it for analysing any sample of used language we may be interested in. Informal examination of a great deal of naturally occurring data of many different kinds supports this view.

In this chapter we will remind ourselves of what those principles are and then briefly consider some of their implications for some of those areas of linguistic study in which, as we suggested in the Introduction, a linear account of grammar might be useful.

Principles

1 Firstly, it is fundamental to an understanding of the kind of grammar we have proposed that it begins with the speaker's perception of what communicative need must be satisfied at the time concerned. It is based on a here-and-now view of what the speaker is doing; and this perception co-operatively takes into account the listener's here-and-now point of view of what needs to be done.

2 We acknowledge that interactants cannot always co-operate successfully. Typically, both are working on the basis of a knowledge of each other's viewpoint that is at best imperfect. Conversational practice does, however, provide ways of sorting

out any misunderstandings that may arise. We have taken it that the working of the essentials of the system will be exhibited in the vast majority of cases where co-operation is successful. The repair of breakdowns is achieved by special use of those mechanisms that have then been described.

3   The stretch of speech that we make the focus of our attention is the increment. Generally, this is something that satisfies a perceived communicative need, in the sense that the hearer will have been told or asked something that is presently pertinent: something that might be acknowledged or responded to. The exception is the kind of increment whose function it is to give information about the discourse, information that is normally not acknowledged.

4   Each increment progresses from an Initial State to a Target State. The Initial State comprises all relevant aspects of the situation in which the increment is produced. Included among these are the speaker's apprehension of the projected Target State: speakers set out with working assumptions both about what the present state of understanding is and about what state of understanding they are seeking to achieve. In assembling each increment, they add one element to another along the time continuum. After the addition of each element except the last, a new Intermediate State is precipitated, a state which results from the way all the elements so far produced have successively modified the Initial State. Each Intermediate State then determines what may come next in further pursuance of the route towards the prospective Target State. The whole set of possibilities for advancement can thus be described in terms of a finite-state grammar.

5   In order to provide a systematic presentation of the grammar, we have found it convenient to begin with a subset of the rules which operate in a strictly linear way and result in the production of simple chains. Other rules extend the capacity of the grammar to produce chains of more complex kinds by allowing two kinds of modification of the simple chaining rules. Extension allows further elements after those provided for by the simple chaining rules have been exhausted, and involves no disruption of the predictable linear sequence that characterizes them. Suspension,

on the other hand, involves a rule which permits the production of certain elements 'out of order' but retains the finite-state property by prescribing a future course of action for each occasion when an element other than one of those allowed by the simple chaining rules has been introduced.

6   The temporal occurrence of elements with respect to each other is thus described without reference to the kind of constituent-within-constituent arrangement that sentence grammars characteristically posit. It follows that, in discussing the communicative values of increments, we cannot postulate any relationship among them other than those that can be related to the way they occur in temporal sequence. Thus the fact that one element occurs at some point after the production of another can be said to have relevance to the way the two are meaningfully related; but a hypothesis that they participate in some kind organization that goes beyond what can be described in one-after-the-other terms cannot. The use of 'bracketing' conventions, for instance, is not available to us.

7   A result of accepting this restriction upon our procedures is that all those differences between increments which a sentence grammar might attribute to differences in constituent structure must be accounted for in another way. This is one respect in which our purpose-driven grammar differs fundamentally from a sentence-based one. The difference arises from the respective aims with which the two types of grammar set out. Sentence grammars usually require that each sentence be capable of being interpreted as a meaningful entity without reference to the situation in which it occurs. In these circumstances, the only way of accounting for particular meaning differences and ambiguities can often be by appealing to supposed relationships among constituents that are identified at various layers in the organization of the sentence. If, instead of doing this, we focus upon the existential value of an increment — that is to say, its meaning in context — and keep in mind the normal co-operativeness of interactants, we can account for the differences in another way. Essentially, they are seen as differences in the communicative need that the increment is produced to satisfy. Since, in a successfully conducted interaction, these needs are assumed to be appreciated by both speaker and listener, alternative interpretations need not be entertained.

8 The potential that many increments have for satisfying two or more different communicative needs—for being appropriate, that is, for two or more sets of circumstances—is recognized by the term 'indeterminacy'. Indeterminacy is taken to be an all-pervasive feature of human language. When speakers make those existentially pertinent sense selections on which all spoken communication depends, they rely upon the hearer's predisposition to orientate to the particular meaning opposition that is intended: that is, the one which makes sense in present circumstances. The general practice of exploiting the existential values of words and other items is made possible only because of our ability to tolerate indeterminacy; other values that might accrue to an item in another situation, but which are not relevant to present conversational business, are systematically left out of consideration.

9 What applies to the values of single items applies also to the relationships that items contract with each other. For instance, when the occurrence of two elements in a chain makes the function of the second with respect to the first indeterminate, as between adnominal and adverbial, an appreciation of present discourse conditions will nearly always enable the co-operative listener to know which is intended.

10 It is often assumed that a grammar is in some sense a representation of what people must know in order for it to be said that they know the language. If we accept this assumption for the moment, we have to recognize that 'knowing the language' can have two different interpretations. Alongside the notion (widely subscribed to) that it comprises the ability to generate all the sentences of the language, we have to place an alternative: that is comprises the ability to satisfy all the communicative needs one may encounter. A conclusion of this is that in doing the latter one is far less reliant upon abstract mechanisms than one would be in doing the former.

The sentence

Our claim that the organization of used language can be described without reference to a formal category called 'a sentence' demands some further discussion, for the sentence has almost always been regarded as a given among those who write grammars. How can we account for the well-nigh universal confidence that recognizing what does and does not amount to a 'well-formed sentence' is a fundamental part of our knowledge of the language?

The word 'sentence' is notoriously difficult to define, and the concept is correspondingly elusive, a fact which might be said to support either of two hypotheses.

One is that the ability to perceive sentences in the language going on around us is innately part of the mental equipment with which we are endowed as human beings. It is something that we bring, ready-made, to our experience of language, and it conditions that experience in such a way that we intuitively compose our own language, and interpret the language of others, along lines determined by the internal knowledge we have of how sentences are assembled. Making that knowledge explicit is a matter of externalizing highly abstract processes, and the tasks of saying exactly what a sentence *is* is correspondingly difficult. This hypothesis has virtually been elevated to an axiom in the work of Chomsky and his followers.

The alternative hypothesis is to adopt the purpose-driven approach we have outlined here. We start with a consideration of a user who lacks technical knowledge which would give conceptual substance to words like 'grammatical' and 'sentence'. For such a person, the question 'Is X a grammatical sentence?' can only be answered if it is taken to mean something like 'Would you ever consider X a proper thing to say?' Furthermore, if knowledge of the language is thought of as the ability to pursue communicative purposes, this in turn can only be taken to mean something like 'Can you conceive of any communicative need that X would satisfy?' It will have been obvious to readers of this book that there is a fair measure of correspondence between what we have called 'increments' and what sentence grammars call 'sentences': consideration of purpose-achieving potential very often results in judgements about particular utterances that sentence grammarians would predict. The correspondence is not complete, however: the fact that a single chain can represent any number of separate increments, for instance, can result in the two approaches segmenting a stretch of speech in different ways. But the important question is not the extent to which the two objects coincide; rather it is whether we think of them as being recognizable because of their real-world potentiality for communicating or because of other criteria which are unaffected by the communicative use they may be put to.

Advancing the purpose-based hypothesis places us under an obligation, of course, to offer some explanation of how the notion of a sentence has come to hold such a prominent place in our thinking about language. We can do this very speculatively by reminding ourselves of the scholarly concentration, for long periods of history, upon the written word. We might reasonably suppose that contemplating and producing written texts tends to promote the notion that a piece of language comprises a sequence of discrete and potentially free-standing entities. Evidence of this is the use of orthographic and other punctuation conventions to separate off one such entity from another. We said earlier, following Halliday, that our experience of writing is, very largely, an experience of products that exist, and historical accident may well have conditioned our thinking against giving much attention to the way communicative processes happen. And once the need for looking upon text as a sequence of potentially free-standing sentences, with nothing left out, has become part of our thinking, certain consequences follow. For instance, the two-increment chain

// P she'd BEEN in TOWN // P SHOPping //

must be regarded as a single sentence because *in town* would otherwise be left as an 'unattached fragment'. The effect of this necessity is not unimportant. The difference in communicative potential between this chain and

// P she'd BEEN in town SHOPping //

and its similarity to

// P she'd BEEN in TOWN // she'd been SHOPping //

are viewed in a way which is determined by the mechanisms of the grammar rather than by consideration of the kinds of communicative use the three might respectively be put to.

The effects of centuries of preoccupation with the written text upon our thinking about language can only have been reinforced by the tendency to think of meaning as a more or less permanently

227

attached feature of each item of language: to follow Saussure (1916) in viewing a linguistic sign as a bringing together of that which is signified and that which signifies. The notion of the sentence has provided semanticists with an alternative focus to the word as an object for their attentions, and any enquiry into 'sentence meaning'— conceived as a predictable relation between a sentence and what it signifies — necessarily excludes consideration of how communicative value depends upon the ever-changing state of understanding between the parties to an interaction. The kinds of question that have been asked have arisen predominantly from an interest in the static, unused object rather than in the dynamic processes of purposeful discourse.

It should be stressed that the rival hypotheses we have discussed arise from approaching the study of language from different starting-points. It may be that it will never be possible to say whether the ability to recognize sentences is a given or whether, when this appears to be the case, we are really recognizing entities that are potentially need-satisfying. We need go no further than to say that the second explanation is as plausible as the first.

A user's model?

The terminology we have adopted is intended to engage the reader's interest in what speakers do rather than in the objects they produce: thus they 'tell' and 'ask' rather than make 'statements' or 'questions'. This is one reason why what we have presented could be said to look like an attempt at a user's model. Speakers have, moreover, been credited with having particular aims and with making moment-by-moment choices in the light of those aims. Listeners, for their part, have been said to interpret what they hear against the background of certain expectations and to respond accordingly. It has been a deliberate feature of the presentation to describe such events in ways which, as far as possible, invoke what might be described as commonsense notions. We have tried to keep in mind the way 'ordinary users' might describe what they were doing, rather than drawing upon the kind of technical knowledge that comes from familiarity with particular linguistic descriptions.

Doing this amounts, of course, to adopting a controversial position with regard to how knowledge about language should be regarded. A fundamental feature of Chomsky's claim is that such knowledge is of a different kind from that which we have of most other features of our world: for him, the 'language faculty', that hypothetical mental equipment which enables human beings to learn language, comprises certain innate dispositions, and these can be described only by devising a technique which puts 'psychic distance' between them and the means we have of dealing with non-linguistic experience (Chomsky 1968: 23). We have set out with a different objective: that of describing the mechanisms that facilitate the purposeful use of speech rather than those which might be necessary for the generation of unused sentences. It is consistent with this view that the abstractness of much sentence grammar, and its apparent inaccessibility to those who are not trained in its methods, arises from an initial act of abstraction, namely the isolation of the language sample from the social context which alone would make it interpretable as purposeful speech.

Psychological reality?

A model which purports to accompany the user step by step through an utterance might be interpreted as an account of what actually happens in some psychological sense. Although little of the decision-making and step-taking we refer to occurs at a conscious level, it would be possible to ascribe some kind of psychological reality to the journey to Target State that our metaphorical treatment has suggested. There is, however, good reason for caution before taking such a step from metaphor to operational reality.

It is important to stress that the real-time presentation of speech we make central to our account of grammar is an observable and incontrovertible fact, not a theory. People just do utter one element and then follow it with another. We have been concerned to show that a grammar which takes this observation is its starting-point is capable of giving a principled account of how people use language to communicate; and in doing so, we have made the claim that no mechanisms which require non-linear explanations are necessary. We can go this far empirically by observing what people do when they use language and then providing theories which link their linguistic behaviour with plausible accounts of what their communicative intentions are. Subsequent questions arise, not about whether speech is actually presented linearly in the way we have suggested, but about what significance the observation has for those who are concerned with cognitive aspects of language production and interpretation.

Purposeful language and psycholinguistics

When we move tentatively across the boundary into psycholinguistics and related areas, we must be clear that the setting up of a model for grammatical analysis has been viewed in this book as a separate enterprise from that of enquiring into what kinds of mental processes might be involved in speaking and listening. Investigating those processes must necessarily involve taking some view of the nature of the phenomenon one is investigating, however. And since the consideration of grammar enters importantly into that view, it is appropriate to say something about the relationship between the kind of approach we have adopted and some of the current work in the psycholinguistic field.

Some general questions can best be raised if we look briefly at a particular body of research: that which has concentrated upon the differing degrees of difficulty people experience in comprehending different kinds of sentence.

The question of the psychological reality of grammars became a central one in the 1960s as a consequence of the interest generated by transformational generative grammar. The alleged existence and putative nature of a 'deep grammar', which was held to underlie the surface structure of a sentence, led to questions about how the processes which were attributed to it were related to cognitive processes. It was suggested that one sentence might be easier to comprehend than another because of the relative complexity of its deep structure and of the transformational rules that related it to surface structure. The issue is no longer a live one, but it is worth pointing out that both those who sought to demonstrate such a connection and those who denied it saw the sentence as the focus of their interest. A fairly typical assertion from the literature of the time is

The description of hearing someone speaking in a language we understand as 'hearing sentences' . . . seems not only natural but fairly illuminating. It emphasises the point that understanding an

utterance involves in some way a knowledge of linguistic structure.
(Thorne 1966: 4)

Syntax is no longer seen as such an obvious starting-point for the psycholinguist as it was at the time, but this perception of language as comprising a sequence of sentences, each of which has a structure, is still very largely taken as a given. Thus, for instance, as recently as 1989, Clifton and Ferreira (1989: 79) expected relative ease of comprehension to involve the operation of a particular kind of 'sentence-processing' mechanism. One strategy which they take to be relevant, and which they call 'minimal attachment' had been described earlier by Frazier (1979) as an instruction to

use the smallest possible number of phrase structure rule applications to attach each incoming word into the structure currently being built.
(Frazier 1979: 76)

We are not, of course, concerned here with evaluating Clifton and Ferreira's findings. Rather, we may use their work as a means of demonstrating the effects of adopting a non-sentence-based approach to the question they address. The argument we have advanced suggests that one way of comprehending an utterance might be to construct for oneself a possible communicative use for it. The statement 'Utterance X is more difficult to comprehend than utterance Y' could be taken to mean 'I can more readily visualize circumstances in which Y would plausibly satisfy a communicative need'. Thus, the way subjects respond to the pair of items

  a. I knew the answer very well
  b. I knew the answer was right

might have something to do with the fact that, experienced as the informants are in taking part in purposeful discourse, they more readily hear one of these as a likely contribution to a probable discourse than the other. It seems relevant to point out, however, that the cognitive demands of this kind of task are not necessarily the same as those of relating an incoming utterance to a communicative need that it was intended to be addressed. The point becomes more important when we look at other examples.

a. Martha will say that it rained yesterday
b. Martha said that it will rain yesterday

or

a. The doctor called in the son of the pretty girl who hurt herself
b. The doctor called in the son of the pretty girl who hurt himself

It is not easy to think of any of these as fitting into the kind of conversation that most informants will be familiar with. In so far as there seems to be a palpable attempt to suggest and exploit potential ambiguities, it might be doubted whether informants would process them as the work of a co-operative speaker. The task set before them will seem rather to be one of solving some kind of linguistic puzzle: trying to find a pattern of relationships among the parts without benefit of context which would normally make one set of relationships self-evidently the intended one. Doing this, of course, makes cognitive demands upon the solver, but it is far from clear that these are of the same kind as those made upon an engaged participant in an interactive event. It seems reasonable to suggest that clarifying which of these is to be equated with 'comprehending' would add to the value of investigations of this kind.

A further point is raised if we look at further examples:

a. The horse raced past the barn and fell
b. The horse raced past the barn fell

a. Tom told the man that he had fired him
b. Tom told the man that he had fired

In both of these pairs it is possible to suggest differences that can be pinpointed by our linear grammar, and that might be relevant to the investigation: example (a) in the first pair does not have suspension while (b) does; in example (a) in the second pair there is no zero realization but in (b) there is. These are more or less random observations and only further experimentation along similar lines would reveal whether looking at differences in this way might cast useful light upon what makes for intelligibility; but if it were true, as we believe, that informants tend towards linear processing, even of uncontextualized stretches of language, this would seem to be a case for supposing that intelligibility might be affected by the way in which the mechanisms we have described are exploited. It might be possible to speak of greater or lesser 'complexity' in this connection.

Language acquisition

The study of how infants become speakers of their native language must obviously be affected in a fundamental way by one's assumption about what it is they have to acquire. The central importance that was given to syntax in the period following 1957 meant that progress from one-word utterances to adult competence was often seen in one of two ways. Either the child was operating a series of rule systems which progressively approximated closer and closer to that which produced well-formed adult sentences; or it was already equipped with the requisite adult system and the emergence of that system in use was delayed only by performance factors (Ingram 1989). In either case, the end-point of the process was assumed to be competence in the operation of a sentence grammar.

How are the results of research conducted in the light of one or other of these hypotheses affected by the possibilities we have raised? What if the goal is not the generation of sentences but the ability to participate in purposeful conversation?

The alternative approach we are suggesting comes closer to Halliday's concept of 'learning to mean' (Halliday 1973: 9–21) than to the various syntax-centred approaches. Halliday sees the child's development in terms of a number of 'functions', a notion which comes very close to what we have been calling 'purposes'. Other primary purposes than telling and asking may be necessary to complete the picture, but we can go a long way towards accommodating, for instance, instrumental, regulatory, and interactional functions in the kind of formulation we have used: speakers can say what they want of others, what they want others to do, and generally interact with others by telling or asking. The fact that, according to Halliday, use of the informative function comes last in order of development is consistent with our observation that neither of our primary purposes is by any means to be associated exclusively, or even principally, with the transfer of information from one participant to the other. We have said that going through the motions of pursuing either end can achieve a variety of secondary purposes.

We might think, then, of the child as learning to tell and to ask and to do so in situations where the need to do one or the other is well appreciated. There is at least a *prima facie* reason for preferring a model of grammar which makes these considerations its starting-point. The task then becomes one of showing how the need for the here-and-now pursuit of communicative purposes affects the element-by-element assembly of utterances at different stages in the child's linguistic development. The machinery we offer for doing this differs, of course, from Halliday's; but we are on common ground in so far as we take 'learning to mean' as what needs to be explained, rather than the putative learning or emergence of the ability to manipulate abstract structures.

Language learning and teaching

The presentation of this book as an exploratory grammar might seem to prevent our discussing its implications for the language classroom in much detail, even if considerations of space did not do so. There is an understandable desire among language teachers and learners for authoritative rulings, for clear-cut guidance on what to do and what not to do. We, on the other hand, have thought it proper in such an exercise as the one we have undertaken to maintain a tentative stance. If we wanted to extract from what we have said a grammar which would be pedagogically useful, we should have to systematize as much of it as we could in a form that could be taken, for teaching purposes, to be definitive. The difficulty of doing this would probably not be so great as would the difficulty of grafting the result upon existing classroom practices. Most grammar teaching materials currently in use follow a broadly traditional pattern, the principles of which have something of the nature of a cultural given. Learners who know anything about grammar almost always know what they have learned from such materials; the knowledge of many teachers is similarly grounded in tradition; and the most conservative influence of all, that of the examination system, perpetuates very clear traditionally derived expectations, not only about what learners should know but about the form in which their knowledge should be expressed. These are facts which one may either applaud or deplore, but in either case they have to be acknowledged, and acknowledging them makes the ready acceptance of a radically different teaching grammar seem highly unlikely.

An exploratory stance is not entirely a bad one for teachers to adopt, however. We can find many ways in which approaching speech as the real-time pursuit of purpose can lead to a salutary reconsideration of those patterns of thinking that we and our grammar books, often unwittingly, pass on.

Seeing the wood for the trees

There is, for instance, the fairly mundane question of where in the textbook, and hence often in the course, certain topics are discussed in relation to the treatment of other topics. Again, tradition has a powerful influence. The need for most grammars to serve as reference books means that they tend to follow a common pattern if for no other reason than that this is the only way to ensure that users can find their way around them. But the organization of the book is the most potent model the learner has of how the language is organized: the patterns of similarity and difference and the generalizations that are presented therein tend to be taken to be unassailable reality. It is proper to question whether the map they are being given is necessarily the best we can provide.

If, for instance, we are right in saying that there is a single way of accounting for all the circumstances in which each of the non-finite forms of English is used (including both those that come within so-called 'verb phrases' and those that don't), it may be desirable for teaching to be directed towards making learners aware of that fact. The usual practice is to offer separate, and largely unrelated, accounts of how each non-finite form is used in different circumstances.

We can illustrate the point by comparing our discussion of verbal elements in Chapters 7 to 10 with the way lessons on verbs are often presented in the textbooks that are in use (see, for instance, Thomson and Martinet 1969: 63–129). There we find a progression through a catalogue of tenses, involving the use of both single-word and multi-word entities, from present continuous and simple present to simple past, past continuous, present perfect, present perfect continuous, and so on. Such presentation obscures two facts that may be considered important. Firstly, it fails to recognize the way individual elements successively affect the communicative value of the complex forms. Secondly, the separation (and much later occurrence) in the book of the much-used non-finite forms discourages reference to what these latter have in common with comparable elements in the verb phrase. They are, in fact, treated as though they were in no way related. While there is certainly a case for breaking down what is to be presented into digestible helpings, there is an equally strong case for doing so in a way which makes it easy subsequently to put the parts together as a coherent whole. It scarcely needs saying that when a rule or instruction is given to a learner, its usefulness will be in direct proportion to its generality. This may involve putting learners in the way of recognizing generalizations that traditional treatments so often ignore.

We can look a little more closely at what this means by considering briefly under the points below parts of the chapter in which Thomson and Martinet (1969: 147–156) set out the uses of the *to* form:

1 A list of verbs which are followed by the infinitive is provided: they include, for instance, *promise, prepare, undertake,* etc. (ibid.: 147) All are verbs which, if they are followed by a verbal element, will be followed by one which signifies an anticipated event. Compare pages 85–86 above.

2 A further list of words which are followed by object + infinitive includes *want* (*I want you to go*) and *expect* (*I expect him to be there*) (ibid.: 147). Here, too, the anticipation of an event or state is involved. The examples demonstrate the truth of our observation that the *to* form can come after NVN as well as after NV. We might add that it can also comes after NVE, as in

   The book is easy to read

a usage which is treated under different headings, and after NVNA as in

   I told him firmly to go

a possibility that is not mentioned at all.

All the examples included in this particular section use the second N of the chain as subject of the *to* form. There are no examples which illustrate a similar re-use of the chain-initial N, as in

   He inspected it to make sure

3 Examples like

   He went to London to learn English (ibid.: 150)

are used to illustrate the use of the *to* form to express purpose. We have said that this implication will always be possible if one event is anticipated at the event time of another, provided that the two events are such that a purpose–outcome relationship might be expected in the 'real' world. The fact that the implication does derive from real-world considerations, and not from the use of the *to* form, can be shown by comparing the above example with

He arrived in London to find it a frightening place

The difference is a matter, not so much of grammar as of the unlikelihood of anyone arriving anywhere *in order to* find it frightening.

4 Under another heading we find other sequentially similar examples where there is no implication of purpose, for instance

He hurried to the house only to find that it was empty (ibid.: 151)

The point about this example is not that *only* causes it, in Thomson and Martinet's words, 'to express a disappointing sequel'; with or without *only* the meaning is that the finding was prospective at the time of the hurrying; but the nature of the two events makes a reference to purpose highly unlikely.

5 Used after *the first*, *the second*, etc. the *to* form produces examples like

He is the first to come and the last to leave

The general principles we have proposed enable us to give the following explanation of such an example: *is* selects an undifferentiated condition, i.e. his condition (or nature?) is such that he will always arrive first and leave last. This paraphrase brings out the fact that a general propensity to do something is regularly expressed in prospective and potential terms. Potentiality rather than actuality is perhaps easier to see in

The best play to perform is . . .

where there is no necessary implication that it will ever be performed at all.

The explanation we have offered for the last two examples may seem rather demanding and not of the kind that all language learners should be expected to grapple with. If the aim is to make as apparent as possible the way the language works, it may be better to focus upon material which enables us to do this without the distraction of difficult examples.

The point of this examination of the Thomson and Martinet treatment, incomplete as it is, is to show that many of the uses of the *to* form that they distribute under various headings, and to which they assign different kinds of note, can be brought together as illustrations of the generalizations we have made, namely that (except where suspension is involved):

a. The *to* form refers to its event in anticipation, that is prospectively with respect to the event time of the preceding verb;
b. The subject of a *to* form may be any preceding noun;
c. Any other meanings that may seem to attach to it can be said to arise from the context in which it is used.

Most examples can be related to this general statement with very little difficulty. Those few that need further explanation can be dealt with later if necessary, as can the modifications that need to be made to cover cases involving suspension. Furthermore, the kind of explanation that is thus provided for the *to* form can easily be expanded to account for the *-ing* and pp forms.

A similar goal of increased generality can be achieved by making use of the observations we have made about open selectors and zero realization in Chapters 12 and 13. The traditional way of dealing with the kinds of chain we examined in these chapters is usually to refer to a rather complicated list of clause types such as in nominal, adjectival, and adverbial, the last being divided into subtypes, such as adverbial clauses of purpose, results, or concession. Apart from the fact that the conceptual framework within which these types are identified is difficult for some learners to master, such presentation can be seen as an unnecessary fragmentation of the field. It amounts to the projection of distinctions upon phenomena to which a single set of principles can be applied. If learners know about what we have called 'open selection' and 'communicative deficiency' and know that utterances are not free-standing, as the presentation of examples seems to suggest, but steps forward in some communicative event, they are well on the way towards knowing how all the clause types work. Furthermore, they will be able to appreciate the mechanisms concerned are very similar to those that produce many other stretches of language that the grammar book does not call clauses.

Learning to use a language or learning about it?

The usefulness of proposals like those we have made in the last section depends upon a decision having first been made that the explicit teaching of grammar is desirable. Teachers of English are by no means agreed that this is so. A division of opinion has existed for some time both among those who are responsible for teaching English to native speakers and those who work with non-native speakers of English. The issues over which both groups have been in dispute can be described in similar terms. One side of the argument goes something like this: native speakers, who already 'know' the grammar of their language, will improve their performance by copious practice in using it rather than by learning about it; non-native learners are better employed in practising the real-world art of 'communication', than in learning about an abstract system. The other side stresses the prior importance of a mastery of the mechanics.

The idea that learning to communicate in a language and learning to manipulate its resources are in some way in opposition has seemed an odd one to many people. The view encouraged by the general drift of this book is that the apparent opposition arises from the nature of the grammars that have been available for teaching purposes. Sentence grammars, deriving as they do from an act of abstraction away from potential use, pose questions about the organization of language that seem to have little to do with those engaging the attention of people who are involved in communicating with others. It seems likely that the use of a grammar which takes account of the fact that language is characteristically used to communicate—that it is *purposeful* in the sense that it facilitates the conduct of all kinds of interactive business—might come closer to satisfying the requirement of both sides. We might say, for instance, that the apparent opposition between grammar and translation methodology and communicative methodology, arises only because grammar has so often been thought of as an activity one pursues without reference to the use to which language is put.

Appendix

The intonation system of English

The term 'intonation' is often applied generally to variation in the pitch of the speaker's voice but not all variation in pitch has the same kind of significance. The term as it is used here means those variations which can be shown to affect the communicative value of the utterance on an either/or basis. In fact, pitch is only one of a number of variables that affect our perception of one or other of a small set of intonational oppositions. Nevertheless, it is possible to regard the phonetic fact of pitch change as signalling the choice, by the speaker, of one such option.

There are a number of competing ways of trying to describe intonation: of trying, that is, to represent it in terms which will enable us to talk about it systematically. As a phenomenon, intonation is notoriously slippery. It is worth noting, incidentally, that our implicit and unselfconscious grasp of its workings seems to enable us both to use it effectively as speakers and interpret it without great difficulty as hearers: describing intonation is really a matter of dredging up to the surface for examination something of which we already have operational control. The particular descriptive framework outlined here, and referred to throughout this book, is one which starts from the same kinds of assumption about spoken communication as does the description of grammar.

Central to those assumptions is the belief that the communicative value of intonation is related to the *purpose* that a particular piece of language is serving in some ongoing, interactive event. Thus, for instance, primary consideration is given to whether speakers perceive a need to tell or to ask, and to what, precisely, they think they should tell or ask. This means that the present state of the relationship between speaker and hearer is kept constantly in mind. Existential considerations determine what is done.

The descriptive apparatus

The essential descriptive categories can be described as follows:

1 Used language is divided into 'tone units'.
2 The tone units of used speech normally have either one or two 'prominent syllables'.
3 The last prominent syllable in each tone unit is the 'tonic syllable', the place at which one of five distinctive pitch movements begins.
4 At all prominent syllables, there is a possibility of choice in a three-term system of pitch level.

Prominence

When, as speaker, you assign a prominent syllable to a word, you indicate that this word represents an existential sense selection. Whether you do so or not depends upon what you take the existing state of understanding to be. In order to made decisions about prominence distribution, speakers must make an assessment of what that understanding is. In this sample transcription, tone unit boundaries are marked with //, and prominent syllables are in upper case characters:

> // i was TALKing to a FRIEND // the other DAY // and she had this most aMAZing story of // FINDing a little old LAdy // in her CAR // in the CAR park // she CAME back from SHOPping and // AS she walked across the CAR park // this old LAdy // was sitting in the CAR //

Many of the words which are made non-selective here would be fairly predictable in any communicative context: *the* in *the other day* and *in* in *in the car* could hardly be replaced by anything else. There are some words that could be replaced by others but the change would not alter the communicative value: if *with* is an alternative to *to* in *talking to a friend* in some dialects, or *the* for *her* in *in her car*, the two words can be regarded as existential synonyms in each case. The second N in *car park* is conventionally made non-prominent, for on nearly every occasion it is used, the specification of *car* would be unlikely to leave open the likelihood of anything other than *park* following. *Little old* . . . are conventionalized epithets for characters in stories and have little reference to size or age: in a certain kind of nursery story all characters are little old men or little old women, and this story clearly draws upon the convention. It is not likely that the friend would be doing other than *walking* to the car, or that the stranger would be doing other than *sitting* in it. One instance of

non-prominence which obviously arises from the special circumstances of the narrative is *story*: the already-established interest is
understood to be in the telling of stories: in this situation, it could
scarcely be an *amazing* anything else (though, of course, the teller
could equally well have used an existential synonym like 'tale' or 'yarn'.

The relationship between prominence and the word stress that is
usually associated with the citation form of items needs to be clarified. In general, if discourse conditions require prominence to be
assigned to a word, it will be located in a syllable that is said to be
stressed, but if a word is not represented as selective, the stressed
syllable it may have will not be prominent: 'walking, 'sitting and
'story all have word stress, but discourse conditions result in one of
them having prominence in this extract.

Tone choice: proclaiming/referring

In describing a tone we attend only to the movement that occurs
after the prominence peak (often there is a step up or a step down to
this point, but that is ignored). After this, the characteristic pattern
is distributed over the rest of the tone unit. Four of the five tones can
be put in two categories on the basis of whether the last part of the
pitch movement is falling or rising. The fall and the rise-fall (both of
them proclaiming tones) and the rise and the fall-rise (both referring
tones) relate the content of the tone unit to the separative and shared
aspects of the speaker–hearer relationship respectively. P or R,
placed at the beginning of the tone unit, refers therefore, for all
practical purposes, to the phonetic treatment from the last
prominent syllable onwards. Its positioning immediately after the
boundary symbol serves as a reminder, however, that as a factor
affecting communicative value, the consequence of the choice is a
modification of the communicative value of the whole of the tone
unit. In transcripts, tonic syllables are shown as follows:

> // R at ONE point // P she took her HAND out from // R i DONt
> know where she HAD it // R in GLOVES or // R and WHEN she
> saw her HAND // P she got REALLy // P FRIGHTened // ... R and
> she was VEry very NERvous // P and thought well WHAT am i
> going to do NOW //

If we look closely at the tone units having R tones, we see that they
all represent a part of the message that the speaker regards as being

already common ground. *At one point*, like *the other day* which occurred earlier, says no more about the timing of events than does 'once upon a time...' in a nursery story, and the tone choice amounts to a recognition that it will be heard as an expected ritualistic expression. It could be taken for granted that the friend didn't know exactly why her passenger's hands had not been obvious earlier: hearers could be expected to understand this without being told. Neither would they need to be told that she was *very very nervous* after the revelation.

Tone choice: dominance

It is actually enough, for the purposes of this book, to recognize the proclaiming/referring distinction in the tone system. Further light is cast upon the functioning of interactive speech, however, if we take into account the alternative means that are available for choosing either of these. If something is proclaimed with a rise-fall (instead of a fall) or referred to with a rise (instead of a fall-rise) an additional implication of 'dominance' attaches to the tone unit.

Dominance can best be explained by observing its use in non-symmetrical speech events, of which the telling of a story is an example. In such an event, there is tacit agreement that, for the time being, control of the discourse is vested in one participant, in this case the storyteller. The most obvious effect of this is that the storyteller, once established in the dominant role, can expect to be allowed to proceed uninterrupted to the end of the narrative. Although the occupants of a controlling role do not necessarily underline their status by using the tone that has dominance implications, it is often expedient or otherwise useful to do so. When we want to take note of this kind of detail in a transcript, we use lower case symbols and the symbol + serves to distinguish the dominant option. A sample which makes much use of r+ tones is:

> // r+ so she aGREED to take her ROUND // r+ she COULDn't leave her STANding in this // r+ FREEZing CAR park // r+ and she GOT back in the CAR // r+ and she STARted to drive OFF // r and was a BIT conCERNED // p that this woman DIDn't SAY anything //

The use of a referring tone in the first five tone units of this extract is not difficult to explain. The teller could rely upon almost any hearer's understanding of how one would respond to the old lady's plea; the hearer would also understand that such response would involve getting in the car and driving off. The reason for the exercise of dominance is, as often, rather more a matter for speculation. Notice, though, that for six tone units in all, nothing is said which advances the story in the sense of telling anything that couldn't be surmised. Under these circumstances, there could be said to be a risk of losing the hearers' interest, and turning on the authority, so to speak, might be a way of holding it.

Level tone

When choosing from among the four tones described above, speakers have in mind the impact of what they say upon particular hearers at particular times in particular verbal communicative events. The value of the tones arises from what we have called the 'interactive' nature of the speech. When this kind of meshing with a second party is not desired, or not possible, a fifth tone, 'level tone', is used.

The use of level tone is common in ritualized or precoded speech. This is not used language in the sense in which we have used the term, because its presentation is not sensitive, in a moment by moment way, to the details of a hearer's perspective. It is therefore strictly outside the scope of this book. In the kind of data with which we are concerned, level tones do occur, however, and most notably at those frequent points where the storyteller needs time to plan the next part of the discourse. Reference to our real-time model enables us to think of these as occasions when the way ahead is not clear, resulting, perhaps, in hesitation and also a temporary disengagement from the kind of person-to-person relationship that the discourse in general maintains. Such disengagement makes it possible for attention to be switched to the non-interactive business of assembling the linguistic resources that the next step will need. The symbol for level tone is 0. A short sample will illustrate its use, and also show how it often alternates with a special use of p tone:

// 0 AND // 0 the WOman // 0 PUT her HAND // 0 BACK // 0 wherEVer it WAS // p VEry very QUICKLy //

We call this kind of disengaged performance 'oblique' discourse, to distinguish it from the 'direct' discourse that is hearer-sensitive. The uses of the five tones can therefore be summarized as follows:

		referring	proclaiming
Direct discourse	Dominant	r+	p+
	Non-dominant	r	p
Oblique discourse		0 or p	

Key and termination

The intonation features that are manifested as changes in pitch level (as opposed to pitch movement) at prominent syllables are not significant for our present description as far as it has gone. Further development of the same kind of analysis would require that we take note of the way they affect communicative value as follows:

The pitch level of the first prominent syllable in the tone unit establishes the key as high, mid, or low. With high key, the matter of the tone unit is presented as being contrary to the expectations of the hearer. With low key, the tone unit presumes that its content will be heard as following naturally upon what has gone before, as being entirely in line with what the hearer would expect. In the case of both high and low key, there is, therefore, an assumption upon the part of the speaker about what the particular hearer's expectations are on this particular occasion. Mid key differs in that the tone unit concerned attributes no special expectations to the hearer, merely adding its content to what has gone before.

Observations of key choice are included in the transcriptions when necessary by placing the first prominent syllable of the tone unit above, below, or on the mid line:

// r and my friend just PUT her FOOT down // p and ^{SPED} OFF // p as FAST as she COULD //

The expectation—of the stranger, if not of the alert listener!—was that she would reverse into the driveway; but she didn't, she *sped off*.

// 0 and SHORTly after THAT // p they came to a ROUNDabout // p an $_{ISland}$ //

245

Here, the last tone unit simply reiterates what the previous one has said, and the existential equivalence of the two expressions, which could safely be assumed to be understood by everyone, is acknowledged by the use of low key.

The level of the last prominent syllable in the tone unit determines the termination of the tone unit as high, mid, or low.

Essentially, the function of termination is to signal the speaker's expectations with regard to the key of any response the hearer might make:

	HIGH anticipates HIGH KEY response (i.e. adjudication)
TERMINATION	MID anticipates MID KEY response (i.e. concurrence)
	LOW sets up no particular expectations

Low termination has the special function of closing a pitch sequence. The pitch sequence is a stretch of speech consisting of one or more tone units and ending with low termination. It represents some discrete part of the discourse. Examples in the data are:

// p a FRIEND // p told me this aMAZing STORy // p the OTher DAY //

This is one of those increments that gives preliminary notice of the status of the subsequent discourse (= 'I am about to tell you a story'), and, as often happens with such preliminary material, it is separated off from what comes after by a pitch sequence boundary.

At first sight, this further example looks similar:

// r+ she WENT into the poLICE station // p and she TOLD them her STORy //

In fact, this is not a forewarning of a story to come: we have already heard it. The break in continuity that this pitch sequence boundary underlines is one between the account of what the friend did and how the police reacted to it:

// r+ they were a BIT surPRISED //...

Glossary

chain
Chains result from a single run through the sequencing rules, including any suspensions (q.v.) or extensions (q.v.) there may be. They often amount to a single increment (q.v.), that is to say, they may end once the Target State visualized at the beginning of the chain has been reached. It is possible, however, for further elements (q.v.) provided for by the chaining rules to be produced in pursuance of (a) further Target State(s).

characterizing (see *identifying*)

commitment
The act of embarking upon an increment (q.v.) commits the co-operative speaker to continuing through the sequencing rules for at least as long as it takes to achieve Target State. The notion of commitment is useful in understanding how suspensions (q.v.) work without the finite-state properties of the grammar being lost.

communicative need
All increments (q.v.) of used language (q.v.) are addressed to a specific need for something to be told or asked. It is awareness of the need that determines the Target State which is the end-point of the increment.

communicative sufficiency
In order to be a sufficient contribution to a discourse, each element (q.v.) in an increment (q.v.) must both be of a kind that satisfies the sequencing rules and also make whatever sense selection present discourse conditions require to be made. If it does not do the latter, it is communicatively deficient, and the deficiency must be made good before further progress is made.

condition
In this grammar, three kinds of finite verbal element are recognized on the basis of whether they specify an event, a condition, or a

probability. It should be noted that, as technical terms, each of these words covers a wider range of meanings than they normally would in common usage.

co-operation
The assumptions underlying conversational practice are that speakers will co-operate by seeking to satisfy a particular communicative need (q.v.) that the listener will assent to; that they will do so in terms that will be interpretable by the latter; and that hearers, for their part, will co-operate by seeking to understand, and if necessary respond to, or seek to have clarified, the speaker's intentions.

differentiated time reference
One of the two forms that finite verbal elements can take signifies that the reference point established by the element is some time earlier than the utterance time (q.v.): that is to say, the two times are different. It contrasts with the form that makes undifferentiated time reference, signifying that the reference point is the utterance time.

element
The syntactic chain is regarded, for analytical purposes, as comprising a small stretch of language called an element. The question of how much speech counts as an element is a matter of convenience. This book begins by treating comparatively large stretches as single elements, but moves towards the ultimate goal of seeing each word (or word-like object) as a separate element. The distinctions made among elements in the earlier chapters (as nominal, verbal, adverbial, and adjectival) follow general linguistic practices, but have no definitive status: they are intended to do no more that provide a working basis upon which to proceed.

event time
An event is anything that happens in time, and the term 'event time', loosely interpreted, can be applied to the referents of most verbal elements. If the element is finite, its form signifies that the event occurs at the utterance time (undifferentiated) or earlier than the utterance time. If it is non-finite, its form assigns the event to a time simultaneous with the reference point of the finite element (the *-ing* form), after it (the *to* form) or earlier than it (the pp form).

exchange
The achievement of a communicative purpose may involve the vocal participation of either one or two participants. Achievement may then be acknowledged by whoever is the recipient of information. The exchange comprises either the one or the two necessary contributions, together with any acknowledgment there may be. Exchange types dealt with in this book serve either telling or asking purposes.

existential value
It is common practice to attach more or less permanent meanings to most words and longer expressions, and often to regard those meanings as deriving from a set of relationships which exist permanently in the semantic system of which the word or other expression is part. The view that underlies this book is different: the relationship among items is a matter of the (often transitory) circumstances of the discourse; participants use and understand them as having a 'this not something else' value which is valid for the peculiar here-and-now circumstances of the communication. The set of choices that can be assumed to be available at any point comprises the existential paradigm. Choice presupposes that there is more than one probability and the item concerned is said to be selective.

exploitation
The general expectation among listeners is that speakers will relate what they say to what the 'real' world of the conversation is like. However, the mechanisms of conversation leave a good deal of room for invention on the part of speakers. The latter are free to exploit those mechanisms, and behave as if the reality of the situation were other than it is, but only within such limits as the listener can be expected to acquiesce in.

extension
This grammar makes a distinction between chains (q.v.) which result from a run through the simple chaining rules and those which involve the use of further elements after one particular route through those rules has been completed. Types of extension that are recognized are reduplication (q.v.), finite second predication, and non-finite second predication.

finite second predicator

Chains are found in which a second (or subsequent) N initiates a subchain (q.v.): that is to say, it is followed by a finite verbal element just as if it were a chain-initial N. This facility is used most frequently when the N concerned is the second of a reduplicating pair.

finite state grammar

This is a rule system in which each successive element (q.v.) is seen as precipitating a new State. Conditions holding in that State then determine what element(s) can be produced thereafter. The linear nature of such grammars distinguishes them from the hierarchical, structure-within-structure framework which is generally regarded as being essential for a sentence grammar.

identifying

The general purpose of nominal elements is to specify the 'things' that the increment (q.v.) is concerned with. This can be done in either of two ways. One may identify the thing(s) — that is to say, specify which thing — or one may characterize it — that is to say, specify what kind of thing. The use of a definite article before the element serves as advance warning that present concern is with *which*, while the indefinite article indicates a concern with *what kind of*.

increment

The sequence of elements (q.v.) required to reach the Target State in a telling exchange is a 'telling increment'. In the case of an asking exchange, the Target State is not reached until the second participant has responded appropriately: 'asking increments' are therefore the product of the co-operative behaviour by both parties. In either case, the number and nature of elements required depends upon present communicative need (q.v.), but no increment is complete unless some part of it is proclaimed.

indeterminacy

In very many cases, it would be possible for a chain (q.v.) to be interpreted in more than one way if it were considered out of context. This indeterminacy is a far more pervasive feature of language than is the phenomenon of 'ambiguity' as it is said to occur in unused sentences. Essentially, nearly all chains are capable, if considered simply as sequences of elements (q.v.), to have a number of potential interpretations. Awareness of the communicative context, and the kind of convergence that results from co-operation (q.v.), enables participants to focus exclusively upon the intended interpretation. Indeterminacy usually constitutes no barrier to successful communication and has the positive value that it makes possible an economical use of linguistic resources. Indeterminacy very rarely results in ambiguity, a condition which will exist only if the speaker's communicative intention is in doubt.

interaction
The used language (q.v.) with which this book is concerned is always produced in pursuit of a purpose in which a second party has an interest. Even when the recipient does not contribute audibly, the assumed state of understanding presently existing between participants influences everything the speaker does. This understanding includes shared apprehension of present communicative need (q.v.).

non-finite verbal element
The non-finite forms of verbal elements are: *-ing* form, *to-* form, past participle form, and plain infinitive. As parts of a chain (q.v.) they have two special features: they have no separately realized subject N; and their event time (q.v.) is given by relating it to the time reference point of another verb.

open selector
A number of elements (q.v.) which would be classified in various ways by a sentence grammar (e.g. *who, when, because*) in fact serve a similar purpose: they indicate that the making of a particular selection is pertinent to the achievement of Target State. They do not, in themselves, make that selection, however, so it remains for one or other of the participants to make it subsequently.

optional element
Some open selectors (q.v.) (particularly *who* and *that*) are sometimes introduced into a chain (q.v.), although they are strictly unnecessary for satisfying either the sequencing rules or communicative need (q.v.).

251

When an element is optional in this way, the chain will contribute to conversational business in exactly the same way without it.

pertinence
A selection is pertinent if co-operating participants see the making of it as material to the usefulness of the increment (q.v.).

post-nominal and post-verbal function
Adverbial elements and various subchains (q.v.) are indeterminate with respect to the element (q.v.) they are notionally attached to. They have post-nominal function if they are to be interpreted as referring to an earlier nominal element. They have post-verbal function if they are to be interpreted as referring to an earlier verbal element. Whenever there are both an earlier N and an earlier V, the element or subchain concerned is potentially indeterminate as to its reference.

probability (see *condition*)

proclaiming tone (see *tone*)

projection
It is the speaker's responsibility to satisfy the listener's communicative needs (q.v.). It is seldom possible, however, to be certain of what they are, and sometimes only a very approximate assessment can be made. We have to think of speakers as generally making the best assumption they can manage concerning the need. This is to say they match their performance to a projected situation in the hope that it closely approximates to the 'real' one. In cases of exploitation (q.v.), the projected situation may have no foundation in reality at all.

prominence
Some syllables are made phonologically prominent by a combination of phonetic means including special pitch treatment, extra intensity, and greater length. Prominent syllables include those which have the additional pitch movement which distinguishes them also as tonic syllables. The function of prominent syllables is to indicate that the containing word represents an existential selection. (See also Appendix, page 243.)

purpose, primary and secondary
This book regards speech as purpose-driven rather than as sentence-oriented. It considers only the primary purpose of telling and asking (though other primary purposes might exist). 'Primary' here signifies that the distinction between the two can be made on the basis of the linguistic organization of the exchange (essentially whether a contribution from one or both participants is necessary for achievement of the purpose). A large number of 'secondary' purposes are pursued by telling or by asking, but there is nothing grammatically distinctive that we can rely upon to know, for instance, whether something is told in order to warn or told in order to amuse. Note that users will often be more disposed to refer to a secondary purpose as their reason for speaking than to a primary purpose.

reduplication
Extensions (q.v.) and suspensions (q.v.) can be initiated after nominal elements and adverbial elements by producing another element (q.v.) of the same kind.

referring tone (see *tone*)

restrictive and unrestrictive reference
Subjects that are either identified or characterized by the nominal element that represents them are restrictive in their reference: they separate out a particular thing or a particular class of things for mention. In the case of some non-finite verbal elements (q.v.), the unrealized subject N refers neither to an identified thing nor to a characterized one but to an unrestricted class of things: the reference is to anyone or anything it might conceivably apply to.

selection (see *existential value, prominence*)

State
States are described in relation to increments (q.v.). The Initial State immediately precedes the beginning of an increment. Here, speakers are informed by all the relevant background that they assume they share with the listener, including apprehension of present communicative needs (q.v.). Satisfaction of those needs is perceived

as the Target State. Each successive element (q.v.) amounts to a step towards Target State; and each results in a new Intermediate State, which we can think of as a reappearance of the Initial State but progressively modified by successive elements as they occur.

subchain
Elements which function as either extensions (q.v.) or suspensions (q.v.) frequently initiate a new run through (some part of) the sequencing rules, the result being a subchain.

subject
The nominal element that always precedes a verbal element in the NV part of a chain (q.v.) is its subject. It is a feature of non-finite verbal elements, whether functioning as extensions (q.v.) or as suspensions (q.v.), that they have no separate realization of their subjects.

suspension
The simple chain sequencing rules prescribe an ordering of elements (q.v.). When any element occurs which is not provided for by those rules it has the effect of suspending production of an element that the rules permit. Suspension continues until the completion of whatever subchain (q.v.) the 'unexpected' element initiates.

tone
The last prominent syllable of each tone unit (the tonic syllable) is the location of the beginning of a significant pitch movement, or tone. For the purposes of this book, tones can be thought of as of two types: end-falling, or proclaiming tones (the fall and the rise-fall), and end-rising or referring tones (the rise and the fall-rise). In telling increments, it is the part that is proclaimed that results in the intended exchange of information: it changes the world of the hearer. The content of tone units which have referring tones, on the other hand, is introduced as part of the background understanding that participants already share, so that their production results in no exchange of information. (See also Appendix, page 244.)

undifferentiated time reference (see *differentiated time reference*)

unrestrictive reference (see *restrictive and unrestrictive reference*)

used language
This term is used for language which is produced in the course of some kind of human interaction. Its distinguishing characteristic is that it results from a preoccupation with satisfying some kind of communicative need (q.v.). In this respect it differs from sample sentences which invite attention primarily as linguistic objects.

utterance time
This term refers to the reference point to which all the time references of verbal elements are related.

world knowledge
Some grammarians make a clear distinction between a specialized knowledge of the rules of grammar on the one hand, and the knowledge that we accumulate as a consequence of our real-world experiences, on the other. The proposed distinction has been taken as a reason for claiming that human minds are uniquely equipped to take on knowledge of the former kind. The strong tendency of this book is to suggest that much less knowledge of the language need be attributed to language users than sentence grammarians often suppose to be the case.

zero realization
The working of the sequencing rules generally requires that every element (q.v.) in the chain (q.v.) will be realized, even when there is no question of its being selective. Under certain circumstances, however, elements which would amount to a second reference in the chain are omitted. The omission rule, when it applies, is observed with the same regularity as is that which, on other occasions, makes realization necessary.

Bibliography

Abercrombie, D. 1964. *Problems and Principles in Language Study*. London: Longman.

Austin, J. L. 1962. *How To Do Things With Words*. Oxford: Oxford University Press.

Bloomfield, L. 1933. *Language*. New York: Holt, Reinhart, and Winston.

Brazil, D. C. 1985. *The Communicative Value of Intonation*. (Discourse Analysis Monographs No. 8). Birmingham: English Language Research, University of Birmingham.

Brazil, D. C., R. M. Coulthard, and C. M. Johns. 1980. *Discourse Intonation and Language Teaching*. London: Longman.

Chomsky, N. 1957. *Syntactic Structures*. The Hague: Mouton.

Chomsky, N. 1962. 'Explanatory models in linguistics' in E. Nagel, P. Suppes, and A. Tarski (eds.).

Chomsky, N. 1965. *Aspects of the Theory of Syntax*. Cambridge, Mass.: MIT Press.

Chomsky, N. 1968. *Language and Mind*. New York: Harcourt, Brace and World.

Clifton, C., Jr. and F. Ferreira. 1989. 'Ambiguity in context'. *Language and Cognitive Processes* 4: 71–103.

Cole, P. and J. Morgan (eds.) 1975. *Syntax and Semantics Volume 3: Speech Acts*. New York: Academic Press.

Coulthard, R. M. 1985. (2nd edition) *An Introduction to Discourse Analysis*. London: Longman.

Coulthard, R. M. (ed.). 1987. *Discussing Discourse*. (Discourse Analysis Monographs No. 14). Birmingham: English Language Research, University of Birmingham.

Enkvist, N. E. 1982. Introduction to *Impromptu Speech: A Symposium*. Åbo: Åbo Akademi, Finland.

Francis, G. and S. Hunston. 1987. 'Analysing everyday conversation' in R. M. Coulthard (ed.).

Frazier, L. 1979. 'On Comprehending Sentences: Syntactic Parsing Strategies'. Unpublished PhD thesis, University of Connecticut.

Grice, H. P. 1975. 'Logic and conversation' in P. Cole and J. Morgan (eds.).

Halliday, M. A. K. 1961. 'Categories of the theory of grammar: *Word* 17/3: 241–92.

Halliday, M. A. K. 1964. 'Syntax and the consumer' in C. E. M. Stuart (ed.).

Halliday, M. A. K. 1973. *Explorations in the Functions of Language*. London: Edward Arnold.

Halliday, M. A. K. 1975. *Learning How to Mean: Explorations in the Development of Language*. London: Edward Arnold.

Halliday, M. A. K. 1985. *An Introduction to Functional Grammar*. London: Edward Arnold.

Halliday, M. A. K. 1989. *Spoken and Written Language*. Oxford: Oxford University Press.

Ingram, D. 1989. *First Language Acquisition: Methods, Descriptions and Explanation*. Cambridge: Cambridge University Press.

Labov, W. 1970. 'The study of language in its social context'. *Studium Generale* 23: 20–87.

Labov, W. 1972. 'Rules for ritual insults' in D. Sudnow (ed.).

Levinson, S. 1983. *Pragmatics*. Cambridge: Cambridge University Press.

Lyons, J. 1968. *An Introduction to Theoretical Linguistics*. Cambridge: Cambridge University Press.

Lyons, J. 1977. *Semantics*. Cambridge: Cambridge University Press.

Lyons, J. and R. J. Wales (eds.) 1966. *Psycholinguistics Papers*. Edinburgh: Edinburgh University Press.

McCarthy, M. J. 1987. 'Interactive lexis' in R. M. Coulthard (ed.).

Malinowski, B. 1923. 'The problem of meaning in primitive languages' in C. K. Ogden and A. Richards (eds.).

Nagel, E., P. Suppes, and A. Tarski (eds.) 1962. *Proceedings of the International Congress of Logic, Methodology and Philosophy of Science*. 1960. Stanford: Stanford University Press.

Ogden, C. K. and Richards, I. A. (eds.) 1923. *The Meaning of Meaning*. London: Kegan Paul.

Robins, R. H. 1964. *General Linguistics: An Introductory Survey*. London: Longman.

Sacks, H. 1967–71. Unpublished lecture notes, University of California.

Sacks, H., E. A. Schegloff, and G. Jefferson. 1974. 'A simplest systematics for the organisation of turn-taking in conversation'. *Language* 50/4: 696–735.

Saussure, F. de. 1916. *Cours de linguistique générale*. Paris: Payot. Translated by Wode-Baskin as *Course in General Linguistics*. (1959). New York: Philosophical Library.

Schegloff, E. A. 1972. 'Notes on a conversational practice: formulating place' in D. Sudnow (ed.).

Schegloff, E. A. and H. Sacks. 1973. 'Opening up closings'. *Semiotica* 7/4: 289–327.

Searle, J. R. 1969. *Speech Acts*. Cambridge: Cambridge University Press.

Sinclair, J., G. Fox. et al. 1990. Collins Cobuild English Grammar. London: HarperCollins.

Sinclair, J. M. and D. C. Brazil. 1982. *Teacher Talk*. Oxford: Oxford University Press.

Sinclair, J. M. and R. M. Coulthard. 1975. *Towards an Analysis of Discourse*. Oxford: Oxford University Press.

Stuart, C. E. M. (ed.) 1964. *Proceedings of the 15th Annual Round Table Meeting.* Georgetown: Georgetown University Press.

Stubbs, M. 1983. *Discourse Analysis.* Oxford: Blackwell.

Sudnow, D. (ed.) 1972. *Studies in Social Interaction.* New York: Free Press.

Thomson, A. J. and **A. V. Martinet.** 1969. (2nd edition). *A Practical English Grammar.* Oxford: Oxford University Press.

Thorne J. P. 1966. 'On hearing sentences' in Lyons and Wales (eds.).

Index

Entries relate to the Introduction, Chapters 1 to 20, the Appendix, and the glossary. References to the glossary are indicated by 'g'.

Abercrombie, D 36
adjacency pair 6
adjectival elements 49–51, 55–6, 161–4
adverbial elements 49, 51, 53–5
  constraint 205, 209
  event time 79
  reduplication 122–3
  suspension 63
  temporal precedence 188
ambiguity 71–4, 77
  modals 118
  reduced by shared
    understanding 127–8
  see also indeterminacy
analysis, hierarchical approach 6
  linear approach 6, see also discourse
    analysis
antonymous relationships 34–5, 94
articles 152, 164, 207–8
asking 13, 15, 22
  increment 39, 223
  interaction 29
  modals 116–18
  purposes 172, 199
  respondent 30–1
  see also exchanges
Austin, J. L. 36, 173–4

be (auxiliary) 107–12, 115
Bloomfield, L. 17

can 113–19
certainty see probability
chains of elements, complex 121
chains of elements in speech 47–56, 167,
  223, 248g
  see also subchains
characterization of nominal elements see
  pre-/post-specification
choice of probability see polarity, sense
  selection, time reference
Chomsky, N. 8–9, 19–21, 228–9
citation forms 95–6

Clifton, C., Jr. 231
commitment in discourse 52–3, 63, 64,
  170–1, 206, 247g
communication versus grammar
  conflict 13, 239
communicative deficiency 104–5
  finite second predication 128
  modals 116
  Practical English Grammar, A
    (Thomson and Martinet) 238
  probable constraints 208, 209
communicative need 31, 52
  constraints 209, 210
  conversational 55
  exploitation by speaker 82
  indeterminacy 203–4
  open selection 142
  principle (7) 224–5
  responses 202
  speaker's perception 222
  tonic syllable 90–1
communicative purpose 39, 93, 230–2
communicative sufficiency 23, 115
  achievement 153–5
  constraints 209, 210
  definition 247g
communicative value 34–5, 203
  intonation 240
  modals 118
  principle 224
  tone 194–5, 196
condition time 108–10
constituent grammar see grammar,
  constituent
constituents, immediate 17–20
constituents, relationship among 69–70,
  203
constituent structure 17, 37
constraint, categories of
  absolute 207–8
  built into rules 204–5
  particular items 205
  particular needs 205, 209–11

constraint, categories of – *cont.*
  see also on-line amendments
conversational needs 206
conversational purpose 26–29, 40
conversational setting of utterances 35
conversational use of modals 116–19
co-operative discourse 31–3, 224–5
  ambiguity avoided 76, 77
  asking exchanges 199
  definition 248g
  lack of 168–9
co-operative value 35
Coulthard, R. M. 5, 6, 7

discourse: what it is intended to count
    as 168–9, 174, 176–8, 181, 183
  see also illocutionary force, labelling
  discourse
  direct 244
  oblique 244
discourse analysis 5
  constituent-within-constituent model 6
  increment-by-increment 6, 7
  separate procedures for 16
  widening scope of 167
discourse, types of 168
do 119–20

element *see under types*: adverbial,
    adjectival, nominal, non-finite verbal,
    verbal
elements, relationship between 69–78,
    225, 248g
Enkvist, N. E. 38
equation in selection 143–4, 145
essential items of talk 171–2
event time 79–80, 83–5
  definition 248g
  -ing and pp forms 164
  possibility 117
event-timing function of verbal
    elements 79
  see also primary event time, selection
exchange between speaker and listener 6
  asking 190–202
  definition 249
  telling and asking 40–6
exclusion in selection 97–8, 99
existential antonyms 94, 98
existential paradigms 93, 97
  constraints 210
  modals 114, 117
  open selection 142
existential selection 93, 141, 241

existential synonyms 94, 177
  modals 114, 118–19
  responses 200
existential value 33–6
  constraints 209
  definition 249g
  intonation 240
  principle (7) 224
  selection 92–4, 145
exploitation by speakers 82–4, 117, 249g
extension 57–61, 121
  definition 250g
  principle 223
  suspensions 67
  V^1-initiated chains 77–8
  zero realization 134
  see also reduplication

Ferreira, F. 231
finding out 193–5
finite second predication 128–30, 133–4,
    138, 250g
  see also non-finite second predication
finite-state account 76–7, 101
finite-state grammar 20–1, 223, 250g
finite-state rule system 51, 196, 203
formalism 8, 19
Frazier, L. 231

grammar 8
  communication conflict 13, 239
  constituent 4, 6, 17–20, 70
  finite state 20–1, 223, 250g
  linear 4, 222–39
  product 10
  purpose-driven 4, 224, 239
  sentence 4, 7–10, 73, 75, 102
    acceptability 207
    constraint 206
    declarative function 192, 195–7
    discrete preliminary labelling 180
    interrogative function 192, 196–7
    open selectors 141, 147
Grice, H. P. 36

Halliday, M. A. K. 5
  grammar as tool 9–12
  intermediate units 19
  language acquisition 233–4
  product and process 37
  theme 187
have
  compared with *be* 108–9
  modals 115–16

have – *cont.*
  selectional possibilities 102–7, 115
hierarchical approach to analysis 6

illocutionary force in speech 173–4
incidental items of talk 171–2
increment
  asking 39
  functional 7, 17
  initiating 190, 191, 192–5
  organization of 99
  preliminary 168–9, 171, 175, 186
  see also labelling, preliminary
  purposeful 38–9, 172–3
  responding 190
  retrospective 173
  telling 39, 41–2, 47, 57, 190
    chains representing more than
     one 61, 126
    differences between 70–1, 73–4, 169
    open selectors 140–1
    principle (4) 223
    tonic syllable 90–2
incremental presentation of language 21,
  22, 26, 111, 116, 223
indeterminacy 22
  definition 251g
  expected 203
  modals 117
  open selectors 141–2
  pp form 109–10
  principle (8) 225
  questions 198–9
  reduplication 123–7
  see also ambiguity
information, transfer of *see* telling
-*ing* forms 57
  adjectives 164
  be 110–11
  event time 83
  feeling 67
  hoping 61
  leaving 59, 60
  looking 66
  meeting 68
  sitting 64–5, 67
  time reference 82
  waiting 60
  wondering 66
Initial State 22, 47–8, 50, 52, 196, 223
interaction (man/machine) 14
interaction (person to person) 16, 29–31
  Abercrombie, D. 36
  definition 251g

existential values 33, 93
  intonation 244
  selection 98
Intermediate State 22
  articles 152
  asking exchanges 190–1
  chains 47–50, 52
  extensions 59
  finite second prediction 128–9
  open selection 141
  principle (4) 223
  questions 196
  redefining 105
  second reference 131–2, 134
  suspensions 63, 77
  time reference 80, 115
intonation 23
  choice of 182–3
  dominance 243–4
  key 245–6
  level 244–5
  pre-specified nominal elements 164–6
  proclaiming 46, 49, 186, 193, 242
  prominence 91–2, 93–100, 241–2
    have 103, 104
  questioning 193–5
  referring 182–3, 194, 242, 243–4
  suspension 179
  system of English 240–6
  telling, requirement for 44–6, 187
  termination 246
  tone units 95–9, 241
  tonic syllable 90–2, 241
  values 33

knowledge, listener's 78, 93, 192, 225
  see also understanding, shared

labelling
  discrete 178, 180
  non-discrete 179–80
  preliminary 179–86, 197, 200, 201
  probable constraints 209
  retrospective 170–1, 188

Labov, W. 36
language acquisition 232–4
learning 234–39 *see also* teaching
Levinson, S. 36
linear approach to analysis 6
linear description of syntax 14 *see also*
  real time
linear time 87–8, 203
'Little Old Lady' narrative 24–6, 29, 33

'Little Old Lady' narrative – *cont.*
  analysis 214–18
  comments on analysis 214–20
local value of utterance 111, 118
Lyons, J. 7–8, 17–18, 36

machine/man interaction 14
making sure in speech 193–5
Malinowski, B. 36
may 113–19
meaning of words 33–4
mismatches in verbal interaction 32, 71–2
modalization 115–16
modals and plain infinitive 113–20
modals, use of 116–19, 208
moment of utterance *see* utterance time
monologue 2, 6, 29, 49

negation time 119–20
nominal elements 23, 49–56, 78
  characterization *see* pre-/post-
    specification
  event time 79
  finite second predication 129
  function in chains 124
  reduplicative N as extension 128
  reduplicative N as suspension 128
non-finite second predications 137, 207
non-finite verbal elements (V') 22,
    57–68
  base form 114–15
  definition 251g
  following more than one
    auxiliary 111–12
  following *be* 109–11
  following *have* 105–7
  indeterminacy 74–6
  suspensions 77–8
  time reference 82–6
  zero realization 131–2, 207
  see also -*ing* forms, *to* forms,
    pp forms
nouns 152–3, 164
now-coding 26, 187

omission of expected element 132–3
on-line amendments 211–13
open selectors 23
  absolute constraint 207
  asking 198
  definition 252g
  functional indeterminacy 141–2
  Practical English Grammar, A 238
  telling increments 140–1

see also W open selector
oppositions 34–5, 94
parsing 18
past participle forms *see* pp forms
pertinence of selection 139–40, 145, 146,
    191
  absolute constraint 207
  definition 252g
  principle (3) 223
phatic function 29, 36, 170
polarity 103–4
  modals 113, 117, 119
  questions 197–9
  see also question types
possibility 116, 117 *see also* probability
post-nominal functions 70–1, 73–4,
    88–9, 252g
post-specification
    (characterizing/identifying) 153–4,
    155–9, 210, 218
post-verbal functions 70–1, 73–4, 88–9,
    252g
pp forms (past participle)
  adjectives 164
  + *be* 109–10
  event time 86–7
  + *have* 105–6
  meant 68
  perfective view 109
  time reference 84
  worried 61
Practical English Grammar, A (Thomson
    and Martinet)
    235–8
pragmatics 36
predication *see* finite second predication,
    selection by predication
preposition/nominal element 123
pre-specification
    (characterizing/identifying) 154,
    159–64, 210
primary event time 103
principles of grammar of speech 222–5
probability 113–14, 115, 116–17, 180,
    207, 252g
  see also polarity, selection, sense, time
    reference
process 10–11, 13, 37–8, 204
product 10–11, 13, 38, 204
prominence *see* intonational prominence
psycholinguistics 230–2
psychological reality 13, 229
purpose, communicative 39, 93, 230–2
purpose, pre-empting 180–2, 201

purpose-driven grammar 4, 21, 26–8
Austin, J. L. 36
communicative need 31, 35
explicit and implicit 175–6, 187
process and product 37
telling 40

quantifiers 164
question types 195–7 *see also* asking

real-time mechanisms 17, 21, 49, 52, 79, 154, 204
see also finite-state account
receipt (acknowledgement of information) 40–1, 170, 198, 201
reduplication 121–30, 133, 136, 143, 149, 158–9
adjectival elements 161
definition 253g
nominal elements 186
probable constraints 208
reference time *see* time reference
responses 197–200
extended 200–2
Robins, R. H. 19
rule system *see* sequencing of rules

Sacks, H. E. A. 6
de Saussure, F. 227
Searle, J. R. 36, 173–4
secondary purposes of increments 172–3, 175
second reference in chains 131–2, 135
selection
and communication 90–100, 105, 139
by equation 143–4, 145
by predication 145–6
primary event time 103, 105
reduplication 126
sense 103, 115, 118, 139–40
selective potential of language 23
selectors, open *see* open selectors
semantics 36
sentence defined by grammarians 5, 22, 225
sentence grammar 6, 7–10, 16
sentence, notion of the 2–3, 16, 20–1, 225–8, 231–2
sequences of elements 66, 101, 204
sequences of words 101
sequencing rules
constraints 204–5
extensions 58–9
implications 51–5

open selection 142, 147–8
pre-nominal specification 159–60
reduplication 125
relationships 69–70
suspensions 63, 65–6, 78
time reference 80
zero realization 136
shall 113–19
should 116–17
Sinclair, J. M. 5, 6, 163, 177
socializing as purpose of speech 28–9, 170
speaker's choice 153–4, 187
speech events 16
speech in time 11–12
spoken data, analysis of 12
State 22, 37–8, 47–8, 52–4, 254g
see also Initial, Intermediate, *and* Target States
Stubbs, M. 5–6
subchains 59–60
absolute constraints 207
definition 254g
probable constraints 208
suspensions 64, 65, 86
zero realization 131, 136, 137
subject of verbal element 75–6, 124, 254g
see also nominal element
sub-sentential level of organization 7, 12, 37
sufficiency *see* communicative sufficiency
supra-sentential level of organization 7, 12
suspension 57, 61–8, 121–2, 134, 223–4, 254g
suspension device 183–7, 203
suspension, non-finite verbal elements 64–6, 77–8
suspensions, subchains as 146–7
suspensive elements
after chain-initial N 207
before chain-initial N 66–7, 122, 207
working of 181–2
Syntactic Structures (Chomsky) 20
syntactic requirement for telling 42–4, 46, 65, 176, 187, 211

talk
essential items 171–2
incidental items 171–2
Target State 22
asking exchange 190–202
be 108

Target State – *cont.*
  chains 47–8, 49, 52, 54
  constraints 207–8
  extensions 57–61
  on-line amendments 211
  post-nominal specification 156–7
  principle (4) 223
  reconsidered 171
  reduplication 122, 124, 128
  suspensions 63, 64
  time reference 80
teaching English 13, 177, 234–9
telling 13, 15, 111
  and asking exchanges 40, 41–6
  interaction 29
  listener 30–1
  minimum requirements 42–6
  preliminary purpose 177, 183
  purpose of story 26–8, 172–3, 177
temporal precedence 187–9, 224
tense 102 *see also be, have,* non-finite
  verbal elements
tense paradigm 102
theme 187
'things' 151–3
Thomson, A. J. and Martinet A. V.
  235–8
Thorne, J. P. 230
time
  communicating in 15–17
  condition 108, 109, 110, 116
  development 6
  discourse 4, 11
  now-happening 37
  reference, differentiated 80–1, 82,
    83–4
    be 110–11
    have 103, 105
    modals 113, 116
  reference, undifferentiated 80–1, 82,
    83–4
    have 103, 105, 116
  see also real time
to forms 57
  arrive 59, 60, 68

be 68, 110–11
do 66
event time 85–6
have 106–7
help 66
look 68
Practical English Grammar, A 238
probable constraints 208
search 58, 60, 68
time reference 84
tone *see* intonation
tonic syllable *see* intonation, tonic
  syllable

uncertainty *see* indeterminacy
understanding, shared 34–6, 77, 78
  asking exchanges 192
  constraints 210
  here-and-now 33, 84
  intonation 182–3
  reduction of ambiguity 127–8
  selection 139
unrestricted reference 76
used language 22, 23, 24–39, 36–7, 48,
  70, 118, 241, 255g
utterance time 79–80, 83, 108, 109, 174,
  255g

verbal elements
  analysis of multi-word 101–2
  event timing 79
  see also non-finite verbal elements
verbs, imperfective 81–3
verbs, perfective 81–3

W open selectors (*what, when, where,*
  which, who) 139–43, 144–5
  see also open selectors, question types
who 134–6, 140, 141, 147–50
will 113–19
would 117
writing, experience of 11–12, 17

zero realization 23, 131–8, 143, 147,
  152–3, 207, 238, 256g